The Reminiscences Of
Vice Admiral Paul D. Stroop
U.S. Navy (Retired)

Interviewed By
Commander Etta-Belle Kitchen
U.S. Navy (Retired)

U.S. Naval Institute • Annapolis, Maryland

Copyright © 1970/1996

Authorization

The U.S. Naval Institute is hereby authorized to make available to individuals, libraries, and other repositories of its choosing the transcripts of five oral history interviews concerning the life and career of the late Vice Admiral Paul D. Stroop, U.S. Navy (Retired). The interviews were recorded on 3 August 1969, 13 September 1969, 14 September 1969, 1 November 1969, and 11 January 1970, in collaboration with Etta-Belle Kitchen for the U.S. Naval Institute.

The undersigned does hereby release and assign to the U.S. Naval Institute all right, title, restrictions, and interest in the interviews. The copyright in both the oral and transcribed versions shall be the sole property of the U.S. Naval Institute. The tape recordings of the interviews are and will remain the property of the U.S. Naval Institute.

Signed and sealed this __20TH__ day of __MAY__ 1996.

Patrick A. Stroop
Patrick A. Stroop for the estate of
Vice Admiral Paul D. Stroop

Preface—1970

This manuscript is the result of a series of tape-recorded interviews with Vice Admiral Paul D. Stroop at his home in San Diego, California during 1969 and 1970. These interviews were conducted by Commander Etta-Belle Kitchen, USN (Ret.) for the Oral History office in the U. S. Naval Institute.

Only minor emendations and corrections have been made to the manuscript. The reader is asked to bear in mind therefore that he is reading a transcript of the spoken word rather than the written word.

Dr. John T. Mason, Jr.

Preface—1996

The oral history transcript of Vice Admiral Stroop was among the first ones to be published by the Naval Institute. As a result, some of the refinements that have later become standard parts of the format were not yet incorporated. This revised transcript has been annotated with footnotes to provide additional information, and the volume has been indexed in the comprehensive style now standard for Naval Institute oral history. In addition to the corrections made originally by Admiral Stroop, some slight editing has been done in the interest of clarity and smoothness. The original version of the transcript is still on file at the Naval Institute.

Paul Stillwell

VICE ADMIRAL PAUL DAVID STROOP
UNITED STATES NAVY (RETIRED)

Paul David Stroop was born in Zanesville, Ohio, on 30 October 1904, the son of John H. and Margaret M. (Jacobs) Stroop. He attended Mobile, Alabama, High School and Werntz Preparatory School before entering the U.S. Naval Academy, Annapolis, Maryland, in June 1922 on appointment from the Seventh Congressional District of Alabama. As a midshipman he was a member of the varsity gymnastics team for four years and captain of the team for one. He was All-Around Inter-Collegiate Champion in gymnastics.

Graduating on 3 June 1926, he was commissioned ensign as of that date. Subsequent dates of rank are as follows: lieutenant (junior grade), 4 June 1928; lieutenant, 30 June 1936; lieutenant commander, 26 January 1940; commander, 15 August 1942; captain, 1 August 1943; rear admiral, 1 November 1953; vice admiral, 25 September 1962.

After graduation from the Naval Academy in 1926, Stroop had preliminary aviation instruction there before joining the USS Arkansas (BB-33) in September. In May and June 1927 he had temporary additional duty under instruction at the Optical School, Navy Yard, Washington, D.C., and the Naval Air Station, Hampton Roads, Virginia. When detached from the Arkansas in 1928, he reported to the Naval Academy as a candidate for the 1928 Olympics; he was selected as an alternate on the U.S. team. Returning from the games the following August, he was ordered to the Naval Air Station, Pensacola, Florida, for flight training. Designated a naval aviator in September 1929, he joined the USS Wright (AV-1) to serve three years with torpedo and patrol squadrons of Aircraft Squadrons, Scouting Fleet, based on that tender.

He returned to Annapolis in June 1932 and there completed courses of instruction at the Naval Postgraduate School in applied communications in the general line. From June 1934 to June 1936 he was attached to Bombing Squadron 5B, based first on the Ranger (CV-4), later on the Lexington (CV-2). Transferring to the USS Portland (CA-33), he served as senior aviator with Scouting Squadrons 10S and 11S, operating in the Pacific, from July 1936 to May 1937. When detached, he was assigned duty in the Bureau of Aeronautics, Navy Department, Washington, D.C., from July 1937 to May 1940.

In May 1940 he joined the staff of Commander Patrol Wing Two, as gunnery and tactical officer, and in November 1940 transferred to the staff of Commander Carrier Division One, to serve as aide and flag secretary, first aboard the Saratoga (CV-3), then the Lexington (CV-2). In July 1943 he became operations officer when that carrier division was changed to U.S. Naval Air Forces Pacific Fleet. He was later assigned to the staff of Commander Aircraft South Pacific. He was awarded the Legion of Merit and received a letter of commendation with ribbon, each with combat "V." The citations follow in part:

Legion of Merit: "For exceptionally meritorious conduct . . . as Flag Secretary . . . For Commander Task Force ELEVEN during the Coral Sea action on May 7-8, 1942, and as Planning Officer for Commander, Aircraft, South Pacific Force, during the period from September 26, 1942, to April 4, 1943. Frequently called upon to make numerous recommendations affecting military decisions of great importance, [he] displayed unerring judgment and excellent foresight in planning. His calm deliberation while under fire of Japanese aerial forces was an inspiration to his subordinates . . ."

Letter of Commendation (Commander in Chief Pacific Fleet): "For distinguished service in the line of his profession . . . on the staff of the Air Task Group Commander in preparation for, during and after the successful engagements with the enemy in the Battle of the Coral Sea, May 7-8, 1942 . . ."

When relieved of duty on the staff of Commander Aircraft, South Pacific in April 1943, he assumed command of the USS Mackinac (AVP-13), a small seaplane tender operating in the South and Central Pacific. In February of 1944 he was ordered to the Navy Department for duty on the staff of Admiral Ernest J. King, USN, the Commander in Chief U.S. Fleet, as aviation plans officer. During this period he attended Allied military staff conferences at Quebec, Malta, Yalta, and Potsdam. Upon completion of this duty he assumed command of the USS Croatan (CVE-25), operating in the Atlantic.

In November 1945 he was ordered to the staff of the Commander Fifth Fleet in the Western Pacific and served as operations officer until February 1946, when he was detached for duty on the staff of Commander in Chief Pacific Fleet as fleet aviation officer. He later served as assistant chief of staff for operations. Returning to the United States in September 1948, he reported as executive officer of the General Line School at Monterey, California. From August 1950 until June 1951 he attended the National War College, Washington, D.C.

In August 1951 he assumed command of the USS Princeton (CV-37) and was detached in August 1952 to assume command of the USS Essex (CV-9), also operating against Communist forces in the Sea of Japan. "For exceptionally meritorious conduct . . . as Commanding Officer of the USS PRINCETON during operations against enemy aggressor forces in Korea from 30 April to 31 August 1952 . . ." he was awarded a gold star in lieu of a second Legion of Merit. The citation further states: "A capable and resourceful leader, he organized a group of recalled reserves, inexperienced recruits and members of the regular Navy into a highly efficient fighting team, thereby overcoming numerous obstacles presented by increasing shortages of trained personnel and deficiencies of material and enabling him to apply the striking power of his vessel against the enemy with maximum effectiveness . . ."

Reporting in October 1952 as Commander Naval Ordnance Test Station, Inyokern, California, he remained there almost a year, being detached in September 1953 for duty as Senior Naval Member, Weapons Systems Evaluation Group, Office of the Assistant Secretary of Defense (Research and Development), Washington, D.C. He became Deputy and Assistant Chief of the Bureau of Ordnance, Navy Department, on 29 December 1954.

He served as Commander U.S. Taiwan Patrol Force, with additional duty as Commander Fleet Air Wing One, from April 1957 until March 1958.

On 14 March 1958, as a rear admiral, he assumed the duties of Chief of the Bureau of Ordnance, Navy Department, and on 9 September 1959, he became Chief of the newly created Bureau of Naval Weapons, activated on 1 September 1959, to combine the functions of the Bureaus of Ordnance and Aeronautics. He remained in that billet until October 1962. He was then promoted to vice admiral and served as Commander Naval Air Force Pacific Fleet from November 1962 to October 1965. He had temporary additional duty as Commander First Fleet from December 1963 to January 1964.

Admiral Stroop retired from active duty on 1 November 1965. From November 1965 to May 1995 he worked for Ryan Aeronautical and Teledyne Ryan as an aerospace consultant and served on numerous government advisory committees. He served for 30 years on the board of trustees of the Naval Academy Alumni Association, including being national president from 1977 to 1979. He died on 17 May 1995 in Coronado, California, and on 23 May was buried at Fort Rosecrans National Cemetery on Point Loma in San Diego, California.

In addition to the Legion of Merit (two awards) and the Commendation Ribbon, each with combat "V," Admiral Stroop received the American Defense Service Medal, Fleet Clasp; the American Campaign Medal; the Asiatic-Pacific Campaign Medal with four engagement stars; the World War II Victory Medal; the National Defense Service Medal; the Korean Service Medal; and the United Nations Service Medal.

Stroop was married to the former Esther Holscher of Baltimore, Maryland, from 18 December 1926 until her death on 23 May 1982. He was subsequently married to the former Kathleen Roeder, who survived him. Admiral Stroop's children, born during his first marriage, are Paul David Stroop., Jr.; Margaret Ann Wells, Barbara Winthrop Draddy, and Patrick Allen Stroop. Stepchildren from his second marriage are Bernard F. Roeder, Jr.; Franke Haimberger; Anne Roeder; and Kathleen Bell.

Interview Number 1 with Vice Admiral Paul D. Stroop, U.S. Navy (Retired)

Place: Admiral Stroop's home in San Diego, California

Date: Sunday, 3 August 1969

Interviewer: Commander Etta-Belle Kitchen, U.S. Navy (Retired)

Q: I am at the home of Vice Admiral Paul D. Stroop, 846 Bangor Street, Point Loma, San Diego. This is the first in a series of biographical tapes concerning Admiral Stroop's long and illustrious career in the Navy. I'm awfully happy that you feel that you can give us the time, Admiral, to do this series. I know that the Institute and the library of the Institute will be enhanced by having the series of tapes concerning your career. Thank you very much for seeing us.

Admiral Stroop: Well, it's a pleasure for me to cooperate with the Institute, and I will do what I can in the way of a biography. I think probably the best way to proceed is to go ahead chronologically and interweave personal affairs with professional items. That seems to be the best way.

Q: I think so too. Begin in the beginning with your days as a midshipman, and if you want to describe your scholastic and athletic activities--I know you were particularly interested in athletics in those days. If we start at the beginning, I think that's the proper way to proceed.

Admiral Stroop: Well, just a few words of my very early life. I was born in Zanesville, Ohio, on 30 October 1904, the only child of John Hoover Stroop and Margaret Stroop. We lived in Zanesville, Ohio, until about 1916, when I was 12 years of age, and my family then moved to Alabama. My father was in ill health and felt that a milder climate would be a better place to live.

I went through high school in Mobile and was appointed to the Naval Academy by the local congressman from Mobile. His name was John McDuffie.* He was a Democrat, the Democratic whip in the House. I received my appointment the year after I graduated from high school. I graduated from high school in 1921. I had a free year and did some preparatory work at Werntz's preparatory school in Annapolis, more affectionately known in those days as "Bobby's War College."†

I passed the entrance examinations with good marks and was told to report to the Naval Academy on the 12th of June, 1922. I well remember the date, because about two-thirds of the way through the physical examination one of the doctors came up and marked on my slip a great big circle around the figures indicating height, 63 and a half inches, and then a great big "NO." So I was not accepted on that day. I immediately went back to Washington and contacted my congressman, who apparently had an interest in my case and some influence in the Navy Department.

We went the next day to the Navy Department and interviewed the Surgeon General and had a very quick and informal physical examination in his office. He said, "Well, this young man is in excellent physical shape, and it's only a military matter, a matter of height. So if the Navy will take him otherwise, we'll approve a waiver." And he wanted me to promise that I would grow if I could, so I promised him I would.

Q: How much did he want you to grow?

Admiral Stroop: I had to be 64 inches at that age, and I had to graduate at 66. I got finally to be 64 and a half inches, so I didn't quite meet its standards, but it seemed to work out all right.

---

* John McDuffie (Democrat-Alabama) served in the House of Representatives from 1919 to 1935.
† Robert Lincoln Werntz graduated from the Naval Academy in the class of 1884 and subsequently resigned his commission in June 1890. He then set up his preparatory school in Annapolis for prospective midshipmen and operated it for many years prior to his death in 1931.

Q: I am sure the Navy's found out it worked out to its benefit.

Admiral Stroop: I reported back to the Naval Academy on the 15th of June and was sworn in on that date and became a midshipman fourth class, in the class of 1926, this being June of 1922. With a rather poor high school background, I expected to have trouble academically. I, as a result, applied myself fairly well and was able to get along quite well as a midshipman academically. I starred every year at the Naval Academy and graduated standing 20.

Q: How many were in your graduating class?

Admiral Stroop: About 550 in the graduating class.[*] The subjects that appealed to me the most were mathematics, the sciences, and seamanship--professional naval subjects--which I thought sort of indicated my interest in the Navy.

I particularly enjoyed the summer cruises. I always did well on the summer cruises and enjoyed them and, I think, profited a lot by them. As a matter of fact, I found the summer cruises the most interesting part of Naval Academy life. We started in '23; that first year we left Annapolis and went to Europe. The second year we had another European cruise, an opportunity to visit London and Paris. And the third year, my first-class cruise, we came around through the canal and up the West Coast. We stopped here in San Diego Harbor in 1925 and then on up to San Pedro and visited Los Angeles, and finally up to Seattle and back down through the canal and back home. It was a most interesting cruise.

At the Naval Academy I went out chiefly for one sport, gymnastics, and was fortunate enough to be able to make the team the first year. In those days, plebes--fourth classmen--were allowed to participate in the regular college meets. I took a few places plebe year. I continued with the sport throughout the four years. Second class year I became intercollegiate champion, all around, and also on the flying rings. It was rather interesting: the Naval Academy had done so well in that particular sport that they were

---

[*] The Naval Academy alumni register indicates 456 graduates in the class of 1926. Stroop was indeed number 20.

asked to not participate in the intercollegiate championships my first-class year, because we had swept so many of the places.* They felt that it was making the sport unpopular and unfair to other colleges.

Q: I never heard of that.

Admiral Stroop: Well, this was rather unusual. We won, I think, 120 meets in succession.

Q: And did the Navy oblige them and not participate?

Admiral Stroop: We continued to participate in dual meets with the colleges, but we were not allowed to participate in the intercollegiate championships my first-class year.

Q: Did that disappoint you?

Admiral Stroop: Yes, I would like to have competed first-class year, because with four years' experience I could have won some more first places, I think. However, I continued training after I graduated, with the thought of trying out for the Olympic Games in 1928. I did try out for them and was just barely able to squeeze on the team as a substitute. I made the trip to Europe, to Amsterdam, as a substitute with the team of 1928. We had two other Navy members, a Marine second lieutenant named Newhart, H. G. "Chubby" Newhart, and then Lieutenant (junior grade) Jack Pearson, now a rear admiral.† Jack had been captain of the Navy team when I was a plebe. He graduated in 1923.

After graduation from the Naval Academy . . .

Q: Before we go on to that, I'd like to ask you a couple of questions. Did you enjoy the Naval Academy?

---

* The first-class year was the equivalent of a student's senior year in a civilian university.
† Second Lieutenant Harold G. Newhart, USMC; Lieutenant (junior grade) John B. Pearson, Construction Corps, USN.

Admiral Stroop: Oh, I enjoyed it very much. It was really a wonderful, thrilling experience to go there. When I was a candidate out in Annapolis, I realized my academic background and training was rather poor. So, as a consequence, I studied quite hard for two and a half months at Bobby's War College. The only time I would take off would be Wednesday afternoon and Saturday afternoon to watch the athletic events at the Naval Academy. I would take in all of these that I could and soak up the atmosphere and aura of the academy. Then I'd go back completely ready to apply myself to my studies, and for those two and a half months I worked very hard.

My preparatory work was limited by the funds I had available to go to school. I saved enough money to go to school for two and a half months at Bobby's War College. I took the examinations in February rather than in April; they gave two sets of examinations in those days. I passed them, of course, and got in, as I said earlier.

Q: Did you feel that the education at the academy suited you for the job that you had to do in your professional life as a naval officer?

Admiral Stroop: Oh, yes, I think so. I think the Naval Academy education in those days was not nearly as complete or detailed or as good as it is nowadays. Everybody took the same subjects, no matter whether you started as I had with only three years of high school or whether you had finished four years of college, which some of my classmates had. We took the same subjects, with the exception that the class was divided in language; one-half took French, and one-half took Spanish. But, even so, with those limitations I think the academy did a fine job of training young officers.

Q: Did you ever feel a lack during your naval career of something that you hadn't had?

Admiral Stroop: I don't think that I could trace it back to the Naval Academy. There were times in various jobs that I had, particularly in the technical fields, where I wished that I had a better technical background in those particular subjects. It would have been better if I had

had more postgraduate work. But, as far as the Naval Academy was concerned, I don't think it made that much difference.

Q: What about the discipline during the time that you were there? Did you think it was more severe or severe enough than it should be?

Admiral Stroop: You always heard, of course, that the Navy wasn't what it used to be, and somebody else said it never was.

Q: I'm sure you heard that when you were there.

Admiral Stroop: That's right. The restrictions in those days were certainly more severe than they have been in recent years. We had not nearly as much freedom. We didn't have as much liberty, we didn't have as much leave, we didn't have as many privileges as the midshipmen have had in recent years and, of course, they have nowadays. But I wouldn't say it was bad. I think it was all right, and certainly I didn't find it much of a burden. I got along real well. I was a flexible youngster and pretty well behaved. I didn't get into too much trouble. With hard work, I had no trouble with the academics. So my four years at the Naval Academy were very pleasant, wonderful years.

Q: Did you know they were good then, or is this looking back in retrospect?

Admiral Stroop: No, I enjoyed them then. I enjoyed being a midshipman. I was proud of the privilege of wearing the uniform. I knew I wanted to be a naval officer, and toward the end of the four years I knew I wanted to be a naval aviator. There was just no other question, no question of resigning or getting out or doing anything differently, and I was being trained for it.

If you want a little personal history then during those four years at the academy before we get into the rest of my career . . .

Q: Yes, I'd like that.

Admiral Stroop: I met my wife at the Naval Academy my youngster or third-class year.[*] She came down as a drag for a friend of mine, and I met her with him in the yard on Sunday afternoon--right after chapel.[†] I remember, as a matter of fact, I had a camera and took her picture. Not long after that, I managed to get a date with her and dragged her down to the academy. We began seeing a good bit of each other, and she became my steady date for various hops and all the events. We essentially went together for at least two years and part of three years.

Q: And she came from where?

Q: Esther came from Baltimore, Maryland. It was quite easy to get down there on the old electric railway, the WB&A, Washington, Baltimore, and Annapolis. She became a regular attendee on the Annapolis scene and was extremely popular with the members of my class. I used to say that she knew more members of my class than I did. Those were the days of cut-in dancing, you know, and she was extremely popular. It was very difficult to get more than a few steps with her at the hops.

Q: Well, she's still awfully cute.

Admiral Stroop: Well, thank you very much. I think so too. We did not get married at graduation, though. We thought we'd be very sensible. She had trained as a teacher and was going to teach school, and I would at least get through my first promotion. We'd wait about five years before we got married. We were actually married in December of 1926 and started raising a family soon after that.

---

[*] The "youngster" or third-class year at the Naval Academy is the equivalent of the sophomore year at a civilian university.
[†] "Drag" was Naval Academy slang for dating girls.

After graduation from the Naval Academy in June of 1926 we had a short period of aviation training.

Q: That was what I wanted to ask you about, because one of the comments that I had was that you had preliminary aviation instruction at the academy, and I wondered what that meant.

Admiral Stroop: When I was finished the Naval Academy, naval aviation was just beginning to feel the need for considerable expansion. The Lexington and Saratoga were just being completed, our first two big carriers.* Patrol aviation was expanding, and they felt the need for more aviators than they had.

Aviation was not particularly popular with the regular line officers. The non-aviators, the battleship types, did not encourage young officers to go into aviation. However, the aviation branch of the Navy was getting stronger and had more influence. It was decided with my class that they would try to interest us especially in aviation--at least give us a background and help us in making the decision as to whether we would go into it or not. So two summers of aviation training were arranged. The first summer took two-thirds of the class in lieu of making their first-class midshipman cruise. That was before their first-class academic year started. That part of the class stayed back at the Naval Academy and took this preliminary aviation training.

The other third of the class, of which I was a member, were graduated in June of 1926, commissioned ensigns, and remained at the Naval Academy throughout that summer to take the same course in aviation training. This was a rather simple course, a certain amount of academic work on aviation subjects and 12 hours of flying in a World War I flying boat called the F-5L. We had various jobs on the flights--navigators, gunners, and system mechanics. A few that were lucky were permitted to get in the cockpit and handle the controls in the air.

---

* The USS Lexington (CV-2) was commissioned on 14 December 1927 and the USS Saratoga (CV-3) on 16 November 1927.

Q: How long was the course?

Admiral Stroop: The course was about 12 weeks, I would say. This, of course, we found to be very interesting in that we had a lot of freedom as young officers. We were allowed to go and come with a lot more freedom than we did as midshipmen. We had a little more money to spend. A good many of us had an automobile or access to a car. It was really a rare privilege in 1926. The work was not nearly as hard and demanding as the four academic years had been.

Q: Where were you based?

Q: All of this training, both periods--the one before I graduated with the other part of my class and the year I graduated--were carried on at the Naval Academy in Annapolis.

Q: Where did you live?

Admiral Stroop: We lived in Bancroft Hall.[*]

Q: Oh, did you?

Admiral Stroop: Yes, as I recall, instead of having a roommate, we all had our separate rooms. We lived over in one of what was then called the new wings and ate, of course, in the mess hall as we did as midshipmen.

Q: But you didn't have to follow the same regulations or restrictions.

Admiral Stroop: No, we had more freedom going out in town, but we had a certain set routine on the average.

---

[*] Bancroft Hall is the large multi-wing dormitory that houses Naval Academy midshipmen.

Q: Because you were still in school.

Q: Oh, yes, we were still in school; we followed a school routine. But I think, as I recall, you could go to town every afternoon and had your weekends off. So this was not too difficult. But, as a result of this aviation training, we didn't join our ships until the fall. It was the fall of that year, 1926, that I reported to my first ship, the Arkansas.* She was a battleship with 12-inch guns, built in 1912. This being 1926, she was just in the process of being modernized. They were putting blisters on her and improving some of her fire control and other improvements. They put a different type mast on her. I joined her in the Navy yard just as she was finishing her year and a half modernization. We were there through the fall and into the winter.

Q: What was your job?

Admiral Stroop: There were, I think, 22 of us assigned to this ship, and it happened that I was the senior ensign of the group. I was assigned to the plotting room, which had to do with gunnery and fire control. The plotting room assignment also called for work on deck. We were assigned as junior division officers, and we also, of course, took bridge watches as the junior officer of the deck on the bridge.

I was on the Arkansas about 18 months and enjoyed it very much. Just toward the end of that period, I managed to qualify as an officer of the deck. I attended two schools during the period. I went to preliminary flight training, as I guess it was called then, at Hampton Roads. We actually flew in training planes and came up to the point of solo. We were not allowed to solo, but they had a solo check, and I managed to get an upcheck. The

---

* The USS Arkansas (BB-33) was commissioned 17 September 1912. Following modernization in 1925-26 she had a standard displacement of 26,100 tons, was 562 feet long and 106 feet in the beam. Her top speed was 21 knots. She was armed with 12 12-inch guns and 16 5-inch guns. She was the oldest U.S. battleship in active service during World War II, eventually being decommissioned in 1946.

other school I went to was range-finder school at the old Washington Navy Yard, and I spent a month there.

During this period that I was on the Arkansas Mrs. Stroop and I got married on the 18th of December 1926 in Baltimore. One of my roommates was head usher, and I had several other classmates as ushers. We had a very nice wedding in St. Luke's Episcopal Church on Carey Street, just a few blocks from where her parents lived, and 17 days' leave.

Early in January we went on our first cruise down to Guantanamo Bay and were gone for four months. During that period, of course, we had gunnery exercises and regular Atlantic Fleet routine for the southern cruise, basing chiefly at Guantanamo.

In the spring of 1928, after I had been on the Arkansas about a year and a half, I received a letter from the Navy Department, inviting me to come back to the Naval Academy and train for the 1928 Olympic Games. This caused a good bit of consternation in the gunnery department. We were getting pretty close to our most important practice of the year--long-range battle practice--and all of a sudden I found out that I was going to be very unpopular if I insisted on going along with the orders that would be mine if I agreed to go. However, I found the executive officer of the ship, and I guess the captain, in favor of letting me be relieved. I went along with the program and went back to Annapolis in February or March of 1928.

In the meantime--I should have mentioned this earlier--our first child was born, Margaret Ann, and we started what was a very interesting growing family.

I came back to the East Coast to Annapolis via Guantanamo. I went overland by a very antiquated railroad to Havana and sea ferry to Key West. Then I went by train from Key West, via Baltimore, to Annapolis and started training for the Olympic Games. During this period my wife and baby lived with her family in Baltimore, and I, of course, had a billet in Bancroft Hall in the Naval Academy.

It was a very pleasant spring getting ready for the Olympic Games. We trained in Annapolis, and finally, toward the end of the period just before the tryouts, we went up to New York City. We billeted on the station ship, the old cruiser Seattle. The three of us that were the Navy entries--Lieutenant Newhart, Lieutenant (j.g.) Jack Pearson, and I--journeyed across Manhattan every day, from the Navy yard in Brooklyn to Union City, New

Jersey. We trained at the Union City Turnverein, where we had reason to believe that we would find the best gymnasts in America. That turned out to be the case, because they placed, I believe, three people on the team, as the Navy did. The trials were held in Union City at the Swiss Turnverein, and the three of us were selected to make the trip to Amsterdam. As I said, I was a substitute gymnast.

Q: Was your size an assistance or a hindrance?

Admiral Stroop: I think generally for gymnastics being small makes the work a good bit easier. Chances are, you had been able to develop coordination earlier than if you had fast growth and you were tall. I think it probably helped.

We went to Amsterdam in July of 1928 and competed in the games.[*] Our team, I think, stood fifth. We had very keen competition, of course. The Swiss, Germans, Swedes, Czechoslovaks--all had very good people. We did reasonably well, though, and we, I think, won one first place and won a couple of other medals, but nothing spectacular.

Q: Did you find that experience an interesting one?

Admiral Stroop: Oh, yes. I particularly enjoyed the trip over and meeting all these outstanding athletes. Johnny Weismuller was on the ship.[†] He was, I think, going to his third Olympics then. And there was a young swimmer, Eleanor Holm, who was only 14 and going to her first Olympics. She was a part of the team. There were several great track stars and a crew from the University of California that had beaten out the Navy in the Olympic trials. They were on there, and the lacrosse team from Johns Hopkins was on the trip.

---

[*] For details, see <u>American Olympic Committee Report</u> (New York: American Olympic Committee, 1928). Page 233 lists Stroop among the 16 finalists for the tryouts held 9 June 1928 at Union City, New Jersey.
[†] Weismuller, a swimmer, parlayed his Olympic fame into the movie role of Tarzan.

One of the interesting facets of the trip was the fact that this transatlantic liner, the President Roosevelt, of course, was used to serving very excellent food, which they had to do in competition with the other Atlantic liners. For some reason or other, nobody had thought about special training-table food for the athletes. We were three days out of port before we discovered that everybody was eating too much and gaining an awful lot of weight. As a matter of fact, our 100-yard-dash man had put on 14 pounds on the trip over and, I might point out, took sixth place. They corrected that. They immediately got out an Olympic menu.

It was interesting also on board ship to watch the athletes trying to train under shipboard conditions. For the gymnasts, and particularly the Navy types, there was no difficulty at all to set up our apparatus on deck. The rolling of the ship didn't seem to bother us at all. The divers had a springboard and a diving board. They would land on mats on top of a hatch. The runners were going continually around the promenade deck and circling it. There was just a constant parade of them. The oarsmen from California had rowing machines set up on deck and worked out there. But it was a continual sense of activity during daylight hours, particularly when people began to feel that they had to work off a little weight. It was very interesting.

I might add that the Olympic Committee had worked with the War Department to have an officer in charge of the whole group, the Olympic team and all the coaches and officials that went over. The senior officer that was named was Brigadier General MacArthur.[*]

Q: The same?

Admiral Stroop: The same. He was on there with his wife.

Q: How many athletes were on the ship?

---

[*] Brigadier General Douglas MacArthur, USA.

Admiral Stroop: I don't really know. I suppose there were a couple of hundred. There were one or two entries for every event in track that they had, and then there were a number of teams. There was the cycling team, a fencing team on which we had a naval officer, and a boxing team which had a naval officer on it--Admiral Harry Henderson.[*] There was a wrestling team. They had a classmate on that, Tex Edwards, who was killed during the war.[†] A soccer team, a lacrosse team, as a mentioned, from Johns Hopkins, a crew from the University of California. There was a decathlon team, a pentathlon team, gymnastic team, and, of course, the swimmers and divers. It was quite a conglomeration, all of them stars in their own right.

Q: It must have been interesting to have personal contact with all of these people, something you wouldn't have any other opportunity for.

Admiral Stroop: And then there were very good coaches. Every event had a coach. The teams had two or three coaches and a trainer. Many of these people had their wives along. They were allowed to make the trip, and some of the athletes were married. They were permitted to bring their wives along if they could afford it. They had to pay their transportation. It was a very interesting trip. We lived on the ship in Amsterdam instead of going to a hotel.

Q: Was the entire ship turned over to the team?

Admiral Stroop: Oh, yes, it was chartered for that purpose. It stayed in Amsterdam throughout the Olympics, and then you came back on the ship if you wanted to, or you were permitted to come back commercially if you preferred that.

---

[*] Ensign Harry H. Henderson, USN, who subsequently retired as a rear admiral in 1960.
[†] Ensign Heywood L. Edwards, USN. On 31 October 1941, Lieutenant Commander Edwards was commanding officer of the four-stack destroyer Reuben James (DD-245) when she was torpedoed and sunk by the U-552 while she was escorting a convoy from Halifax, Nova Scotia.

After the Olympic Games were over and we got back to New York, I had orders waiting for me to go to Pensacola to become a naval aviator.

Q: Had you requested that?

Admiral Stroop: Oh, yes, I was ready to go; I wanted to go. I picked up my little family in Baltimore, my wife and young daughter who was a year old. She was a very cute little curly-headed girl that I didn't know very well. We had to turn in the roadster that I bought, a snappy roadster, because it wasn't suitable for a family. We got a four-door sedan secondhand and drove to Pensacola. I was able on the way, of course, to visit my old home. My mother and father were living in Mobile, Alabama. We spent some time with them. This was an opportunity that occurred many times again during the year at Pensacola. We were able to go back and forth and visit my family, and then they would visit us in Pensacola.

The flight training at Pensacola was, of course, a good bit simpler and not as extensive as it is now. We usually competed the course in 12 months. It consisted of ground school for half a day and flying for half a day. We had a very general course and were really trained in all types of Navy airplanes. In those days a naval aviator was supposed to be able to serve on a carrier as a carrier aviator, or in the patrol planes, or on battleships or cruisers. That was the general career pattern. Actually, following your graduation from Pensacola, in succeeding years you were alternated through these various assignments.

I found Pensacola very interesting. I had very little trouble getting through the course. I think I got what was called a "down" on my first check in primary seaplanes. With three more extra hours I passed that and then went on through the course without any trouble. We trained in five squadrons. The first had the primary seaplanes, about 30 hours. The old squadron commander is a neighbor of ours here in San Diego now, Jerry Bogan.[*]

---

[*] Vice Admiral Gerald F. Bogan, USN (Ret.), whose oral history is in the Naval Institute collection. He was a lieutenant commander while stationed in Pensacola in 1928.

Katie Bogan and Admiral Bogan live out in La Jolla. One of the other instructors was Admiral Bob Hickey.*

My particular primary instructor was an admiral named Johnny Hoskins, who was a lieutenant in those days.† He was the man who got me through preliminary flight raining. Johnny's the one, you know, who lost a leg during World War II and was finally given command of a carrier--the one I commanded later, the Princeton--and became an admiral.‡ He's dead now.

The next squadron, of course, was primary land planes, and then you went into . . .

Q: What kind of plane were they using?

Admiral Stroop: We had a plane called an NY, built by Consolidated.§ Both the landplane and the seaplane were the same type--one with floats and one with wheels--small, two-seat biplanes. The instructor sat in the front seat and the student in the rear seat. Then, of course, when you got into the service types, you occupied the front cockpit. That was the pilot's cockpit, and your observer was in the back seat.

The next three squadrons--three, four, and five--were service types. Usually they were the older service types, but they were actually service-type airplanes. You were preparing yourself for flying any type of plane that the Navy had, so that you would have flexibility when assigned into a squadron.

Q: Did you do any carrier landings during this . . . ?

---

* Lieutenant Robert F. Hickey, USN; he retired in 1959 as a vice admiral.
† Lieutenant John M. Hoskins, USN, who retired in 1957 as a vice admiral.
‡ In October 1944 Captain Hoskins was on board the light carrier Princeton (CVL-23), ready to take command. During the Japanese attack that sank the ship on 24 October, Captain Hoskins was wounded and lost his right foot. After he recovered and was fitted with an artificial foot, he was the first commanding officer when the new Princeton (CV-37) was commissioned 18 November 1945.
§ The Consolidated NY trainer was the Navy version of the Army PT-1. It entered Navy service in the mid-1920s. The NY-2 model was 28 feet long, wing span of 40 feet, gross weight of 2,627 pounds, and top speed of 98 miles per hour.

Admiral Stroop: No, in those days the students at Pensacola did not do carrier landings. Nowadays, you see, they specialize in their own types. A carrier aviator is trained essentially from the start as a carrier aviator, and he actually does carrier landings at Pensacola. The chances are that his whole flying career will be in carrier-type planes.

Q: But you had the whole range. Every type plane the Navy had, you learned to fly it then?

Admiral Stroop: Well, I wouldn't say exactly that, but I was prepared to fly it, and I did fly most of the types. It is rather interesting, when I retired here and they went through my logbooks and found that I had qualified or flown over 100 types of airplanes over this total period of time.

After Pensacola I was ordered to an East Coast squadron: Torpedo Squadron Nine, VT-9. Home base was Norfolk, Virginia, and the ship that we used as a tender was the old USS Wright.*

Q: And the Wright was the . . . ?

Admiral Stroop: The Wright was the tender which we based on when we went on our cruises. In addition to the Wright, we had some bird-class tenders. They were World War I minesweepers converted for aviation tending. They looked like large seagoing tugs. On our cruises down to Guantanamo Bay and Panama we based entirely on those and the Wright for the cruise periods.

When I joined VT-9, I found that I had one other classmate in there, Paul Watson.† We also had a number of very colorful naval aviator types, probably the most colorful one

---

* The seaplane tender USS Wright (AV-1) was commissioned 16 December 1921. She had a full-load displacement of 11,500 tons, was 448 feet long, 58 feet in the beam, and had a top speed of 15 knots. Renamed San Clemente in 1945, she remained in service until her decommissioning in 1946.
† Ensign Paul W. Watson, USN.

being Dan Gallery.* Dan, as a matter of fact, was executive officer of the squadron. I was assigned to flying in his section, which turned out to be a very interesting experience, because Dan was always trying to find something colorful to do--like flying under a bridge, or having the section zoom a ship, or screaming down 50 feet over a highway, or watching the tourists going to Florida in the wintertime when we were heading south. Great guy, and a wonderful man to work for, great leader and great fighter. I was very fond of him, have a great admiration for him.

Q: How much older was he than you?

Admiral Stroop: Well, Dan was the class of '21, and I was '26, so he was about five years older than I was. There was a younger man who was number three in the squadron, operations officer. He was Joe Bolger, who has been a close personal friend of mine all of my life.† He became a vice admiral and now lives on Long Island in New York.

Q: Where did your patrols take you?

Admiral Stroop: Actually, when we were based in the East Coast, we were doing mostly gunnery work and training and were not making long-range patrols. During the winter cruises, when we went south, we participated in war games and patrolled out from Guantanamo Bay, Cuba, and from Panama.

Q: You were in seaplanes, of course.

---

* Lieutenant Daniel V. Gallery, Jr., USN. Later, while in command of the USS Guadalcanal (CVE-60) in June 1944, his forces captured the German submarine U-505. Gallery eventually became a rear admiral and wrote a number of popular books about the Navy. His oral history is in the Naval Institute collection.
† Lieutenant Joseph F. Bolger, USN.

Admiral Stroop: Yes. We started out with a type of plane called the T4M, which was a single-engine, twin-float seaplane launching torpedoes or bombs.[*] At that time we were called VT-9, Torpedo Squadron Nine. At the end of that first year we received new planes, and our designation was changed to Patrol Squadron Ten. We received PM-1s, the first Martin flying boats from Baltimore.[†] The third year we received another type of airplane, the P3M-2, also built by Martin, called the Sesqui plane, and also a twin-engine flying boat.[‡]

I think the most interesting times during those three years were the long flights down to Cuba and to Panama.

Q: Did you take that long flight in a single-engine plane?

Admiral Stroop: Oh, yes. We did it in increments, of course. For example, when we left Norfolk on the first cruise, we only went to Charleston. We found the Wright in Charleston, waiting for us with buoys all planted. We tied up to the buoys and went aboard the Wright. The next day we left Charleston and went to Miami, Florida. We also had an emergency station where we would stop at, either Jacksonville or Titusville on the Banana River, close to where Cape Kennedy is now. We had fuel available. Then we went on to Miami; some of us would make it nonstop to Miami. When we got to Miami, we found that we had two of the small bird-class tenders in there.

Q: Was that the picture you showed me in the hall, the bird-class tender?

---

[*] Martin T4M torpedo planes first entered the fleet in 1928 on board the Lexington (CV-2) and Saratoga (CV-3). The T4M-1 was 41 feet long, wing span of 57 feet, gross weight of 9,503 pounds, and top speed of 109 miles per hour.
[†] Martin PM-1 torpedo planes were production versions of the Naval Aircraft Factory's PN-12. The PN-1 was 48 feet long, wing span of 73 feet, gross weight of 16,964 pounds, and top speed of 116 miles per hour.
[‡] Martin P3M torpedo planes first entered the fleet in 1930 with Patrol Squadron Ten. The P3M-2 was 62 feet long, wing span of 100 feet, gross weight of 17,977 pounds, and top speed of 115 miles per hour.

Admiral Stroop: No. I haven't got a picture of that. This was just a great big seagoing tug. Having arrived in Miami, we found a very convenient arrangement. We had to stay there four days while the Wright then went on down to our next stop. She had to have time to proceed from Charleston to south Cuba. One of the bird-class tenders was sent on to a place called Mariel on the north of Cuba. Also in Miami, since there was not enough space on the tenders to stay, we were billeted ashore in a hotel, which was very nice. During the four days we were there, the All-American Air Show was held. We were not participants in that as fleet operating seaplane squadrons, so we had four free days and had an awful lot of fun.

We left Miami and went on to Mariel, Cuba, which was west of Havana about 40 miles. We landed there and spent the night, and then we hopped across Cuba. This was a great daring flight of 90 miles overland in seaplanes.

Q: It really was, wasn't it?

Admiral Stroop: Oh, yes. We got all prepared for it and briefed. We had one lake in the middle of Cuba, a big reservoir where we could land if we had engine trouble. But nobody ever had to do that. Then we went to . . .

Q: Excuse me, were these single seaters as well as single engines?

Admiral Stroop: No, they actually had three cockpits and they carried the fourth passenger down below. They were rather large planes designed for carrying heavy loads, 1,800 pounds. They had two pilots in tandem, the mechanic, and a radio operator. Actually, there was room enough you could carry many more people if you needed to. I've carried as many as eight people in it, just on a ferry trip to transport personnel.

Q: Were you always the pilot?

Paul D. Stroop #1 - 21

Admiral Stroop: Oh, yes. I qualified as soon as I got in the squadron and became a first pilot right away.

Q: You didn't carry any torpedoes, did you, of course, on any of these flights?

Admiral Stroop: No, you only carried torpedoes on gunnery training flights.

Q: Did you love it all the time?

Admiral Stroop: Oh, yes, it was very interesting--particularly with Dan Gallery as the leader and thinking up screwy things to do that you could get court-martialed for nowadays, if you got caught.

Q: But that really was wonderful experience those three years.

Admiral Stroop: Yes, it was a fine preparation for a career in aviation. After the three years in Torpedo Nine and Patrol Squadron Ten, I was then selected for postgraduate work at the Naval Academy.

Q: And had you applied for that?

Admiral Stroop: Yes, I put in a letter and asked to be assigned to a postgraduate course at the Naval Academy and went there in . . .

Q: June of 1932, wasn't it?

Admiral Stroop: Yes, June 1932. Postgraduate School in those days was located at Annapolis, Maryland.

Q: On the grounds?

Admiral Stroop: Yes, in the Naval Academy grounds. We all took what you called the line course. This was preparation for specialization and a second year's course or a third year's course.

Q: And you were what grade now?

Admiral Stroop: I was lieutenant (junior grade). I had made lieutenant (junior grade) while I was in Pensacola, as a matter of fact. You were three years an ensign in those days. A rather interesting thing happened, though, at this time. Here I was, going to shore duty and had a growing family. We were in the midst of the Depression, and Congress and the Navy Department and the War Department decided that we should all take a 15% pay cut, which we did.* Our base pay was cut 15%, and also all promotions and automatic increases in pay were frozen for a period of, I guess, 18 months or two years.

Q: Where was Mrs. Stroop living then?

Admiral Stroop: Mrs. Stroop, of course, during the first sea cruise had lived chiefly with her family in Baltimore. So, in view of these rather drastic economic circumstances, she continued to live there. I commuted from Baltimore to Annapolis daily, which was quite a chore.

Q: It was in those days. The roads weren't like they are now.

---

* Following the crash of the New York Stock Exchange in late October 1929, the United States was plunged into the Great Depression, from which it did not recover until the nation geared up for World War II at the beginning of the 1940s. The Depression was marked by high unemployment and many business failures.

Admiral Stroop: I rode the electric train for about a year. Then I bought a small automobile, and I commuted in that for about three or four months. Then her father died, Mr. Holscher. We decided that since she was an only child--and, incidentally, I was an only child--that we would pull up stakes and move with her mother to Annapolis. This was in early 1934. We spent the last six months of my postgraduate work living in Annapolis. It was a beautiful little house in Wardour, which we got for $50.00 a month.

Q: Bud Bowler lives in Wardour.[*]

Admiral Stroop: It's a very pleasant community, part of Annapolis. We lived there then, and I finished my postgraduate work at the Naval Academy.

Q: That was a two-year tour, wasn't it?

Admiral Stroop: A two-year tour, both years spent at the Naval Academy. The first year was in what was called the general line course, and the second year in a course called applied communications.

Q: What did that mean?

Admiral Stroop: Well, the practical side of Navy communications: that is, the administration of communications with just enough technical material thrown in so that you could understand and administer communication organizations. It was actually a very fine course, I thought, because every subject that you took was applicable to the naval profession. In my case, it was quite applicable to the duties I had immediately following the course at the Naval Academy.

I missed one important event. I think it was in early 1931 our second child was born, Paul D. Stroop, Jr., who was later to go to the Naval Academy and graduate in the

---

[*] Commander Roland T. E. "Bud" Bowler, Jr., USN (Ret.), was the secretary-treasurer of the Naval Institute at the time of this interview.

class of '54 to become a submarine officer.* So when we moved down to the Naval Academy, there were five of us in the family: my wife and I and two children and Esther's mother.

Q: Did Mrs. Stroop's mother live with you most of her life from then on?

Admiral Stroop: Mrs. Stroop's mother lived with us from then on until the day she died, which was just about a year and a half ago.

Q: You must be a kind man.

Admiral Stroop: That was from 1933 to 1968. She was a great addition to the family. She was a wonderful person to have around. We never had a baby-sitting problem. She worked well with the family and really smoothed out the affairs of the household, so we were able to take trips and do things that we wouldn't have been able to do otherwise. For example, later on in life we took a 12 weeks' trip to Honolulu together, just my wife and I. We left the family here in San Diego. So this was no burden at all.

Q: Many men of a different character than you, however, would find it a burden.

Admiral Stroop: Well, it just wasn't. It was very pleasant.

We left Annapolis in 1934, and I had orders to my first carrier squadron, Bombing Squadron Five on the Ranger.† This was the first Ranger that was an aircraft carrier. It was the sixth ship in the Navy to be named Ranger. It was a very small carrier. We were

---

* Paul D. Stroop, Jr., was born 29 June 1931. Following his graduation from the Naval Academy in 1954, he remained on active duty until 1963, when he resigned his regular commission and went into the Naval Reserve.

† USS Ranger (CV-4) was commissioned 4 June 1934. She had a standard displacement of 14,575 tons, full load of 17,577, was 769 feet long, 80 feet in the beam, an extreme width of 110 feet on the flight deck, and had a draft of 22 feet. She had a top speed of 29 knots and could accommodate about 75 planes.

still working within the limitations of the treaty with Japan and England, and they were trying to save tonnage. So the Ranger was built as light as possible, as small as possible, to accommodate the airplanes of those days. It was sort of an experiment which I don't think worked out too well. On the other hand, it showed us that we could operate from small carriers. From having the Ranger's experience, I think we were able to do a better job with the smaller ships that we converted during World War II.

Q: What was the Ranger's number?

Admiral Stroop: She was CV-4.

Q: That means the fourth aircraft carrier in the Navy?

Admiral Stroop: That's right. The first one, of course, was the Langley; the second one, the Lexington; the Saratoga was CV-3; and the Ranger was CV-4.

Q: And where was the Ranger?

Admiral Stroop: The Ranger was built at Newport News, and her squadrons were assembled at the naval air station in Norfolk, Virginia. So in June of 1934 we went to live in Norfolk, Virginia.

Q: And what were your duties there?

Admiral Stroop: I was number seven in seniority in a bombing squadron. This was a dive-bombing squadron.

Q: And this was a new experience for you, was it not?

Admiral Stroop: Well, except that I had this kind of training--a little bit of it--in Pensacola. But, yes, it was a new experience. It was a new type of airplane. As a matter of fact, we started out with some old airplanes while we were waiting for delivery of some new ones. We had an airplane called the F4B-4, a little single-seater built by Boeing.* It was actually built as a fighter, but it could do dive-bombing work. All dive-bombing squadrons in those days were sort of alternated between being fighters and bombers.

We got an allowance of these, only 9 for an 18-plane squadron. While our new planes were being completed, we were actually assigned a new type of plane called the BF2C, built by Curtiss up in Buffalo, New York.† It was one of our early retractable landing gear planes. It was a larger airplane than the F4B, it had more power, carried a heavier weight of bombs, was faster, and, of course, had the retractable landing gear. It was a biplane, a large upper wing and a shorter lower wing.

We trained in Norfolk while the Ranger was shaking down and got the squadrons all assembled and working together. Gradually, during the winter of 1934 or early 1935, we took delivery of our new planes, the BF2Cs, up in Buffalo, New York. I guess probably March we started operating the new planes on the Ranger. We found that the BF2C was not a particularly good carrier airplane and had some rather interesting experiences getting started in carrier operations.

Q: Had they been tried out before they were ordered? How did anyone know they would work on a carrier?

Admiral Stroop: Remember that times were tough in those days, and we didn't have too many airplanes of any kind. This particular model, the BF2C, we had ordered only one

---

* Boeing F4B-4 fighters first entered fleet squadrons in 1932. The F4B-4 was 20 feet long, wing span of 30 feet, gross weight of 2,750 pounds, and top speed of 176 miles per hour.
† Curtiss F11C-2 Goshawk fighters entered squadron VF-1B in 1933. The following year the plane was redesignated BF2C to indicate its dual role as both fighter and bomber. The BF2C-1 was 23 feet long, wing span of 32 feet, gross weight of 5,086 pounds, and top speed of 225 miles per hour.

squadron of 18 planes. We actually ordered 27 planes. The order was for 27 planes to keep an 18-plane squadron operating. So this, in effect, was a new experience.

    I well remember the day of the first landings. I went out with two other pilots to make our first landings of the BF2C, and I had a little difficulty. I had made up my mind that I would never fail to get down on the deck. In this particular case, I found myself coming in fast and would have gone into the barrier. I put the plane down on deck; I insisted on getting down on the deck. It hit hard enough to bounce the plane back in the air again, and at the same time my throttle jammed on. By the shock of hitting the deck and the engine revved up, I cleared the barrier but expected to catch it on my hook. I didn't quite and continued flying and went on around and then came back and landed.

Q: Was this your first experience with landing on a carrier?

Admiral Stroop: I had gone out to qualify earlier in the F4B. Actually, as the communicator and squadron navigator, I would not be a regular pilot of either one of those planes. I had what was called the navigation plane, which was a twin-seater Grumman with a radio operator in the back seat. But it was expected that I would fill in in the fighters, too, so I had to qualify in all three of these types: the F4B, the BF2C, and the SF-1.

Q: And did you land all of them on the carrier?

Admiral Stroop: Yes.

Q: How does that feel the first time you ever land a plane on a carrier?

Admiral Stroop: Well, it's a pretty interesting experience. Of course, you feel that the signal officer is making you fly too slowly, because all your life you've been trained to keep plenty of airspeed so you don't spin in. And the signal officer insists on bringing you down to about five knots above stalling speed so you can land as slowly as possible. The old saying goes, "Five knots for you and five knots for your wife," so usually the married officers fly a little faster than the others. Then, of course, the deceleration when you catch the hook is a pretty interesting experience.

Q: The use of the word "interesting"--would it even be scary?

Admiral Stroop: Oh, I suppose if they do like they do the astronauts and take the heartbeat, you'd find it was a little faster. As a matter of fact, this has been done in recent years. It is an interesting point. Out in Vietnam they have adopted some of these techniques that they use with the astronauts for measuring heartbeats. They found that our pilots in Vietnam had a higher heart rate for a carrier landing than they did from the attack they made against enemy targets.

Q: Well, that is certainly noteworthy, isn't it?

Admiral Stroop: Yes. I think carrier aviation even then, certainly today, is the most demanding individual performance of any operation in the military service. The work that these young pilots are called upon to do--the landings, the instrument flying, and the bad weather they fly in now--is just miraculous.

Q: They must have to have a certain kind of personality to make them able to do it at all.

Admiral Stroop: Well, you certainly have to be able to keep your head and be cool and function in an emergency and not panic. You have to have a certain amount of calmness and personal courage.

Q: We're on the Ranger now.

Admiral Stroop: Yes, and Bombing Squadron Five is just qualifying.
    The next day, I recall, the first landing was made by the skipper of the squadron. He skipped all the wires and ran into the barrier and wrecked his airplane. The next man got

aboard all right, Victor Soucek, who was flying there too.* And number three did the same thing the skipper did. His name was Rufus Young, and he hit the barrier.†

Well, this was pretty sad. I had had the experience the day before, you know, going clear over the barrier. Then there were these two planes in the barrier. They decided something was probably wrong either with the training we had had or with the airplane itself. So they stopped the qualifications, and we went back and did some more training. We found a small malfunction; the hook was not staying down close to the deck but would actually snap up and lay against the fuselage. So you were sometimes landing without benefit of the hook. It might catch the wire, and, again, it might not. But with some additional training and some rework of the tension on this gear that held the hook down, we were able to become a successful carrier squadron.

We came around to the West Coast on the Ranger then and came in here at San Diego in 1935. I left Mrs. Stroop, the two children, and her mother in Norfolk. She was about to have another baby. When I left, she was almost due to go to the hospital. Actually, she was two or three weeks late when the baby was born. That was Barbara, our second daughter, who is now married to a submarine officer.

Q: I must say that, as only children, you and Mrs. Stroop both have done very well with your children and your children's children.

Q: Yes, we're 4 and 11 now.

I left Mrs. Stroop in Norfolk with the job of having a baby, packing up the house, and getting the children aboard a transport. When the third child was 27 days old, she got aboard this transport in Norfolk and started around toward California through the canal. In the meantime, I had preceded her and gone on the Ranger and had come through San Diego. We had done some training at San Diego and had gone out to a war game in the Pacific.

---

* Lieutenant (junior grade) Victor H. Soucek, USN.
† Lieutenant Rufus C. Young, Jr., USN.

When she arrived, Mrs. Stroop was without anybody to greet her. But I had rented a house over on Adella Avenue in Coronado and arranged to rent some furniture in addition to what we had coming. We had had the car delivered, so she had her car from the East Coast. That was here, and I brought the dog around on the Ranger. The dog was in a residence down at the boathouse at the naval air station. It was a little cocker spaniel. I had all these preparations made when Mrs. Stroop came with our family and had a place to move into. She was here when I returned from the cruise.

I might mention my first landing on North Island.[*] We had four squadrons, and the senior squadron commander was a man named Felix Stump.[†] In those days, we all thought that occasionally Felix made mistakes, and in this particular case he did make a mistake. We decided we would have a rather spectacular landing, something you never see nowadays. We landed each squadron of planes all together; 18 planes were landing on the field at the same time.

Q: At North Island? I wouldn't think there was that much space.

Admiral Stroop: Oh, for planes in those days it was pretty simple. So we came in, and Felix led the flight in. They had certain field rules that we were briefed on. Many of us had never been on North Island before. Felix brought us in on the wrong course, so we no sooner landed on North Island than we found we were on the mat for violating operating instructions.

Q: Did you all land safely, however?

---

[*] North Island Naval Air Station is on the end of the Coronado peninsula, across the harbor from San Diego.
[†] Lieutenant Commander Felix B. Stump, USN. Later, as a four-star admiral, he served as Commander in Chief Pacific and Commander in Chief U.S. Pacific Fleet, 1953-58.

Admiral Stroop: Oh, yes. The wind wasn't that bad; it was a cross-wind. Felix was coming in on what was called a two-ball course, and he should have been coming in on a one-ball course. I always thought that was rather interesting.

Well, after arriving there . . .

Q: Excuse me. When you were out on the Ranger, you were participating in war games, did you say?

Admiral Stroop: Yes, we had war games in Panama. They, I guess, had all the carriers down there--the "Lex" and "Sara" and the Ranger.

Q: Well, the war games were on your way out here.

Admiral Stroop: Yes, on the way around.

Q: Who was the enemy?

Admiral Stroop: We split the fleet up into two parts, you see, and we always had at least one carrier on one side and one or two carriers on the other side. The patrol squadrons operated too. We worked up a war game that would last about five to ten days.

Q: Your job was flying. Your job did not have anything to do with administration at that time.

Admiral Stroop: No, except within the squadron. I was communication officer for the squadron. I had charge of all the technical gear on occasions, and I was also squadron navigator. I had charge of training the pilots in navigation, and on the long, over-water hops I did the navigating.

In my particular squadron the squadron commander would always have me come up and take the lead and bring the squadron back to the ship. We had very little electronic assistance in those days. As a matter of fact, it was a matter of pride that you didn't even use what you had. We had a homing compass in the airplanes, and it required the carrier to put out a radio signal, and you would home on it. But it was a matter of pride to me that I never needed to use it. With sufficiently accurate dead-reckoning navigation, I always got back.* But I had the advantage of having a radio in the second seat, and I had worked pretty hard at this navigation business. So we always got back all right.

Q: Well, that was probably the most important job in the squadron.

Admiral Stroop: Well, it was interesting.

I had two years in that squadron, flying various types of airplanes and operating from various ships. It was during this period that I operated briefly from the Lexington and also from the Saratoga. Unfortunately, I never had the opportunity to operate from the Langley personally. We were, however, in the same formations with her.

Q: That would have made you have the experience of all the carriers.

Admiral Stroop: That's right. There are almost no aviators left, you know, now that had been on the Langley--the old Langley crowd.

Q: I would wonder if there are any left.

Admiral Stroop: I don't think on active duty. There are some 20 alive who operated from the old Langley.

I came back from that first cruise and found my family here all settled in Coronado and quite happy. It was their first experience with California, and they really loved it. The

---

* Dead reckoning (short for deduced reckoning) is a method of navigation whereby one plots a direction and amount of progress from the last well-determined position. The result, known as the DR position, amounts to the best estimate of one's actual position at a given time.

routine, of course, in those days, 1935 and '36, was extremely pleasant. You worked five days a week, had Saturday and Sunday off, and occasionally they had a Saturday inspection. So you had a lot of time at home. Cruises were not too long: two, three, or four months at a time, not any more than that.

Q: Did the ships go out each day or not?

Admiral Stroop: You would go out just periodically. You'd go out, say, on a Monday and back on Friday. Sometimes you'd go out as long as ten days, but then that was always followed by a period in port. The carrier squadrons and the carriers themselves didn't go out as frequently as the destroyers did. Also, the carriers would go out for their own gunnery practice, and they wouldn't have the squadrons on board. So the squadrons which were based here on North Island had a very good home life. We were very pleased with it. You could consider yourself very fortunate being on sea duty and certainly a lot better than the experiences that the carrier aviators have these days with tremendously long cruises and very hard work in between cruises.

Q: When did flight pay start?

Admiral Stroop: Well, it started as soon as you started flying. We had flight pay that aviation summer after we graduated, for example. Then, when I went for a short period of training, for about six weeks to Norfolk, I had flight pay. The day I reported in to Pensacola I started on flight pay. And I had flight pay from that day continuously until the day I retired. It was a matter of pride that I--even though in later years I wasn't required--got at least four hours every month and usually a good bit more. I think I made my last flight and my last landing the day before I retired. I flew the plane up to L.A. and back.

Q: Did you? I think that's exciting. And what were your duties on the Lexington and how long were you aboard?

Paul D. Stroop #1 - 34

Admiral Stroop: Well, the Lexington was just a platform for an exercise. I don't know just why it is mentioned in there. We went on a little cruise. I don't remember now what it was all about, but I was interested in becoming qualified as an officer of the deck again, so I stood bridge watches on the Lexington as a squadron officer, and I had written into my record that I was qualified as officer of the deck. I had already qualified on the Arkansas, and here I qualified again on a carrier, and I qualified the following year on a cruiser.

Q: I'm sure you asked for all these things.

Admiral Stroop: Oh, yes.

Q: It's interesting, but, of course, you have observed it, too, in people who were successful. They always look out for doing the right thing and for continuing to make the effort to improve their career, rather than sitting and waiting until somebody says, "Why don't you do so-and-so?"

Admiral Stroop: Well, of course, officer of the deck qualification, I always thought, was particularly important, because the ultimate job, really, in the Navy is command of a ship. You have certainly got to have officer of the deck experience before you can go out and command a ship.

Q: Well, the Evans that just had the collision down here with that Australian ship, certainly somebody wasn't watching who should have.[*]

Admiral Stroop: That's right.

---

[*] At 4:15 on the morning of 3 June 1969, during a SEATO naval exercise in the South China Sea, the U.S. destroyer Frank E. Evans (DD-754) was struck and cut in two by the Australian aircraft carrier Melbourne. The bow section of the destroyer sank, resulting in the loss of 74 of her 273 crew members.

Q: So it's really the basic thing, but it just interests me, and it's obvious as you describe your career, that you took every occasion to improve your knowledge and your position to help you become better qualified professionally. You were aware of that, I am sure, every step in your career, were you not?

Admiral Stroop: Well, I don't think you work at it particularly. It just had to become a habit, you see. It was a very natural thing. Well, anyway, that experience on the Lexington was quite short. Not mentioned in your outline here is the fact that I had some little time on the Saratoga.

Q: No, it isn't, not until considerably later is it in mine, not until 1940.

Admiral Stroop: No, it was during the same summer that we operated one time from the Saratoga. Quite frequently in those days, and nowadays the carrier that you normally are attached to is not available, for she might be in the yard for overhaul or out doing something else. Those squadrons are quite flexible, and they must get aboard ship every now and then. So it is quite common nowadays, and it was then, to find squadrons operating temporarily off another ship, maybe just for a day at a time, maybe just going out qualifying pilots for landing. The deck would be made available out here off San Diego, and they'd run half the planes on North Island through it. The "Lex" and "Sara" were big enough that they could operate an extra squadron if need be. I've forgotten just why I was assigned to the "Lex" during that period. Probably the Ranger was in the yard or something like that.

Q: And in the Saratoga was that the same situation?

Admiral Stroop: Yes, the same situation. But, as I recall, I don't think I ever spent more than one or two days on her during that period. But I remember it well, because here I had accumulated another carrier to land on. As a matter of fact, one of my first squadron commanders, McGinnis, was air officer on the Saratoga.* I remember waving to him as I went by.

Q: Then, after this particular period, you were ordered to the USS Portland?†

Admiral Stroop: That's right. I think, as I told you earlier, in those days naval aviators were trained and expected to be versatile. I had had, up through this point, a cruise in seaplanes, flying boats, and I was just completing a two-year cruise on a carrier in carrier aviation. And in those days they operated small seaplanes from cruisers and battleships. So it was my turn, and this was the next thing I needed to do to complete the entire circuit. I might add that generally this type of duty was not very popular with naval aviators. As a matter of fact, Dan Gallery, who was rather colorful, used to call it the year in "purgatory."

So I got ordered to the Portland as senior aviator. We had assigned four airplanes.‡ They were little, single-engine, single-float, twin-seat seaplanes built by Curtiss in Buffalo, New York, and called the SOC-1.§ My number-two aviator was Red Raborn, now Vice Admiral Raborn.** I had another man named Bill Darnell, who retired soon after the war, and another young officer, an ensign at that time, Jimmy Smith.†† There were four of us. We were the four aviators on board, four planes, and I think a very small group of people-- about 18 enlisted men.

---

* Lieutenant Commander Knefler McGinnis, USN.
† The USS Portland (CA-33) was commissioned 23 February 1933. She had a standard displacement of 9,950 tons, was 610 feet long, and 66 feet in the beam. Her top speed was 32.7 knots. She was armed with nine 8-inch guns and eight 5-inch guns. She was eventually decommissioned in 1946 after service in World War II.
‡ This four-plane unit was a detachment from Scouting Squadron 10 (VS-10S).
§ The SOC Seagull was 31 feet long, had a wing span of 36 feet, gross weight of 5,437 pounds, and maximum speed of 165 miles and hour. It was armed with two .30-caliber machine guns.
** Lieutenant (junior grade) William F. Raborn, Jr., USN. From 1955 to 1962, Raborn served as director of the Special Projects Office, which developed the Polaris fleet ballistic missile system. He was promoted to vice admiral in 1960. His Polaris oral history is in the Naval Institute collection.
†† Lieutenant (junior grade) William I. Darnell, USN; Ensign James A. Smith, USN.

Of course, we were intimately concerned with the shipboard life, and we were a minority on board and, in some cases, unpopular. But, here again, I found this to be extremely interesting. We, of course, had an experience being launched, catapulted off the high catapults and being recovered at sea while the ship was under way. You landed as close as you could to the ship, and they had a sled towing from the boom rigged out amidships, with a sort of a net made out of pieces of line all knotted together in the form of a large cargo net which was towed through the water. You drove your airplane up on that, and you had a hook underneath the keel which hooked into the net. Then you cut the engine, and you drifted back and into the net and were picked up by a crane.

Q: You and the plane and everything in the net.

Admiral Stroop: No, not in the net. Then you were attached to the ship through the net, towed along by this hook on the bottom of your float. Then your rear-seat man stood up in the cockpit and unbuckled his belt. A hook was lowered from a crane, and he shackled that hook to a bridle which you had permanently attached to the airplane, and then you were . . .

Q: I see, the net was just to hold you and protect you while you were being . . .

Admiral Stroop: The net towed you through the water and kept you at a constant position with regard to the ship.

Q: So you could be hooked on to it.

Admiral Stroop: So you could be hooked on to it, yes.

Q: What kind of catapults did they use?

Admiral Stroop: These were powder catapults. The early catapults maybe were air catapults, and . . .

Q: Steam?

Admiral Stroop: No.

Q: What do you mean by air catapults?

Admiral Stroop: Well, compressed air. Air was compressed and held in tanks. Then, when a valve was opened, the compressed air was forced against a piston, and the motion was multiplied through cables and sheaves so that the car with the plane attached to it was forced down the catapult track at an accelerating rate of speed.

Q: Was this on the Ranger and the Lexington and on the Saratoga--the same type of catapult?

Admiral Stroop: They had catapults, yes, but they were almost never used. The only ships that used catapults regularly were the cruisers and the battleships because they had to. You see, you couldn't get the flying speed otherwise.

Q: The one on the cruiser--was it on a turntable that itself moved?

Admiral Stroop: That's right. The catapults were mounted on large mounts, and they could be trained in or out. They could be trained parallel with the ship for cruising. If you wanted to launch, you trained them out about 45 degrees on either bow. The ship would be under way when you catapulted, and the ship would take a course which would let you be catapulted, of course, into the wind.

Q: And that was powder?

Admiral Stroop: A powder-actuated catapult; it had a powder charge.

Q: That was the second device. They first used air and then later powder.

Admiral Stroop: And, of course, later steam.

Q: Did you ever hit the water on takeoff?

Admiral Stroop: Oh, no, you were way up high out of the water. We were at the level of the ship's bridge.

Q: Oh, so you did not have the problem of going down and then . . . ?

Admiral Stroop: No. The catapult always gave you plenty of flying speed. That was the standard method of launching and recovery. As I say, you either recovered with the ship under way at sea, or, if the ship went into port, by then you could land on the water and taxi up to be picked up.

Q: That must have been quite an exciting experience--to be picked up while you were still in your airplane.

Admiral Stroop: Oh, it's not really.

Q: Maybe not to you. Well, obviously you had to like it and have an affinity for it, or you couldn't have done it well.

Admiral Stroop: Well, all these three general aspects of aviation, I found them all extremely interesting and challenging.

Q: You use the word "interesting" so frequently that I wonder what it means to you.

Admiral Stroop: Well, just that, I guess. Something that keeps you pleasantly occupied.

Q: Intrigues you mentally and emotionally; you must be sympathetic with it.

Admiral Stroop: The cruiser aviation was, of course, somewhat different from carrier aviation in many respects. On the other hand, here was an opportunity to . . .

Q: And you were in charge of all the planes, and this is the first time you had been actually number-one man.

Admiral Stroop: That's right. This was my first small command.

Q: But it had the perquisites that I'm sure you found pleasant.

Admiral Stroop: Oh, yes. I was sort of department head aboard ship.

Q: Who was the skipper of the Portland?

Admiral Stroop: Captain Willis Bradley.[*] He retired as a captain and later, I believe, became a congressman from the Long Beach district.

Q: And did you have to coordinate your activities with him, or how did the operations actually go?

---

[*] Captain Willis W. Bradley, Jr., USN.

Admiral Stroop: Well, of course, it was a very normal shipboard operation. You had the commanding officer and the executive officer of the ship. We were in the gunnery department.

Q: You were part of the gunnery department?

Admiral Stroop: Part of the gunnery department, because, you see, one of our principal jobs was spotting for gunfire. The other job, of course, was scouting on ahead of the cruiser. We had those two jobs. And I might add . . .

Q: What were you scouting for?

Admiral Stroop: Well, one of the cruiser's jobs was scouting ahead of the fleet, you know. We were looking for submarines, or we were looking for enemy ships?

Q: How far out would you go?

Admiral Stroop: In those days about 200 miles. Now you could go farther. You could go out, say, 250 or 300.

Q: But you were extending the cruiser's facilities an awfully long way.

Admiral Stroop: That's right. And during the time you were gone, you might be flying for four hours, and the cruiser would only move 100 miles, you see. So you were getting out 200 ahead, and we carried in the back seat an observer who was a trained ensign. Most of these people later became naval aviators. This was the way they started out.

Q: And what were you at this time? I had forgotten to ask.

Admiral Stroop: I was still lieutenant (junior grade).

Q: It was interesting that you were still a part of the gunnery department.

Admiral Stroop: Well, this didn't bother me as much as a lot of other people, because I had been in the gunnery department before, you see. I had been in the gunnery department on the Arkansas. When I took the postgraduate course, I had been associated with the gunnery people there in this particular general line school section, so I always had a leaning toward weapons during my early career. So I got along fine with the gunnery department people.

Q: Well, and also again, I think it's interesting to relate it to your subsequent assignments. Every one of these things that you learned certainly fit into the picture of making you qualified to do . . .

Admiral Stroop: I joined the Portland up in Long Beach, and I elected at that time to leave my family to continue to live in Coronado, because we didn't want to be faced with moving, and we were very pleasantly situated. So I lived aboard ship most of that time, except for weekends, when I could get home and for a period in Honolulu.

The Navy Department made the decision that they would start overhauling large ships, one at a time, at the Navy yard in Pearl Harbor. The Portland was the second ship selected. This, of course, was a very fine decision, because it enabled the Navy to build up facilities in the yard at Pearl Harbor that were needed later on. It was considered quite a hardship, because here was a ship which normally would go to a yard in the United States, and the families could be there. You were faced with a personal bill for transporting your family to Honolulu if you could do it at all.

Q: Plus the fact, I would imagine, there might have been some politics involved, and this took work away from the mainland shipyards.

Admiral Stroop: Oh, sure, but, of course, we were not concerned with that. We were ordered to go to Pearl Harbor and went. We solved our personal problem by Having Mrs. Stroop come out. She rode out, I think, on the Lurline, tourist, for $85.00.* I remember this was quite a struggle to scrape that together. We left her mother and our three children back here in Coronado. We had a full-time maid. The maid had a husband that we allowed to live on the place. He did the gardening, and also the pay freeze had been lifted. We got our 15% back, and I think I had gotten one or two fogies by that time.† Since we were still in the Depression of the early '30s, we were doing quite well financially and were able to swing it.

---

* The Lurline was a Matson Lines passenger ship that made regular runs between Hawaii and the West Coast of the United States.
† "Fogy" is slang for an increase in pay because of length of time in service.

Interview Number 2 with Vice Admiral Paul D. Stroop, U.S. Navy (Retired)

Place: Admiral Stroop's home in San Diego, California

Date: Saturday, 13 September 1969

Interviewer: Commander Etta-Belle Kitchen, U.S. Navy (Retired)

Q: I believe we were talking about your assignment on the USS Portland, which was in 1937, I believe, and you were describing going out to Pearl Harbor. Do you want to continue with that, please?

Admiral Stroop: Yes, actually the date we went to Pearl Harbor was in 1936. The Portland was a heavy cruiser. I was senior aviator. We had four airplanes. They were Curtiss scout observation planes called SOC-1s. We were attached to the gunnery department and were considered, of course, regular ship's officers. The commanding officer of the Portland was Captain Willis Bradley. The executive officer was a very wonderful, fine officer named Dan Callaghan. Dan Callaghan was a commander then. He became a captain, naval aide to President Roosevelt.[*] He was an early selectee for rear admiral and was lost off of Savo Island early in the war.[†] He was a wonderful officer.

Q: I think you told me that you didn't have any objection to being attached to the gunnery department because of your previous experience, previous duties.

---

[*] Captain Daniel J. Callaghan, USN, served as naval aide to President Franklin D. Roosevelt from July 1938 to May 1941.
[†] On the night of 12-13 November 1942, Rear Admiral Callaghan was killed during a surface action against Japanese warships near Guadalcanal and Savo islands in the Solomons.

Admiral Stroop: That's right. I had had a good bit of experience in gunnery, and I understood most of their problems. Of course, the job of the planes on board was to spot their main battery, as well as to scout ahead for the ship, scouting operations.

We went to Pearl Harbor to go into overhaul in the Navy yard there. Our ship was the largest ship that had ever been sent to Pearl Harbor for overhaul in the Navy yard. The purpose, of course, was to get that yard into the business of overhauling large ships. I think it was a very sound thing to do, because, of course, the yard and the capabilities were built up, and they were able to repair battle damage at Pearl Harbor much better for this. We spent, I think, four months out there during the overhaul period. It was quite enjoyable.

Q: Where were the planes in the meantime?

Admiral Stroop: The planes were put ashore at Ford Island, right across the harbor from the Navy yard. We operated there as seaplanes. In addition, of course, to our little planes there were, I think, five patrol plane squadrons also based on Ford Island, all operating as seaplanes.

Q: Did you still act as commanding officer of the four planes?

Admiral Stroop: Oh, yes, I was commanding officer of what was called the Portland unit. We lived over there in the BOQ, except, of course, that those of us who were married and had wives out there were living in town.[*] My next junior aviator was Lieutenant (junior grade) Red Raborn and another one named Lieutenant (junior grade) Darnell, and the most junior one was Ensign James Smith, Jimmy Smith. They were all very fine pilots, all different types of individuals. Of course, you know Red Raborn's history. He went on to become father of Polaris and became a vice admiral. When he retired he became the head of the CIA.[†] We are still quite good friends. I see him quite frequently.

---

[*] BOQ--bachelor officers' quarters.
[†] CIA--Central Intelligence Agency.

Q: Is he in this area now?

Admiral Stroop: No, Red is living in Washington. He is vice president of Aerojet General Corporation, and he lives in Washington. He comes out here quite frequently, or I see him back there.

Well, the time in overhaul was very pleasant. We had what in those days were called tropical hours. We went to work at 7:00 o'clock and finished at 1:00. We had every afternoon off and the weekends off.

Q: What were your duties then?

Admiral Stroop: We would start flying around 7:30 in the morning and did familiarization flying and also some gunnery training. It wasn't very difficult. We operated our own schedule and were able to be pretty much our own bosses there. It was an extremely pleasant summer. After we finished overhaul, we came back to the States, based in Long Beach, made trips up and down the coast, and up to San Francisco and down here to San Diego.

Finally, in May 1937, I was detached and went to the Bureau of Aeronautics for my first tour of shore duty.

Q: BuAer was the first shore duty that you had had since you had gone to the Postgraduate School, wasn't it?

Admiral Stroop: Yes, I went to Postgraduate School for two years, but then, of course, you must remember I had a year at Pensacola learning to fly. So that was really shore duty too. You might say that I had had a total of three years of shore duty in 11 years of commissioned service.

Q: What was BuAer like then?

Admiral Stroop: BuAer was a very small outfit. It had been commissioned, of course, in 1921. It was the youngest of the naval bureaus. And it had, compared to today, a handful of officers and civilians.

Q: Was it still making its way in the Navy?

Admiral Stroop: To a certain extent, yes. As a matter of fact, the Bureau of Aeronautics in those days was probably more self-contained than any other bureau. We had our own personnel division, and the allocation of aviators, orders for aviators, were generated right in the BuAer office. And also the airplane programming and budgeting and all that.

Q: The deciding of what planes were to be built? For procurement?

Admiral Stroop: Absolutely. That was all done in the bureau. The Chief of the Bureau of Aeronautics in those days was a very powerful man. He handled all of his own programming, all of his own budgeting. He made his own decisions in selection of airplanes.

Q: Selection of officers as well? Not selection of officers but assignments.

Admiral Stroop: Assignment of officers. The chief of the bureau was Admiral A. B. Cook, who was not an old-time aviator.[*] He had gotten his wings as a captain, I believe, and he was later relieved by Admiral Jack Towers.[†]

Q: You were still there?

---

[*] Rear Admiral Arthur B. Cook, USN, served as Chief of the Bureau of Aeronautics from 12 June 1936 to 1 June 1939.
[†] Rear Admiral John H. Towers, USN, served as chief of the bureau 1 June 1939 to 6 October 1942.

Admiral Stroop: Oh, yes, I worked for Jack Towers. That was the first of three different tours that I served with Jack Towers.

Q: Did the bureau also do its training? Were they also in charge of Pensacola?

Admiral Stroop: Oh, yes, they had a training division, and they handled everything that had to do with naval aviation.

Q: I would think so.

Admiral Stroop: Because here you had one man, the Chief of the Bureau of Aeronautics, in charge of everything that had to do with naval aviation. The success or failure of it depended on him and on his organization, the Bureau of Aeronautics.

Q: And this was men and assignments and training and, in addition, the selection of the airplanes and the building of those and their . . .

Admiral Stroop: That's right, and also the running of the various shore stations. Naval air stations also came under the bureau. All of their appropriations for public works and all of this was the responsibility of the chief of the bureau.

Q: What about the carriers?

Admiral Stroop: The carriers, of course, were built by the Bureau of Ships.* But the aviation characteristics of the carriers were all handled by the Bureau of Aeronautics. We had a section called the Ships Installation Section of the bureau. I had a classmate down in

---

* Effective 20 June 1940, the Bureau of Construction and Repair was merged with the Bureau of Engineering. The new organization was known as the Bureau of Ships.

that outfit, Admiral Jim Russell--Lieutenant Jim Russell then.* He was a very fine, competent officer who had finished the postgraduate course in aeronautical engineering.

My job in the bureau was airplane programming. I had the job of making long-range plans for procurement of aircraft and the immediate job each year of preparing the budget and helping the chief of the bureau to defend the budget. He and I would go up to Congress alone. I would carry a briefcase with the supporting papers and sit behind him and assist him in his testimony before the congressional committees. It was a very fine experience for somebody who was later to become the chief of the bureau.†

Q: Do you remember any anecdotes relating to that, any problems you had?

Admiral Stroop: Well, let me see. We sometimes had some unusual questions. I remember one time Admiral Towers was asked by Congressman Darrow from Pennsylvania about how many parts there were in an airplane.‡ He was trying to lay a foundation for a larger inspecting force, jobs for civil service employees. The admiral turned to me and said, "Do you have any idea how to answer that one?"

I recalled that I had seen some figures in respect to the fact that the dollar cost of the airplane pretty much corresponded with the estimated number of parts. In other words, a $100,000 airplane, which was about the most expensive we had in those days, would have 100,000 parts. So that was the admiral's answer. It brought a little chuckle.

Q: That's interesting, though. Can you pursue that any further? Was that really factual?

Admiral Stroop: Yes, it was really factual. It wouldn't be factual today, because airplanes cost so much more. These airplanes were comparatively inexpensive. I remember a first-

---

* The oral history of Admiral James S. Russell, USN (Ret.), is in the Naval Institute collection.
† Effective 1 December 1959, the Bureau of Aeronautics was merged with the Bureau of Ordnance. The new organization was known as the Bureau of Naval Weapons. Rear Admiral Stroop was the first chief of the new bureau.
‡ Representative George Darrow of Pennsylvania.

run fighter in those days was $50,000. Today the first-run fighters run--well, there's a model of the F-4 there that runs over $2 million. Of course, there's a lot more sophistication, higher speed, more power, and all that.

Q: They didn't know any different.

Admiral Stroop: I remember another incident that impressed me very much. We appeared in those days for authorization of our programs before the Naval Affairs Committee; this was in the 1930s. The chairman of the Naval Affairs Committee was Carl Vinson, who still had many more years to serve in Congress, although he was chairman of the committee when the Democrats were the majority party.[*] It was not Admiral Towers who was testifying that time. There was another admiral who was being asked some questions by a young committee member on the laws relating to tonnage. You remember there were tonnage-limiting laws by agreement with Japan and agreement with Great Britain.

Q: Of ships.

Admiral Stroop: Of ships; that's right. And back of that particular law there were other, earlier laws. Each year, or every two years, the Congress would authorize a certain tonnage of ships for the Navy in various categories. Well, the admiral who was being questioned by the young congressman didn't have really very good answers, and the congressman who was questioning him didn't know anything about it either. So Mr. Vinson banged his gavel down and held school for the admiral, the whole committee, and witnesses. He went back to about 1890 and reviewed all the laws relating to naval tonnage. It was really quite an experience to hear this very learned, capable man--who was a great power in Congress even then--tell all of us just how laws are brought about. He told what they meant, how they

---

[*] Carl Vinson of Georgia entered the House of Representatives in 1913 and was appointed to the Naval Affairs Committee in 1917. He became the ranking Democrat in 1923 and chairman in 1931. When the Armed Services committee was formed in 1947 Vinson became chairman and held that position, except for two short periods when Republicans held the House, until his retirement from Congress in 1965.

were affected by subsequent legislation, and brought us up to date on just how much tonnage was left in the various building categories. Of course, that was what it was all about--authorization for new ships that year.

Q: It's kind of reassuring, though, to think that somebody in Congress has that much knowledge, isn't it?

Admiral Stroop: Well, this man, Vinson, was a remarkable individual. He was very powerful, he had lots of friends, he was very sincere.

Q: A friend of the Navy, I always thought.

Admiral Stroop: A friend of the Navy and a friend of the armed forces. He later became chairman of the Armed Forces Committee. He was a strong advocate of air power, too, for the Air Force.

Q: I was able to get a new barrack for the WAVES in Bainbridge, Maryland, through Mr. Vinson. That was in 1962.[*]

Admiral Stroop: Well, those three years in the Bureau of Aeronautics were extremely busy ones and very interesting ones.

Q: Can you tell me, do you know how many planes the Navy had in those days?

Admiral Stroop: The Navy had 2,000 and the Air Force had 2,000--the same number of planes in each service.[†] One of my jobs, in addition to procuring the planes, was distributing them among the squadrons.

---

[*] WAVES--Women accepted for Voluntary Emergency Service.
[†] At that time it was known as the Army Air Corps. In 1941 it was renamed the Army Air Forces, and in 1947 it became a separate service, the Air Force.

Q: How did you do that?

Admiral Stroop: When the new ones were delivered, I assigned them to squadrons. When they came up for reassignment, I would reassign them, allocate them throughout the Navy. It was fairly simple. I kept charts of the organizations--the carriers, the cruisers, the shore stations--and we had a column of allowances. That is, so many training planes, so many fighting planes, so many dive-bombers. And against that column of allowances I would have figures showing the exact number of planes of each type on board. You tried to keep the allowances and the actual number on board matched up.

Q: Did you work up the table of allowances?

Admiral Stroop: Well, it was worked out by mutual meeting of minds with regard to the shore stations. The assignment of aircraft to squadrons was pretty well fixed. All the carrier squadrons were 18-plane squadrons in those days. The cruisers each had four planes. The battleships had three or four; I've forgotten which.

Q: That was pretty much limited to what they could carry.

Admiral Stroop: That's right, and, of course, the number of planes determined the number of people they had, the number of pilots they had, and that sort of thing. The training squadrons were a little bit different. They came in for negotiations each year, and it depended on the number of hours they had to fly and the number of students that were training. These allowances would vary from year to year.

Then each shore station where naval aviators were stationed would have a number of airplanes for familiarization flying. Every pilot in those days had to fly at least four hours a month for flight pay purposes, and he was encouraged to fly more than that, at least 100 hours a year. So we had to have assigned to these shore stations enough planes to handle that program too. Actually, that's where I had most of the argument, because nobody ever figured they had enough airplanes. They would come in with a letter or personal visit to try to get their allowances raised. Allowances were also determined pretty much by the availability of planes. It was no use to have an allowance of 20 planes when you could assign only 10, you see.

Q: Did you have trouble getting the allocation from Congress?

Admiral Stroop: Generally no. We had a rather simple system of justifying airplanes. The normal age of planes was six years, except the patrol planes ran out a little bit longer. The year before a plane became obsolete we would anticipate its going off the books, and we would ask for new planes that preceding year and get the money. It was rather simple arithmetic.

Occasionally we would run into a situation where a group of planes could be bought one year or the following year. I remember specifically USS Wasp was being built at that time.* Her complement of airplanes--together with the spare planes that we would buy-- amounted to 105. This happened in the year that I left the Bureau of Aeronautics, 1940. Admiral Kimmel was budget officer at the Navy Department, and I remember almost the last appearance I had with him was to argue for inclusion of these 105 planes in the fiscal year 1941 budget, and I lost the argument.† The 105 airplanes were deferred out of that budget.

Q: How did the Wasp ever get any?

---

* The keel for the aircraft carrier Wasp (CV-7) was laid 1 April 1936; she was commissioned 25 April 1940.
† Captain Husband E. Kimmel, USN, served as the Navy budget officer from 1935 to 1938, being promoted to rear admiral in November 1937. From 1938 to 1941 he served at sea in cruisers. In February 1941 he became Commander in Chief U.S. Pacific Fleet and was in that billet when the Japanese attacked Pearl Harbor in December 1941. It is likely that this discussion took place earlier than Admiral Stroop remembered, because the Wasp joined the fleet in 1940.

Admiral Stroop: Well, they were put into the next year, you see. The theory was that by the time the Wasp came along, we would not be delayed, because in those days we were very quick in our purchase and building of airplanes. In the meantime, which happened frequently, squadrons would go into commission without new planes. We would take older planes, and we would use those maybe for two or three months until delivery of new aircraft started.

Q: Were the Navy and Congress sold on aviation by this time in history?

Admiral Stroop: I think the answer there is yes. There were still people who had reservations, but after Pearl Harbor there were no reservations. This was just before Pearl Harbor.

Speaking of Admiral Kimmel, I had the very unusual experience of attending a ceremony where Admiral Nimitz took over as commander in chief of the fleet. Admiral Kimmel, of course, had been relieved summarily by the President, but he came to this ceremony, which I thought was a fine thing for him to do.*

Q: Yes, I'm sure.

Admiral Stroop: After the ceremony was over, I had an opportunity to chat with him and wish him well. He very oddly remembered this incident of the 105 planes for the Wasp, and he said, "Stroop, I surely wish I had let you buy those planes." That's the last time I saw him.

Q: It's a sad thing.

---

* Following the Japanese attack on 7 December 1941, Admiral Kimmel was relieved as Commander in Chief of the Pacific Fleet on 17 December. The interim commander in chief was Vice Admiral William S. Pye, USN. Admiral Chester W. Nimitz, USN, took command on 31 December. For a photo showing the ceremony, see Air Raid: Pearl Harbor! (Annapolis: Naval Institute Press, 1981), page 258.

Admiral Stroop: That tour of duty lasted, I think, a trifle over three years, maybe 37 months.

Q: I had one question. When you told me the number of airplanes, how many aviators were in the Navy in those days?

Admiral Stroop: I don't believe I can answer that. I would say probably 3,000. I don't think any more than that. That's a matter of record. You could get that record, of course.

In the spring of '40 it was obvious that I was going to be leaving the bureau. I was anxious to get away, because I wanted to get back to sea, doing some active flying.

Q: Before you do that, though, did you meet any other people in Washington? You've spoken of Kimmel and Towers and Cook and Vinson. Are there any other people about whom you had anecdotes?

Admiral Stroop: Well, one of the people I worked with rather closely was Commander Savvy Cooke.[*] He was over in the office of the Chief of Naval Operations. He would come to me to help look over some of his long-range plans: how we'd use airplanes, what kind of numbers of airplanes we would put in the long-range war plans. Admiral Cooke was a very brilliant man. He was relieved in 1940 by Commander Forrest Sherman, and I had the same relationship with Forrest Sherman.[†]

Also, rather interestingly enough, the General Board was in existence in those days. The General Board had the job which we now assign the Ship Characteristics Board. They had one officer usually assigned to working on the aircraft side of the business. We had a

---

[*] Commander Charles M. Cooke, Jr., USN. During World War II Cooke was one of the Navy's top planners and eventually became a vice admiral.
[†] Commander Forrest P. Sherman, USN, joined the War Plans Division of OpNav in early 1940. In World War II he was a top planner for Admiral Nimitz in the Pacific. From 1949 to 1951, as a four-star admiral, Sherman served as Chief of Naval Operations.

few admirals over there who had gotten their wings late in their naval careers. One was Admiral Ernest King.[*] Another was Admiral Frederick Horne.[†]

I remember Admiral Horne was working on numbers of airplanes for future war plans, and I thought he was really out of his mind. He came to me and asked how would we work up a 5,000-plane program: "Where would you assign them?" I think that program had just hardly gotten under way in the training stage. Of course, the war was coming, and we were in a limited emergency. Just as I was leaving the bureau to go to sea, they were working on a 10,000-plane program.

Admiral Horne was a very smart, hard-working officer. He was then a rear admiral on the board, and I remember the only other aviator on the board at the time was Ernie King. And Admiral King, of course, had a reputation of being pretty rough and tough.

Q: He was an admiral then?

Admiral Stroop: He was a rear admiral. Admiral Horne was two years younger than Admiral King and two years senior to him at that time.[‡] Both of them being rear admirals, he said one of the things he could do for the Navy was to keep Admiral King under control. It was very interesting to note that within two years Admiral King was four-star Admiral King, commander in chief of the fleet and Chief of Naval Operations, and Admiral Horne was his deputy.

Q: At this time, war had already begun, of course, in Germany.[§]

---

[*] Rear Admiral Ernest J. King, USN, who later, as a four-star admiral and five-star admiral, served as Commander in Chief U.S. Fleet from 1941 to 1945.
[†] Rear Admiral Frederick J. Horne, USN. As a four-star admiral, Horne served as Vice Chief of Naval Operations from 1942 to 1945.
[‡] Horne, who was born 14 February 1880, was in the Naval Academy class of 1899; King, born 23 November 1878, was in the class of 1901.
[§] War was officially declared between Germany and the Allied Powers on 3 September 1939.

Admiral Stroop: Oh, yes, the war had begun in Germany, and we were in what was called a limited emergency. We were actually beginning to build up forces, and that was the reason for the 5,000-plane program and the 10,000-plane program.

Q: Would you explain that more, because you said there were 20,000 planes in the Navy.

Admiral Stroop: No, 2,000. By actual count, there were about 2,020.

Q: I see, and the Air Force had 2,000.

Admiral Stroop: That's right.

Q: And now they were talking about going to 5,000 and 10,000.

Admiral Stroop: That's right. Well, you see, the number of airplanes was authorized by Congress just the way ships were.

Q: Two thousand seems so small I can hardly imagine the Navy having that few.

Admiral Stroop: That's right. Now, I don't know what the legal limitation was in those days, but it was around that 2,000 figure. But you had to keep within that envelope, and what we were talking about when we talked about the 5,000-plane program and the 10,000-plane program was going to Congress, again before Mr. Vinson, and getting legislation passed to authorize this number of airplanes.

You see, in all this budgetary business before the Congress, even today, you have to have authorization for the big purchases before you can even go before the appropriations committees to get the money. Each one of these big items annually is heard four times in Congress, once each before each committee for authorization by each house and once before the House and Senate appropriations committees. You have to pass through all of those hearings to get favorable reports out of Congress before they can even get on the floor of Congress to have the appropriation voted on.

Q: How did you react to Admiral Horne's query about a 5,000-airplane Navy?

Admiral Stroop: Well, it was sort of like pie in the sky. It might be a good idea, but you'd never get it. However, of course, history showed that we did get it. My successor in the Bureau of Aeronautics was a man who drew up all of these plans for expansion of naval aviation, as far as airplanes went. That happened to be Lieutenant George Anderson.[*] I had the great pleasure of having George relieve me on two different jobs. I was asked to go out and pick the best officer I could find for my relief. Since we had the detailing job right there in the bureau, the chief of the bureau could get the man he put his finger on, and it was George Anderson in this particular case.

I remember the last day we were together in the bureau, we had a hearing before Mr. Vinson's committee again. Admiral Towers was the principal witness, the Chief of the Bureau of Aeronautics, and I was, as usual, his principal assistant up there for the hearing. We took George Anderson along. Admiral Towers had my orders for detachment in his office, but he hadn't signed them yet. I had gone ahead with my personal planning and actually had my household goods all packed, and the house was bare. My wife and family were practically sitting on the front steps waiting for me to come home, and yet my orders weren't even signed.

We went up for this hearing before Congress, and I purposely let George Anderson do all the assisting for the admiral in answering the questions. Of course, he did a perfectly splendid job. We went back in a taxicab. (We didn't have official cars then; we rode taxis back and forth to Congress and paid our own way, by the way.) Admiral Towers looked at me and said, "Well, I'll sign your orders." This was because Anderson had done the fine job that he always did.

---

[*] Lieutenant George W. Anderson, Jr., USN. As a four-star admiral, Anderson served as Chief of Naval Operations from 1961 to 1963. His oral history is in the Naval Institute collection.

Q: Isn't it interesting that all of the people who became so very famous and well-known, you really almost all grew up together, didn't you, in your professional life?

Admiral Stroop: Well, the Navy, of course, was a lot smaller then, and I knew practically all the naval aviators in those days--most of them personally and all by name or reputation.

Q: Where was BuAer located?

Admiral Stroop: BuAer was located in the eighth and ninth wings of the old Main Navy Building, right where the Air Systems Command offices are today.[*] As a matter of fact, my office in those days was within 40 feet of the office I occupied later as chief of the bureau.

After that tour of duty in the Bureau of Aeronautics that totaled about 37 months, I was asked if I would join the staff of Captain Aubrey Fitch. Captain Aubrey Fitch had been commanding officer at Pensacola, and he was being ordered to Patrol Wing Two, based in Pearl Harbor, Hawaii.[†] This appeared to me to be a most interesting and pleasant assignment, and, of course, I accepted the nomination with alacrity.

So the spring of 1940 found us headed for Pearl Harbor. We drove across the continent and had commercial passage for my family, consisting of Mrs. Stroop and her mother and three children and myself on the Lurline sailing from Wilmington, California. It happened to be the year of the fair in San Francisco, and we were fortunate enough to ride the Lurline up to San Francisco and stayed there for two days.[‡] We lived on board alongside the dock and went over to the fair. It was very pleasant, and, of course, we went on out to Pearl Harbor.

---

[*] The Navy Department building was at 17th Street and Constitution Avenue in Washington, D.C. The building remained in use until the early 1970s, when President Richard Nixon directed that it be demolished.

[†] Captain Aubrey W. Fitch, USN, became Commander Patrol Wing Two in April 1940. During World War II he reached the rank of vice admiral and served as Deputy Chief of Naval Operations (Air).

[‡] The Golden Gate International Exposition of 1939-40 was staged on man-made Treasure Island in San Francisco Bay. The Navy took over the island in World War II.

This was a very pleasant prospect. We were to get quarters on Ford Island.* I remember Captain Fitch lived in Quarters K, which was still the flag officer's quarters at the head of the island, and we lived right next door in Quarters L. These were new buildings that had been built during my tour of duty in the Bureau of Aeronautics. I had the floor plans and knew that they were very pleasant and adequate. We lived, of course, right on the shore. I was looking forward to a long tour, maybe a couple of years on what was then called sea duty, even though we had quarters. Then I'd probably go to shore duty in Pearl and have maybe four years out there altogether. Well, this didn't happen. We had four very interesting months--124 days, I think it was--before I was ordered back to San Diego.

During that period with Captain Fitch we made some interesting trips. We were just beginning to put some construction on Palmyra Island, Johnston Island, and the Midway islands. This construction consisted of bases for our seaplane squadrons. So the captain, who had responsibility for the seaplane squadrons, called Patrol Wing Two, took us out to visit these places several times. This was very interesting going to these islands, which were then frontiers and later important names in history in World War II.

Q: What was the concept? Was the atmosphere there of a buildup for impending trouble, or what was the . . . ?

Admiral Stroop: Yes, we were beginning to think about the limited emergency, and we were building bases on each one of these islands. We started out at Midway and Johnston islands, building just seaplane bases, because they all had a natural harbor or lagoon. The concept was to be able to base up to a squadron or, in an emergency, two squadrons of seaplanes. Then in the beginning they also planned on putting landing strips on them, particularly on Midway, and, of course, that construction came along quite fast.

Q: Was any of that done during your time?

---

* Ford Island is in the center of Pearl Harbor; it was then the site of a naval air station and contained berths for carriers, battleships, and cruisers.

Admiral Stroop: Well, they were starting it during our time. But, as I say, a good bit oriented toward seaplane operations.

Q: Was your trip just to take a look?

Admiral Stroop: That's right. The construction thing was being done by civilian construction companies, and it was being actually supervised in detail by the Navy Department. The Civil Engineer Corps was in charge, but since we were going to operate the bases, we were very much interested in how it was going and so forth.

Q: What kind of planes did you fly out--seaplanes?

Admiral Stroop: We had a large experimental four-engine plane called the XPBS, Sikorsky, and that was the flag plane for our group. They used that on two occasions, and another time we took our flagship, which was the tender Wright, and actually went by ship. This, of course, took several days to take that trip around.

Q: What was the limit, at this time, that these planes could make?

Admiral Stroop: Well, let's see. They were capable of flying from the West Coast to Honolulu, over 2,000 miles.

Q: When was the first Pan Am flight that went? Was that '37?[*]

Admiral Stroop: Pan Am was flying in those days. As a matter of fact, it was rather interesting to note that we sort of shared the base at Midway with Pan American. Pan American had gone ashore there and built a seaplane base and had a small hotel. This was, of course, in 1940 when we went out there to inspect. We even had some limited seaplane

---

[*] An S-42 flying boat made the first San Francisco-to-Honolulu flight for Pan American World Airways in April 1935.

operations. In war gaming we would base at Midway and actually stayed in the hotel at Midway.

Q: But didn't the first Pan Am flight go nonstop in '37 to Pearl?

Admiral Stroop: That would be about right. They had been flying about that long, I guess. They were operating the clippers then, the big Martin clippers.

Q: This was very early in the time when a plane could even fly that far, when you were out there in '39 or '40.

Admiral Stroop: This was still unusual, but Pan American had service to Guam and the Philippines in those days.

Q: Did you have a war atmosphere feeling of your own?

Admiral Stroop: It was beginning to come up. We had what was called a limited emergency. As a matter of fact, soon after we left Pearl Harbor, the following year they set up long-range seaplane patrols out at Pearl Harbor. These were the patrols which missed the Japanese fleet coming in.

Q: How far did they go?

Admiral Stroop: They were going out about 400 miles--about 400 miles out and 400 miles back. A long day's flight in those days.

Q: How did you happen to have such a short tour there?

Admiral Stroop: Captain Fitch, when he went out, was on the selection list for admiral. About two months after he got there, he made his number and became a two-star admiral.

He was ordered back to San Diego to be commander of Carrier Division One, the Lexington and the Saratoga. He was relieved by Admiral Patrick Bellinger, who was still in command at the time of the Pearl Harbor attack.[*] Admiral Fitch selected as his chief staff officer Lieutenant Commander Cornwell, later to become Rear Admiral Cornwell.[†] His flag lieutenant and aide was Lieutenant Monroe.[‡] The three of us--Cornwell, Monroe, and Stroop--were asked to come back to San Diego to form the nucleus of the staff for Commander Carrier Division One.

Q: Did that disappoint you, to come back so fast?

Admiral Stroop: Yes, we were enjoying life in Pearl Harbor and enjoying our first set of government quarters, you know. I had gotten my children in school, and the dog had just finished quarantine, which took 120 days. The dog had been home four days.

Q: That's why you can remember the days without any trouble.

Admiral Stroop: And four days later we were on a ship coming back to San Diego. We came back here in the fall of 1940, took the children out of school, and reestablished them in the Coronado school. We rented a house over on Adella Avenue, and that's where we were located when Pearl Harbor came along. We were operating from the Saratoga and the Lexington.

Q: What was your job on that staff?

Admiral Stroop: I was flag secretary and tactical officer for Admiral Fitch. Lieutenant Commander Cornwell was still the chief staff officer, and Jack Monroe was still the flag lieutenant. Of course, the staff got a little bigger. We had Captain Bowen--Lieutenant

---

[*] Rear Admiral Patrick N. L. Bellinger, USN.
[†] Lieutenant Commander Delbert S. Cornwell, USN.
[‡] Lieutenant Jack P. Monroe, USN.

Bowen then--as communication officer, I remember.* I remember a number of ensigns for communication duties. We were occupying the administration building at North Island, where I later had my office as Commander Naval Air Force Pacific Fleet before I retired.†

Q: Were you ashore?

Admiral Stroop: We had an office ashore at San Diego, and we were not only doing the job of Commander Carrier Division One but also doing some of the work for what is now Commander Air Force Pacific Fleet. That was because during this period of limited emergency the main command, which was at that time Admiral Halsey, had shifted out to Pearl Harbor.‡ He had established his headquarters at Pearl Harbor and left some of his logistics people back in San Diego. So we really had two jobs there, and in order to carry out those jobs properly, we had to be based ashore except when we went aboard the ships for operations at sea.

Q: Which was the first ship you were aboard, the Saratoga?

Admiral Stroop: I believe so. We shifted from the Lexington to the Saratoga, depending on what the operations were. We also had headquarters ashore.

Q: Can you describe the operations of the Saratoga and the Lexington?

Admiral Stroop: In those days those two ships were the only two modern carriers we had. They were homeported in Long Beach, and the squadrons were based over here at North Island.

---

* Lieutenant John B. Bowen, Jr., USN.
† Vice Admiral Stroop served as ComNavAirPac from 30 November 1962 to 30 October 1965.
‡ Vice Admiral William F. Halsey, Jr., USN, served as Commander Aircraft Battle Force and Commander Carrier Division Two from June 1940 to April 1942, when his title was changed to Commander Carriers Pacific.

Periodically the squadrons would be called upon to go out aboard ship and participate in maneuvers. But generally it was a shore-based situation. Then, as tension grew greater, at least one of the ships was always out at Pearl Harbor, so we didn't have her here under our control.

Actually, at the time of Pearl Harbor you may recall the Lexington was out operating off of Pearl Harbor.[*] The Saratoga on Sunday the seventh of December was actually at sea off San Diego, qualifying aviators right here off Point Loma, which was a rather unusual situation on a Sunday.[†] That's a sort of a working day job you would have done during the working week. When we got the news of Pearl Harbor, we stopped the qualification and brought the Saratoga back in port and got her ready to deploy, which we did the next day, Monday.

Q: Who was the commanding officer of the Saratoga?

Admiral Stroop: His name was Douglas, and the commanding officer of the Lexington was Ted Sherman.[‡] Ted Sherman was to remain in command until she was sunk.[§]

Q: There were both part of Carrier Division One.

Admiral Stroop: That's right. Those were the two ships.

Q: The two made Carrier Division One.

Admiral Stroop: They made Carrier Division One. That's right.

---

[*] On 7 December 1941 the Lexington was transporting Marine Corps aircraft to Midway Island.
[†] On 7 December 1941 the Saratoga was just entering San Diego after a period in dry dock at the Puget Sound Navy Yard.
[‡] Captain Archibald H. Douglas, USN; Captain Frederick C. Sherman, USN.
[§] The Lexington was sunk 8 May 1942 during the Battle of the Coral Sea.

Q: Where were you when Pearl Harbor happened?

Admiral Stroop: I was in Coronado.

Q: Can you remember the day and what you were doing?

Admiral Stroop: Very much so. I was playing golf with the communications officer, Bowen. We were on the sixth hole over here at the Coronado Golf Course, which is now made up into a housing development. We had each hit very good drives, and we saw a man come running across the golf course and wondered what he wanted. It was Admiral Fitch. He knew approximately where we were. He had parked his car by the fence and had gotten out and came running across the golf course to tell us that the attack had occurred.

Q: What did he say? Do you remember his words?

Admiral Stroop: I think probably, "The Japs are bombing Pearl Harbor. We're at war. Come with me." I remember that because I got in the car with him and went right to the office in my golf shoes. I remember I had my golf shoes on all day long around the office there at North Island.

Q: Can you remember how you felt at that time, what your thoughts were?

Admiral Stroop: Well, of course, we were surprised and shocked and particularly concerned about the damage reports that were coming in and wondering what kind of a follow-up attack there would be. Then, of course, we were concerned about what we should be doing.

Q: Did you know how much damage was done? How long did it take to find that out?

Admiral Stroop: We didn't know the extent of the damage, really, until about the third day after that.

Q: But you did know that soon.

Admiral Stroop: Yes. We got the word at sea.

Q: Was there any exhilaration about it--that here it is, finally it has come, or . . . ?

Admiral Stroop: I wouldn't say there was exhilaration. We just knew that we were in for a bad fight, and it was probably going to be a bad war. We had every feeling that we would ultimately win, but on the other hand we didn't have any overconfidence about a quick victory, particularly after the Japs had been able to do what they did in the initial blows.

I remember as the day wore on there, we felt that we should be getting the Saratoga out to the war zone. I personally wrote up the dispatch that was what you might call a self-killer. It said that unless otherwise directed, ComCarDiv 1 and staff would embark in Saratoga and proceed the next day for Pearl Harbor, which we did. I don't recall that Commander in Chief Pacific Fleet even replied to that dispatch, but we had sent it and assumed he had gotten it.

We brought the Saratoga into San Diego, alongside the dock, and began loading right away to go to Pearl Harbor. We sailed about 8:00 or 9:00 o'clock Monday morning for Pearl. We put an extra squadron of planes on board. We didn't have enough destroyers around San Diego to give us ASW protection going out to Pearl; they had all deployed with the Hawaiian detachment.* So we took four destroyers from what was called the sound school there, the forerunner of the ASW school, and these were four very old four-pipers.

---

* ASW--antisubmarine warfare. In October 1939 the Navy Department directed the establishment of a Hawaiian Detachment of the U.S. Fleet, which was then based in California. In the spring of 1940 the bulk of the fleet remained in Hawaii after going there for Fleet Problem XXI. Thus the major ships of the U.S. Pacific Fleet were operating out of Pearl Harbor at the time the Japanese struck in December 1941.

Paul D. Stroop #2 - 68

Q: Could they keep up with you?

Admiral Stroop: Oh, yes, they always managed to match our speeds. But they, of course, were very short-legged. They had to be refueled on the way out. They made very fine sonar or ASW destroyers, because their mission in life was running the sonar school there. They had fine technicians on board operating sonar, so we felt quite good about that. That was included in our dispatch to Commander in Chief Pacific Fleet. It said we were also going to take these destroyers out with us to Pearl Harbor.

Q: Who made the decisions that day?

Admiral Stroop: Well, Admiral Fitch made the decisions. The staff recommended them. You see, I wrote the dispatch which . . .

Q: Whose was the idea to take the destroyers from the sonar school?

Admiral Stroop: Well, it was the only sensible thing to do. Admiral Fitch was senior officer present in San Diego, so he issued the orders. There was no problem over that. We got under way the next morning with the destroyers and headed out.

Q: What lights? Dark lights? Did you have any running lights during the trip?

Admiral Stroop: We would darken the ship at night, but we left San Diego in daylight.

Q: How long did it take you to get there?

Admiral Stroop: It took, I think, about seven days. We started naturally for the shortest trip to Pearl Harbor, which takes you between Oahu and Molokai--they call it the Molokai Channel. About halfway out they said we were to approach south of Hawaii. They didn't want the ships to be seen, and they figured that if there were any Japanese submarines around they would be in those channels. So we then laid a course to the island of Hawaii 100 miles distant so we couldn't be sighted from shore, from up high in the mountains, and came into Pearl Harbor from the southeast.

I remember we were approaching Pearl Harbor just about dark in the evening. That evening--I think about the seventh day at sea--we were told to stay at sea during the night. We had to keep up speed for submarine protection, you see, so I laid out the courses to follow during the night and to be at the entrance again early in the morning.

Q: Like a familiar holding pattern of airplanes.

Admiral Stroop: That's right. Exactly the same thing. We had a rather unusual incident, which I am sure never made any of the history books. About midnight the night we were off Pearl, waiting to enter the next morning, the chief engineer of the ship came up to the flag bridge. That was quite unusual, because usually he communicated through the captain. He was shaking and white and he said, "You know, we're never going to make it."

We asked him, "What's the matter?"

He said, "We haven't got enough fuel to get into Pearl Harbor." He explained that in the years gone by in the engineering competition some of the tankers had been systematically cheating the Saratoga on oil. He said they had been pumping in salt water, and that was his story. Anyway, the tanks which he thought had plenty of oil had salt water. This was a pretty horrifying thing, you know, because . . .

Q: He had just discovered it at that time?

Admiral Stroop: I think he had known about it, but he kept quiet about it, because he had figured we were going to be in the night before. If he had gotten into Pearl Harbor, I think we would have been all right. I had to change my plans for the rest of the night, and I started back for Pearl Harbor immediately. We got the ship turned around, started back for Pearl. We began some rather desperate measures. The Saratoga had lots of small oil tanks all throughout the ship that had been used just for ballast. We began pumping oil out of those and found some of this was sludge. It had to be heated up with steam, you know, to make it flow. Then, of course, they had some tanks full of diesel oil for the ship's boats. They took advantage of that, and we finally made it into Pearl Harbor.*

Q: Was it your job to meet this emergency?

Admiral Stroop: No, it was the job of the ship. My job was as tactical officer. I was the staff officer, and I laid out the courses to get back into Pearl as quickly as possible. That was my job.

Q: Then you did make it, of course. Was it close?

Admiral Stroop: We got back in; yes, it was very close. The Saratoga had 12 boilers, as I recall. We had had eight on the line during the night, and just as we got a couple of lines over, these boilers all lost their oil. It was that close.

Q: Good heavens. I surely never read it in any of the things . . .

Admiral Stroop: Oh, no, you'll never see it. It was just an incident early in the war, something that would go unreported.

Q: But if you hadn't made it, it would have been tragedy.

Admiral Stroop: Well, I don't know. That would have put the Saratoga under tow, and in a very disgraceful manner we would have been towed into Pearl Harbor.

---

* The executive officer of the Saratoga at the time was Commander Alfred M. Pride, USN, who eventually retired as an admiral. He told a somewhat different version of this story in his Naval Institute oral history. A portion of it was published in U.S. Naval Institute Proceedings, May 1985, page 382.

Q: But also you would have made yourself a very handsome target.

Admiral Stroop: That's right, but I don't think that there were Japanese submarines around there. I don't know, of course. A ship dead in the water out there was a dead duck for any enterprising enemy submarine skipper, and they could let us have it.

So we came into Pearl.

Q: Why did you say they didn't want you to come in until then?

Admiral Stroop: I never knew why they kept us out the previous night. Maybe the berth wasn't ready. I said that we got the news on Pearl about three days out. Actually, we got it just before we rounded Hawaii. Some other ships from Pearl Harbor joined up. There was a cruiser which joined up with us and a couple of other destroyers. I remember either the skipper of the cruiser or the admiral on board sent a long personal message over, describing the damage, because he had witnessed it, you see, at Pearl Harbor. And Pearl Harbor, of course, was a very shocking sight to witness when we finally entered in.

Q: No matter what you had been told, I am sure you weren't prepared for it.

Admiral Stroop: Of course, one of the things you noticed immediately was the oil on the water. You see, the battleships had been torpedoed, and the tanks had ruptured. There must have been one or two inches of oil sludge all over the surface of Pearl Harbor. Everything was black. As you came in, the first ship that you noticed was the Nevada. She had started out of the harbor with the chief quartermaster at the helm and just a watch on board, you know.

Q: I didn't know that any ships tried to get under way.

Admiral Stroop: Yes, she got under way, and she was bombed just as she was passing Ford Island. The acting commanding officer, whoever he was, ran her aground abeam of Hospital Point.

Q: An enlisted man?

Admiral Stroop: I heard it was a chief quartermaster who did this, though actually I am sure there were officers up there too. Anyway, there was a chief quartermaster at the helm, and he was the one that spun the wheel and ran her ashore there to keep her from sinking. They didn't want to block the channel, which was probably a very smart thing to do.

Then we came on in and saw all the rest of the damage. The West Virginia, I remember, was sitting on the bottom. I've got a picture here someplace of all that damage, taken by the Japanese. The Oklahoma had been torpedoed and turned over. The Arizona, of course, was the most badly damaged. She was a hulk. But her hull is still sitting on the bottom, of course, and is a national memorial. All of the bodies are still in the ship.

Then, on the other side of the island, the Utah had been sunk. She was a former battleship used as a target. She had special strengthening sheathing on her deck to stand practice bombs. The tender Oglala had been sunk. A couple of destroyers in dry dock had been badly damaged. The California was sitting on the bottom, right close to the office that was later to become our headquarters. I remember that so well, because we watched the salvage operations with much interest. We would walk over there every evening at dusk to see how they were coming along.

Q: She was eventually towed back to the West Coast, wasn't she?

Admiral Stroop: I think so.* Every one of those ships except the Arizona and Utah were raised. They, of course, are still there. The Oklahoma was the last one to be floated. They

---

*On 25 March 1942, the California (BB-44) was refloated and drydocked at Pearl Harbor for repairs. On 7 June she departed under her own power for repairs and reconstruction at the Puget Sound Navy Yard.

had to turn her over, because she was upside down, and they rotated her hull. This took many months. They finally got her afloat and put her out in Pearl Harbor. After the war they started her back to the States to be salvaged, and she was lost on the way back.[*]

Q: Can you remember your feelings? Can you describe them?

Admiral Stroop: Well, of course, we had been prepared by a few dispatches and also by the message which we had gotten when the ship joined up, so that we knew pretty well what to expect, but it was still pretty shocking what had happened there.

Q: Were the men lined up on the deck as you went in?

Admiral Stroop: I don't think so. I don't recall. They weren't much for ceremony at that particular time.

Q: I mean to just be looking.

Admiral Stroop: Oh, yes, everybody was out and watching to see what they could see. We found a very, very dispirited group of officers around Pearl Harbor. Really, they were discouraged. They were still in a state of shock, and it was not a pleasant situation.

Q: Do you remember any of the officers?

Admiral Stroop: Admiral Kimmel, of course, had been summarily relieved by the President, as had General Short.[†] Vice Admiral Pye, who was Commander Battle Force, the

---

[*] The Oklahoma (BB-37) was refloated on 3 November 1943 and put into dry dock for repairs. Her hull sank on 17 May 1947 while being towed to the West Coast. For details on the ship's salvage, see "OKLAHOMA: Up from the Mud at Pearl Harbor," U.S. Naval Institute Proceedings, December 1975, pages 46-59.

[†] Lieutenant General Walter Short, USA, had been the commanding general of the Army's Hawaiian Department.

commander of all battleships, was acting commander in chief of the fleet. He was to be relieved in a few days, or maybe a week, later by Admiral Nimitz, who was promoted from Chief of the Bureau of Navigation to this particular job. I said earlier that I was privileged to attend that little ceremony.

Q: Where did that take place?

Admiral Stroop: That ceremony took place late in December, right in front of the Submarine Force headquarters building in Pearl Harbor.* The only people that were asked to attend the ceremony were the principals, one or two members of the admiral's staff, and all the flag officers in the area. The flag officers each took an aide over, and I went as an aide to Admiral Fitch. There weren't more than 12 of us involved.

Q: That was a memorable experience, of course.

Admiral Stroop: On this occasion, as I recall, Admiral Nimitz read his orders for commanding the fleet, and Admiral Kimmel came down in a suit of whites and just sort of stood in the background. He wasn't a part of the ceremony, just a sort of a witness. But after the ceremony was over--the official part of it didn't last more than five minutes-- Admiral Kimmel made a little speech about the state of the fleet and tried to inspire people, especially to tell them that everything was going to come out all right. It was after that that I went around to shake his hand, and he told me he was sorry he hadn't bought those planes for the Wasp when he was the budget officer.

Q: It must have been an extremely sad experience.

Admiral Stroop: It was a very sad thing, because, of course, the general situation was bad, and Kimmel had been summarily relieved by President Roosevelt, which we all felt wasn't

---

* Commander in Chief Pacific Fleet had his headquarters in the Submarine Force headquarters building at the time.

called for. He was a fine officer and very sincere, very capable. He may have made mistakes in interpreting intelligence, but I think the major mistakes were made right back in Washington in the interpretation of intelligence.

Q: Or in failing to get this to him.

Admiral Stroop: That's right. They had more information in Washington than he certainly had.

Q: Did you ever feel that it was permitted to happen?

Admiral Stroop: No, I don't think so. I've heard that theory too. No, I don't think it was permitted to happen. I don't think our people could have planned it that way.

Q: I don't mean military people, but historians maybe distort . . .

Admiral Stroop: No, I don't think so. They talk about this and about the possibility of it, and, of course, the fact that it did accomplish a purpose. It mobilized the whole country immediately, cemented everybody into a unified position. We were going to go to war, we were going to mobilize and suffer whatever we had to and work hard and win this war. It did that, and so the historians, some of them, are apt to surmise that this was planned on the part of high officials of our government. I don't think so.

Q: You say you think the summary dismissal of Kimmel wasn't called for.

Admiral Stroop: I don't think so. He was a very fine naval officer, he was conscientious, he worked hard, he was a good leader, he was respected, and I think eight officers out of ten would have been caught in exactly the same way.

Q: You feel the fault was not his. Do you think he would have been able to organize and plan and carry out the war in the Pacific to its conclusion as well as Admiral Nimitz did?

Admiral Stroop: No, I don't think so. Admiral Nimitz was a very fortunate choice.

Q: Do you know why Admiral Nimitz was selected or how he was selected? After all, he was the chief of the bureau, immediately selected over the heads of how many officers?

Admiral Stroop: Well, he must have been about halfway up on the flag list at that time. The chief of the bureau in those days was a rear admiral. So there were vice admirals, and there were even full admirals ahead of him that had to be considered.

Q: Do you know why he was selected or who selected him or how he happened to be selected?

Admiral Stroop: I suppose he was selected by the Chief of Naval Operations, the Secretary of the Navy, and the President of the united States.

Q: Why him?

Admiral Stroop: Well, I think his abilities were to a certain degree recognized. He happened to be on hand there in Washington, and he could be spared. I don't know what he did personally about it, but I am sure he was highly honored to get the job.

Q: Do you think he volunteered?

Admiral Stroop: Of course he did.

Q: Of course he did?

Admiral Stroop: Why wouldn't he? I'm sure he did.

Q: I think anyone would be terrified of that responsibility.

Admiral Stroop: Well, Admiral Nimitz was a modest man, and I think "volunteer" is probably the wrong word, but he surely didn't shy away from it. I think he was personally very honored to get the assignment. Knowing Admiral Nimitz, I'm sure he didn't come up and say, "I'm the only man who can do it." He wouldn't do that. It wouldn't be like him at all, but on the other hand he was there and available, and he sure didn't turn it down or anything like that or argue against going. He was a fine choice for the job.

Q: Do you remember what he looked like on that day and what he said?

Admiral Stroop: Well, I never did see much change in Admiral Nimitz. I think it was the first time I remember ever seeing him. I saw him later on during the war a number of times, and he looked to me about the same as he did the last time I saw him up here in San Francisco. I had a number of very interesting experiences with him later on, which I will get to as time goes by.

Q: Everyone was in whites that day, however.

Admiral Stroop: Yes, we were in whites, and, as I say, it was quite a short ceremony, and everybody went back to their duties.

Q: What time of day was it?

Admiral Stroop: I think about 10:00 o'clock in the morning.

Q: Was the weather . . . ?

Admiral Stroop: Nice, beautiful day, a pleasant day.

Q: Things were already being started to be cleaned up, I'm sure.

Admiral Stroop: Yes. You'll have to check the date on it, but it must have been around . . .

Q: I have the date as Christmas Day in 1941 that he took over the base.

Admiral Stroop: No, it wasn't Christmas Day, because I wasn't there Christmas Day.

Q: Could he have arrived on Christmas Day and then taken over on the 31st? Would that be . . . ?

Admiral Stroop: That might have been right. It might have been between Christmas and New Year's, because it was about the middle of December. No, it was about the 20th of December when Admiral Pye was still in command of the fleet that we held a conference with Admiral Fletcher's flagship, I think, and received orders to go out to relieve Wake Island.[*] On this occasion we sailed on the Saratoga and went out with the Tangier, one of the aviation tenders in company with radar aboard which they wanted to put up on Wake Island and with some more military personnel for Wake Island.[†]

We had a squadron of Marine fighters loaded on the Saratoga to take out there. We headed for Wake and were within one day of carrying out our mission when the attack occurred on Wake Island. I remember this very distinctly, because around 2:00 o'clock in the morning, after we laid plans to have an early morning launch of aircraft to get onto

---

[*] Rear Admiral Frank Jack Fletcher, USN, Commander Cruiser Division Six.
[†] The Saratoga's task force left Pearl Harbor on the morning of 16 December, bound for Wake Island.

Wake Island and to attack the Japanese forces, we were ordered by Admiral Pye to turn around and go back to Pearl Harbor.

Q: Who was the skipper on Saratoga then?

Admiral Stroop: Still Captain Douglas, as I recall.

Q: How did you feel when you got these orders to come back?

Admiral Stroop: Well, we were very, very much disappointed. Actually, as far as we knew and I think it's right, we were unsighted, and we were in about the same relative position to Wake Island as the Japanese were to Oahu at that time of the morning, northwest. We were running in with our deckload of aircraft all loaded and ready to go, plus an extra squadron of Marine fighters who were to carry out their attack and then land and be based at Wake.

I felt that we were going to surprise the Japanese forces which were coming up from the southeast and probably had superior air power, plus the element of surprise. It would have been a very modest victory, but we would have sunk some Japanese cruisers and probably some other ships in their attacking force--landing craft and that sort of thing. I think we would have gotten our forces ashore on Wake Island and probably would have gotten the large group of civilians off. That was one of our jobs, you know, to remove all the civilian workmen that were there carrying out this construction work that I mentioned earlier.

Q: I have friends that were taken as prisoners there on Wake Island.

Admiral Stroop: Well, I know that we would have done a lot of good if we had gone in. Whether we would have been able to successfully get the civilians off, I don't know. That would depend on how the early part of the fight went. But the plan, of course, was to relieve the garrison, to destroy what we could of the attacking force, to get the civilians all off, and to leave ashore for early warning that very important radar which we had in pieces on the AV.* But we were ordered to turn around and come back. The reason for it, of course, was to make sure that what carriers we had left in the Pacific remained afloat. The Saratoga was there, the Lexington was one day behind us, and I think the Enterprise was one day behind her.

Q: All going on the same post?

Admiral Stroop: Yes, they were all headed for Wake Island. This development--the attack on Wake--of course was not anticipated when we left Pearl Harbor for that day. We knew we were in a precarious position, but the intelligence on the attack began to develop as soon as we got out there. Then, I think about 2:00 o'clock in the morning before we were to go in that day, we began to get positive knowledge of the attack.

Q: How do people act when they are disappointed?

Admiral Stroop: Well, they are very glum. There were pretty bitter words about the people who ordered this, specifically Admiral Pye.

Q: Well, what did they say?

Admiral Stroop: We thought it wasn't the thing to do. We felt we could have carried out our mission. Well, at any rate, it was a heart-breaking thing to listen to the results of what went on that day and, I guess, the next day. Actually, we were on the ship when the message came in that the enemy had landed and "issue in doubt." This was the Marines' last message: "Issue in doubt."†

---

* AV was the designation for a seaplane tender.
† For details on the plight of the Marines, see Robert J. Cressman, "A Magnificent Fight": The Battle for Wake Island (Annapolis: Naval Institute Press, 1995).

Q: Were you flying then?

Admiral Stroop: No, I was attached to the admiral's staff.

Q: You were still tactical officer.

Admiral Stroop: We came around after . . .

Q: What was your rank? What grade were you?

Admiral Stroop: Lieutenant commander. I took my examinations for lieutenant commander just before I left the Bureau of Aeronautics. It was rather interesting--there were two or three of us who were coming up. Jim Russell was another one. We studied hard and took our examination. This was the last promotion examination given until after the war.

Q: I was on the board that gave the first Navy WAVE promotions after the war. So I remember that that was true; they felt kind of cheated.

Admiral Stroop: We felt pretty sat upon. We took the examinations, and we got promoted a few months later, during this very short term of duty at Pearl. I was a lieutenant commander at this time. I guess it was a year later I made commander. Two years later I made captain. Things moved along pretty fast.
    We came back in to Pearl and were pretty glum about the whole business.

Q: Did the people in Pearl know what had happened also?

Admiral Stroop: Well, the people I was associated with did, because I had been working with Admiral Nimitz's staff. They all knew. Of course, there were reasons for it.

Q: That had been really just almost immediately before Admiral Nimitz took over.

Admiral Stroop: Yes.

Q: I wonder if Admiral Nimitz had been in charge then, if he would have given those orders.

Admiral Stroop: I doubt it. I like to think that Admiral Nimitz would have taken a chance and let us go on in. He might at least have let us make the initial attack and see how things were going. He might not have carried on through all the plans that we had to relieve the garrison on the island and get the civilians off.

This would have depended on many things--among other things, the fate of the AV. This was the slow ship--18 knots, you know--that was supposed to take these people off. I personally felt that under the circumstances we probably would have lost the AV. I think if we had tried to run her in to Wake Island and put her in that area where the Japs would know where she was from their shore-based planes, she had very little chance of carrying out her mission. But we would have gone ahead and tried to do it and tried to give them protection from the carrier. Of course, they could move pretty fast. They wouldn't have had to stay anchored there at Wake Island very long, probably only a few hours.

Q: As far as the Japanese, I would assume, based on what we did later in the war, we could have done an awful lot of damage because of the surprise.

Admiral Stroop: Of course, we had only one carrier in the force. How effective we would have been that first day, I don't know. The following day, the Lexington was right behind. We would have had her, and I don't think it would have lasted over two days. I think the issue would have been decided and the Japanese forces at sea would have been defeated and turned back. What the decision would have been, I don't know, but we might have rather properly decided to evacuate everybody from Wake Island rather than leave a garrison there at all, because it was essentially indefensible, really, with the forces we had over a continued period of time. We might have held control of it for two or three days. But this is all conjecture. I think that Nimitz would have told us to go ahead, but he hadn't taken command. Pye was in command. It was when we came back during this next week that Pye was relieved by Nimitz.

Q: He's a name that unless you just happened to have known of his time in history is pretty much unknown.

Admiral Stroop: William S. Pye. He had a son in the class of 1928, Bill Pye.[*]

Well, we came back into Pearl. Admiral Halsey was shored-based at Pearl and was Commander Aircraft Battle Force. That's the title that is now called Commander Naval Air Force Pacific Fleet. He had taken a part of his staff and embarked in Enterprise. Although the job that he had was sort of a material job, a supporting job, a training job, he had sort of summarily cut out this job at sea himself. So he went to sea with the operating part of the staff.

He ordered our staff--Admiral Fitch and the rest of us--over to fill in the void on Ford Island. So we had all of the material people. We had to work for Admiral Halsey, plus our little tactical staff, and for the next three months we performed shore jobs there and we based actually at Pearl Harbor. Admiral Fitch moved back into Quarters K, where he had been the year before, and set up a bachelor mess. I was part of the mess. There was Cornwell and Jack Monroe and a classmate, Fitzhugh Lee, who's retired over in Coronado.[†] He joined the staff at that time. We were there about three months.

Q: So you weren't on the Saratoga when she was torpedoed.

---

[*] Lieutenant William S. Pye, Jr., USN, was killed in an airplane crash in 1938.
[†] Lieutenant Commander Fitzhugh Lee, USN. The oral history of Lee, who retired as a vice admiral, is in the Naval Institute collection.

Admiral Stroop: No, and this was a rather bitter pill. The Saratoga was sent out toward Midway Island, and they put on board a non-aviator, Admiral Fairfax Leary, and his staff.* It became obvious that the fleet tactics were going to be centered in this war around the carrier. It would be a sort of a carrier task force with carriers, cruisers, and destroyers. The center of action, the center of command, and the fighting would all be done from the carriers. So there was a little competition about who would get these fighting jobs. Of course, there was the continuation of the competition between the aviators and non-aviators. At that stage of the war, they thought, "Well, we'll let some of the non-aviators have these jobs."

Admiral Leary was aboard the Saratoga. He went out just on a patrol out towards Midway and had some of our staff aboard. As a matter of fact, Cornwell was with him. Apparently there was some argument about how fast they would run at during the night, and, of course, the aviators wanted to run it at a higher speed. The ship was actually making 15 knots when she got her torpedo.† I'll give Admiral Leary credit for this: after that experience he came in and said that only aviation-experienced admirals should be in command of these carrier task forces. I'll always admire him for saying that.

Q: It was a heck of a lesson to have to learn that way.

Admiral Stroop: I don't think it was based as much on getting the torpedo as the fact that he realized that he didn't know personally very much about airplanes and the operation of airplanes. Now, maybe the torpedo incident sort of forced the issue, the fact that he had apparently been wrong. But the real reason for him saying this was the fact that he wasn't experienced in flying airplanes, and most of the war was to be fought with the airplane carrier being the capital ship.

---

* Vice Admiral Herbert Fairfax Leary, USN, Commander Task Force 14.
† On 11 January 1942, a Japanese submarine torpedoed the Saratoga when she was 500 miles southwest of Oahu, Hawaii. Six of the aircraft carrier's crew members were killed.

Q: Did you have any other experiences with non-aviators having problems trying to run aviation shows?

Admiral Stroop: Well, you can read Jocko Clark's book, you know, and get a criticism of Spruance which I don't go along with.* I think Spruance did all right.

There were two other flag officers involved in carrier operations at that time in the Battle of the Coral Sea, which I participated in later when Frank Jack Fletcher was in command. The morning of the action he handed tactical command to Admiral Fitch, who was the aviator. I remember that quite well, because as tactical officer I laid out the courses and all that and the concept of operations. And there was another who flew his flag in Lexington for a while, Admiral Brown.† He went down to the South Pacific theater very early and came back. Our staff finally put to sea on the Lexington, relieving this other non-aviation flag officer. From then on, the carrier forces were always commanded by aviation-experienced flag officers.

Q: I notice that Admiral Clark criticizes Nimitz for not earlier in the war recognizing the proper utilization of the carrier, as opposed to battleships. Do you have any feeling on that? Do you remember where he said that he and other aviation people thought that carriers should go in and out and not stay in shore to support a landing, and that as a result they suffered some damage. Finally, Nimitz realized that aviators knew how to handle the ships better. But I think he was critical of Nimitz in that regard. I wondered if you had any feelings on that.

Admiral Stroop: Well, actually, of course, he was more critical of Admiral Spruance and then, I suppose, inferentially Nimitz because he supported Spruance and put him in command. There were two or three instances during the war when decisions had to be

---

* Admiral Joseph J. Clark, USN (Ret.), with Clark Reynolds, Carrier Admiral (New York: David McKay Company, Inc., 1967). Admiral Raymond A. Spruance, USN, commanded the Fifth Fleet in 1944-45; he was not an aviator.
† Vice Admiral Wilson Brown commanded some of the early carrier task forces while embarked in the Lexington.

made one way or the other--that is, to stay and support the landing area or to go after the main units of the Japanese fleet. Spruance usually decided to stay in and support the landings, and that's what he was criticized for. I don't recall a specific criticism of Admiral Nimitz for this, other than the fact that he did have Spruance in charge. But remember also that Spruance had relieved Halsey and went to the Battle of Midway. Spruance did a pretty good job there, although I understand there are some arguments about use of the Hornet there at Midway with Pete Mitscher aboard.[*] How far you were going to chase the Japanese and you were running into difficulty there, too, with fuel. They had already sunk the four carriers of the Japanese fleet.

Q: But you didn't have the feeling then that he expressed being critical of Nimitz.

Admiral Stroop: No. I don't know what I would have done under the same circumstances. But obviously the way Jocko Clark spoke, he's a very gung-ho fighting type person. I served under him off Korea too. I know him quite well. I still see him a couple times a year.

Q: I didn't know, and I couldn't tell from reading the biography whether you had been on the Saratoga when it was torpedoed.

Admiral Stroop: No, I was not. I was ashore on Pearl Harbor, and she came back and then had to go to the States, to Bremerton, to be overhauled and repaired.[†]

Q: I was in Bremerton in the shipyard when she came in, and I remember the crew members just really criticized the civilian workmen. But in those days they really gave everything they had to get that ship repaired and back into action.

---

[*] Captain Marc A. Mitscher, USN, was commanding officer of the carrier Hornet (CV-8) during the battle. For specifics see Lisle A. Rose, The Ship that Held the Line: The USS Hornet and the First Year of the Pacific War (Annapolis: Naval Institute Press, 1995).
[†] Puget Sound Navy Yard, Bremerton, Washington.

Admiral Stroop: The Lexington, I think, during this same period made a cruise down to the South Pacific and came back. Here it was decided to relieve the non-aviation flag officer with a flag officer that had aviation experience, Admiral Fitch. So after a few months being ashore there at Pearl, we went to sea on the Lexington and then went down to the South Pacific. We left Pearl Harbor about the 15th of April, 1942, and we went with a small task force down to the Coral Sea.

Q: What were you part of then?

Admiral Stroop: We were what was called then a carrier task force. I don't recall all the ships in the task force. We had some cruisers.

Q: Was it Task Force 11?

Admiral Stroop: I don't remember the number. We had a cruiser admiral with us who, I think, was senior to Jakie Fitch. Jakie was the commander then in that situation. We were headed for the South Pacific and the Coral Sea, and we were to join up with the Yorktown, which was down there ahead of us. She had been brought around summarily from the East Coast, and she was already operating down there.

So we arrived down there in the Coral Sea, joined up with some British ships. It was quite a sizable task force: two U.S. carriers, the Yorktown and Lexington, about four of five U.S. cruisers, a couple of British cruisers, Australian destroyers. Just before we arrived down there, the Yorktown went on a foray against Florida Island.* The Japanese also had some carriers in the area. They had found the Sims and the Neosho and sank them just the day before we entered the Coral Sea.† We joined up, I think, on the sixth of May,

---

* On 4 May 1942 the carrier Yorktown (CV-5) sent three attack groups against Japanese troops debarking troops on Tulagi Island, near Florida Island in the Solomons.
† On 7 May 1942, Japanese aircraft sank the oiler Neosho (AO-23) and the destroyer Sims (DD-409), apparently mistaking them for a carrier and cruiser.

1942. Then we fueled that night and were ready to operate on the seventh of May. We expected to be within carrier aircraft range of the Japanese fleet on the seventh, which we were.

Q: How did you know the Japanese fleet was there?

Admiral Stroop: Well, we had considerable intelligence. We had very special intelligence which helped us also at Midway Island.*

Q: Was this the situation when . . . ?

Admiral Stroop: And also, of course, the Japanese had sunk the Neosho and the Sims, so here was concrete evidence. And, of course, they had landed on the north coast of New Guinea, and there was pretty good evidence that they were going to come around the east end of New Guinea after they had landed on the north coast of New Guinea. They then were coming around the eastern tip of New Guinea, we thought, and that's what actually happened the next day. We joined up with our British friends with the Lexington and the Yorktown and prepared for the Battle of the Coral Sea.

Q: You didn't know it was the Battle of the Coral Sea then, did you?

Admiral Stroop: No, but we thought there was going to be a fight.

---

* Word of the special intelligence--derived from decrypting Japanese radio messages--did not become generally known until the mid-1970s, a few years after this interview.

Interview Number 3 with Vice Admiral Paul D. Stroop, U.S. Navy (Retired)

Place: Admiral Stroop's home in San Diego, California

Date: Sunday, 14 September 1969

Interviewer: Commander Etta-Belle Kitchen, U.S. Navy (Retired)

Admiral Stroop: Early in, I believe, April of 1942 we were still in Pearl Harbor, and Admiral Fitch was designated to go to sea in Lexington. Our orders were to carry us down into the South Pacific and ultimately into the Coral Sea action. In preparation for the upcoming events, Lexington was put in the Navy yard at Pearl Harbor, and I remember a considerable number of 20-millimeter guns were mounted on her gallery decks, around the perimeter of the flight deck. There were some other changes in the ship.

We sailed, I think, finally from Pearl Harbor about the 15th of April. We were in company with some cruisers--I believe it was Admiral Kinkaid's cruiser division--and some destroyers.[*] We continued towards the South Pacific, where we were ultimately to rendezvous with Rear Admiral Frank Jack Fletcher, who was flying his flag in Yorktown. At the same time, we were to rendezvous with a force of Australian ships under Rear Admiral Crace, Royal Navy.[†] We didn't realize, of course, that we were going into a carrier action with the Japanese, but intelligence we received on the way down indicated that there was a great deal of Japanese activity, particularly along the coast of New Guinea.

Q: What was your mission as you left Pearl?

Admiral Stroop: Our mission was to go down and strengthen the U.S. forces in the South Pacific and probably to make some raids on Japanese installations ashore.

---

[*] Rear Admiral Thomas C. Kinkaid, USN, Commander Cruiser Division Six, served as Commander Task Group 17.2 for the operation.
[†] Rear Admiral John G. Crace, RN.

Q: Did you see these orders? Were they sealed orders? Did you know what you were going to do when you left Pearl, or was it something you found out after you got under way?

Admiral Stroop: I did not personally see the orders. I remember a number of conferences were held at the flag-rank level, which I didn't attend. All I really knew personally was that we were to embark in <u>Lexington</u> and proceed to the South Pacific. I was still flag secretary, tactical officer, flag navigator, and also assumed the job of intelligence officer. In other words, I would receive the intelligence dispatches each day and prepare a summary for the admiral's benefit of the situation and what the enemy was probably doing.

Q: You evaluated them and . . . ?

Admiral Stroop: That's right. This was based on the dispatches that came in, particularly during the night. This called for early reveille in the morning, and I tried to have a summary ready for the admiral at breakfast time.

Q: Where were these coming from--Pearl or various other places?

Admiral Stroop: Practically all this intelligence was at least relayed through Admiral Nimitz's headquarters at Pearl Harbor.

Q: And were they in code? Did you have to interpret them?

Admiral Stroop: Oh, yes. Practically all of them were classified, and the business of just decoding these and getting them ready kept our communications staff very, very busy.

Q: How many would you get during the night?

Admiral Stroop: I would say probably a dozen each night relating to enemy activity, and maybe a few others relating to our own forces, but most of them were intelligence dispatches. We were in the business of getting ready to fight a battle, and intelligence was uppermost. Administrative traffic was held, of course, to a minimum--practically nonexistent, as a matter of fact.

We entered the Coral Sea around the first of May, 1942. I remember quite distinctly the first communication we had from our Royal Navy friends, Admiral Crace, had to do with his evaluation of the importance of the Coral Sea area. He said in his first communication to Admiral Fitch and Admiral Fletcher that he considered this area of the greatest importance and that our combined forces should do everything they could to keep the Japanese from coming into the Coral Sea area. Of course, at this time the Japanese had landed on the north coast of New Guinea, and there was strong evidence that they were going to come around the eastern tip of New Guinea and make a landing at Port Moresby, which was an important outpost of the British Empire.

The <u>Yorktown</u>, of course, with Admiral Frank Jack Fletcher, had preceded us with her air group and accompanying cruisers and destroyers into the Coral Sea and about the first of May did raid the new Japanese installations at Tulagi Island. We read of this, of course, with a great deal of interest and noted that they had caused some damage to the Japanese, including sinking one ship. This all is a matter of history. After that raid, that force was to join up with the force of which we were a part. As I recall, we lined up along with the Australian ships about the fifth or sixth of May, 1942.

The night of the sixth of May was spent in refueling, topping off destroyers, refueling the carriers, and getting ready for what was to be the Coral Sea battle. I recall that as the staff navigator I was concerned that the optimum refueling course, which was probably going to take all night, wasn't the best course to get us into the position we wanted to be in on the morning of the seventh of May. We did a very deliberate slow change of course during the night, changing just a few degrees at a time to a new course to head us from a westerly to a northerly direction and get us closer to the area where we thought we might find Japanese carriers.

The morning of the seventh of May we sent out our scouting planes from the Lexington and from the Yorktown on a regular planned search, which we had laid out the night before. We were searching not only for elements of the striking force--the two Japanese carriers, Zuikaku and Shokaku--but also we were quite interested in the invasion force, which was, according to intelligence, coming around the eastern tip of New Guinea.

Q: Can you tell me how you actually laid this out? This was your first occasion to think of being in battle, was it not, other than Wake?

Admiral Stroop: The plan was quite standard. It was something that we had used in peacetime maneuvers. We simply drew a limited circle in the direction of the area of interest and assigned planes to go out on radii, so that at the outer end of their search they would be twice visual distance apart. In other words, the objective was to cover the outer limits of your search sector completely--this, of course, eyeball search, using the scouting planes.

Q: What was the limit that the planes could go, several hundred miles?

Admiral Stroop: I think in this particular case they went out about 250--not any more than that. Unfortunately, on the seventh of May the Zuikaku and the Shokaku had the advantage of weather cover, and they were not discovered by our forces on that day. The Lexington and the Yorktown also had some weather cover, and we were not discovered by the Japanese until very late in the evening, too late for them to make an attack. However, as I recall, we did get a contact report, I think from an Army Air Corps B-17, of the invasion force coming round the coast of New Guinea.* So we sent our attack forces in that direction to hit the invasion force.

We assumed that the Zuikaku and the Shokaku were out of range. We didn't really know where they were, because we hadn't seen them. We sent our attack force, torpedo

---

* Admiral Stroop is here using the former name of the Army's air arm. On 20 June 1941 the U.S. Army Air Corps was officially redesignated the U.S. Army Air Forces.

planes and dive bombers, up to the eastern end of New Guinea and found the invasion force: a certain number of ships plus a converted carrier, the Shoho, and, I believe, one cruiser. Our forces immediately went in to attack, and it was a very successful attack, except that we had an overkill on the carrier. I think probably we put 14 torpedoes in the carrier and many bombs, and it was sunk immediately. Looking back on this, it was too bad that the attack hadn't been better coordinated and some of the force spread around on other ships. But this being our first battle of any kind, why, everybody went after the big prize, and they sank this rather soft carrier very quickly.

Q: Who had been responsible for that actual planning?

Admiral Stroop: Well, we had a couple of squadron commanders airborne. We didn't really know what we were going to find when we got there. The initial contact report from the Army Air Corps aviator was not very complete. It read something like this: "A large number of boats headed in several directions."

Q: Which isn't very clear, is it?

Admiral Stroop: And that was about all that we had to go on until our attack force got there.

Q: And then they didn't have time to make any change of plan, I presume.

Admiral Stroop: That's right. The great majority of them did head for the carrier and, of course, sank her very quickly. I remember my friend, Lieutenant Commander Bob Dixon, was leading one segment of the attack force.* As a matter of fact, he was probably senior. We were out of voice communication with the force during the time of the attack, and on part of the return trip on account of the distance. But as soon as Bob Dixon could get a

---

* Lieutenant Commander Robert E. Dixon, USN, was commanding officer of Scouting Two, an SBD squadron flying from the Lexington.

message through, he called the ship, and he sent that message that became rather famous, "Scratch one flattop." He was the author of that one. Well, we got our attack force back.

Q: All planes recovered?

Admiral Stroop: I don't recall, but if there were any lost, it was extremely minor. Very few that day, and it was, of course, a very fine, successful day. We hadn't found the main body of the Japanese, and up until that afternoon they hadn't found us either.

On the evening of the seventh of May, we had recovered all of our planes. Our search planes had returned, and we were running a cruising formation at dusk when we sighted some lights coming over the horizon. On our carrier, the Lexington, we thought that probably these were some of our own planes from the Yorktown returning. We were not sure that they had all their planes back. We knew that the Lexington planes were all aboard. These planes were in very good formation. I remember noticing the port running lights of the formation all in a beautiful echelon. One of the things that struck me as odd was that the red color of the port running light was different from the shade of running lights that we had on our own planes. They had a sort of a bluish tint, red-blue tint to it.

About the time that we sighted these lights, one of our screen destroyers began firing at the planes. I remember a voice message went out over the TBS to the skipper of the destroyer, a friend of mine, Lieutenant Commander Chillingworth, telling him to stop, that these were undoubtedly friendly planes coming in.* This of course, was not true. These were Japanese aircraft.

Q: Who had said these were friendly planes?

Admiral Stroop: I guess our air officer of the Lexington. I remember the message went out.

---

* Lieutenant Commander Charles F. Chillingworth, Jr., USN, commanding officer of the USS Dewey (DD-349).

Q: Everybody heard it?

Admiral Stroop: Oh, yes. And Chillingworth came right back on the TBS and said, "I know Japanese planes when I see them."

Q: You yourself had recognized the color of . . .

Admiral Stroop: Well, I just subconsciously noted there was a difference, and at the moment I thought--I didn't consider them enemy planes. I thought they were probably Yorktown planes returning. Well, actually, these were Japanese planes which had mistaken the Yorktown and the Lexington formation for their own ships. They came in with their lights on and were ready to get into the landing formation. Of course, there was a lot of confusion, but after Chillingworth identified them as enemy planes, everybody began shooting, and there were a lot of fireworks. The Japanese planes broke up their formation, turned out their lights, and disappeared.

Q: Did you get any?

Admiral Stroop: I don't think we hit any that night, no.

I might mention an important part of this day's action. We were under a rather heavy cloud cover late in the afternoon, after our scouts had returned with no luck. We'd gotten our own planes back from the attack on the invasion force. We began getting indications on the radar screen of unidentified aircraft in the vicinity. So we put fighters in the air and vectored them out. The Lexington fighters were led by Lieutenant Commander Paul Ramsey, who was skipper of the fighter squadron on the Lexington.[*] The Yorktown put their fighters up. They were also in the air and led by Lieutenant Commander Jim

---

[*] Lieutenant Commander Paul H. Ramsey, USN, commanding officer of Fighting Two.

Flatley.* At any rate, the Lexington fighters were vectored in the direction of the unidentified aircraft. Ramsey, according to his story, came out of a cloud deck, and under the clouds he found a formation of Japanese attack planes which apparently had been sent down in our direction and had not found the Lexington and Yorktown.

Q: He was on top of the planes?

Admiral Stroop: He came out behind them. He was in perfect position. He immediately was able to shoot down the two following planes--the last two planes in the formation--and got two kills right away. I don't recall the details of the rest of the engagement, but I remember Ramsey came back to the Lexington. During the cruise south he'd grown a luxuriant mustache, and he had said that as soon as he shot down his first Japanese plane he would shave this mustache off. When he came to the Lexington, he made a quick circle around the ship, with his canopy open. He was stroking his mustache, indicating that he wasn't going to have it much longer. Of course, he landed aboard and shaved it off that night.

Q: How did you feel after the really first successful thing that the Navy had done?

Admiral Stroop: Well, of course, we felt very good and very confident.

Q: I mean you personally.

Admiral Stroop: I felt very good about it. I also was disappointed that we hadn't contacted the striking force. We were apprehensive about their location, because we knew they were close around. We had two contacts with Japanese aircraft during the course of the afternoon and evening.

---

* Lieutenant Commander James H. Flatley, Jr., USN, commanding officer of Fighting 42.

Q: And particularly when they came out on top of this group that was searching for them.

Admiral Stroop: That's right. Well, to go on with this fiasco at dusk when the Japanese planes broke into our formation and apparently mistook us for Japanese carriers . . .

Q: Too bad they didn't land.

Admiral Stroop: We followed them on radar and lost them at about 40 miles. I always figured that the Japanese carriers and American carriers had gotten quite close to each other after dark.

Q: Would that had indicated when you lost them that they would have landed?

Admiral Stroop: Well, there were other indications. Of course, they began going off the radar screen at 40 miles. Now, radar was not very well developed in that day, and they might have gone over the radar horizon. But the other indication that came up was the fact that our intelligence unit tuned in on their airplane landing frequency. We could hear the Japanese carriers talking to the pilot in the air, and this was another indication that the Japanese carriers were not too far away. As a matter of fact, I even discussed with the admiral the possibility of having a destroyer attack that night, but he felt that the distance was probably too great, and it would be difficult to locate them.

Q: Could you understand them?

Admiral Stroop: They were talking in Japanese. I remember one conversation that was repeated to me. One of the Japanese pilots couldn't get his wheels down, and the carrier told him that if he couldn't get his wheels down, he'd have to land in the water. They wouldn't take him aboard, didn't want to clutter up their flight deck with a crash when they had other planes coming aboard.

Q: Did you have someone who interpreted the Japanese?

Admiral Stroop: Yes. So after he got this order from his air group commander or the captain of the Japanese carrier, he then requested that the carrier shine a light on the water so he'd have a spot to land on. This was one little incident, but it indicated that they were quite close, much closer than we thought they were, and certainly somewhat surprising. We hadn't been able to find them during the day's scouting operations, because the weather was not good.

Q: The planes could have flown right over them and just not seen them?

Admiral Stroop: That's right.

Q: Was there any night fighting at this point in the war?

Admiral Stroop: No, night fighting came on later, but we had had rather limited experience in night operations. Most of the pilots were night qualified for carrier landing. They'd done this, of course, in the early '30s, and it was a part of our training. We felt that we could have limited night operations, but it wasn't a matter of routine at all.

    Well, that ended the action on the seventh of May, and it was quite obvious, of course, to the Japanese--and to us, too--that the carriers were fairly close to each other, and that we probably would have an engagement the next day. I think history will show that the Japanese carriers went north during the night, and the Yorktown and the Lexington went south during the night. They were getting their air groups prepared for the next day's operations.

Q: Did anybody sleep that night?

Admiral Stroop: Oh, yes. I went to sleep, but I wakened early. I remember I had to get up in a hurry when a bundle of intelligence dispatches were made available to me. I didn't have time to shave, and I put my electric razor in my pocket, thinking I would shave some time on the bridge the next day. I never did get an opportunity to shave. I still had the razor when I abandoned ship. On the morning of the eighth of May, reveille for me was probably 3:30 in the morning, and I began analyzing dispatches and getting ready for the launching of the search group, which again was led by my friend, Lieutenant Commander Dixon.

Q: Who was analyzing the data and messages with you?

Admiral Stroop: Well, naturally, the chief of staff, who was Lieutenant Commander Cornwell. And Admiral Fitch read all the dispatches, and we discussed them. The communications officer, Captain Bowen, who lives over here in Coronado, was also going over them, and I had an assistant intelligence officer, an ensign, who was getting very familiar with everything that was going on, and he was also quite helpful.

We started our search groups out right at daylight, and the commanding officer of the search squadron, Lieutenant Commander Bob Dixon, took what he thought was the most likely sector. It turned out that he was practically right. The first sighting was made probably around 8:00 or 9:00 o'clock in the morning by one of Dixon's squadron pilots, a younger officer, who sighted the Zuikaku and Shokaku and sent the message back. Dixon himself then moved over into that sector and sent the young pilot back. He stayed as long as he could in the vicinity of the Japanese carriers, giving us locations, speed, and direction of their movement. He did a perfectly classic job of shadowing these carriers, taking advantage of cloud cover when he could and reporting back to us.

I might add that Bob Dixon, in my opinion, was one of the great heroes of this two-day operation. He had led the attack on the Shoho, and that was very successful. And then he did this tremendously fine job of shadowing the Zuikaku and Shokaku and surviving, although this was always considered a very dangerous thing to do--to remain around in the vicinity of enemy carriers, where you could be the target of much higher-performance fighter planes. Dixon did it and got away with it. He had been a test pilot at Anacostia and had learned early in the game how to economize on fuel and get the most out of an engine. This certainly stood him in good stead that day, because he stayed in the vicinity of the carriers much longer than anybody thought he could.

When all the search planes came back and Bob Dixon hadn't arrived, why, we figured that something had happened to him. We hadn't heard from him. About an hour after everybody thought he would be out of fuel, he showed up all by himself over the horizon, came back, and landed aboard--simply because he had floated around in the sky in the vicinity of the Japanese carriers and conserved his fuel and came back. He was a great guy and an outstanding naval aviator.

Well, after the initial report came, the decision, of course--the obvious decision--was made to send off the attack planes from the Yorktown and the Lexington and to make a coordinated attack on the Zuikaku and the Shokaku. The distance was a little greater than we wanted, or would like to have had--I've forgotten how much it was, maybe something over 200 miles--for all our air group, particularly the TBDs, the torpedo planes, which were carrying the heavy torpedo loads and would not have too much range.

We sent them out at about maximum range, and an attack was scheduled to take place at about 11:00 o'clock or 11:15 in the morning. The Lexington and the Yorktown then remained in the vicinity on various courses and speeds, waiting for the return of the scout planes, which they took aboard. Then they waited for the attack planes to come back. They were scheduled to have their attack about 11:15 to 11:30 and scheduled to return about 1:30 in the afternoon.

About 11:00 we began getting indications on the radar of a large group of planes approaching us, and we figured, of course, that the Japanese were doing the same thing we were. They had their attack planes coming down. The Lexington and the Yorktown were in an area of good visibility, whereas the Zuikaku and the Shokaku still had the advantage of cloud cover. That, to a considerable degree, affected the action, because a good many of our attack planes could not ever make contact with the Zuikaku and the Shokaku--just a few of them. Those that did were quite effective. They damaged one carrier, the Shokaku, considerably, and the other one a slight amount. However, the Japanese managed to control the damage and to get away.

My memory is hazy about the details of the arrangement, but I do recall that the air group commander, Commander Bill Ault, arrived over the enemy carriers with, I think, only four aircraft in his particular section.* In other words, the attack was not a coordinated attack. Each squadron was led separately by its squadron commander. The air group commander was not in contact with them or lost contact, but he did have in his own section three or four planes that were accompanying him. When he got over the enemy carriers, he went on in and attacked. He himself claimed, as history will show, a 1,000-pound hit with his own particular bomb.† A combination of the weather and uncoordinated attack, I feel, made us less successful in attacking the Zuikaku and the Shokaku. We should have been more effective than we were. I don't know whether we got any torpedo hits or not on those carriers.‡

As I said earlier, at 11:00 o'clock we began getting radar indications that the enemy aircraft were approaching, and I remember making an entry in the war diary at that time, because I thought maybe later on I wouldn't be able to make entries in the log. I was keeping the war diary in longhand, in a ledger on the bridge. I made an entry at 11:20: "Under attack by enemy aircraft." That turned out to be exactly right. At 11:20 we began seeing enemy aircraft overhead, and they came down in a very well coordinated attack. They attacked with torpedo planes and dive bombers.

Q: How did it feel to be under attack? I can't possibly imagine. Can you describe how . . . ?

Admiral Stroop: Well, you're a little curious, and you're a little scared, and you don't think that--well, you wonder what the outcome is going to be. I can remember standing on the

---

* Commander William B. Ault, USN, commander of the Lexington's air group, was lost at sea while trying unsuccessfully to return to the carrier. The destroyer USS Ault (DD-698) was subsequently named in his honor.
† Ault made this claim in a radio transmission during his unsuccessful attempt to find a U.S. carrier on which to land while returning from the mission.
‡ For details on the battle, see John B. Lundstrom, The First Team: Pacific Naval Air Combat from Pearl Harbor to Midway (Annapolis: Naval Institute Press, 1984).

bridge and watching the enemy dive-bombers come down. These were fixed-landing-gear dive-bombers--I've forgotten the code name for them.* You were convinced that the pilot in the plane had the bridge of your ship right in his sight; you knew it, and this didn't look good. Fortunately, they were not strafing, because if they'd been strafing I'm sure that they would have made the topside untenable, but they apparently didn't strafe in their dives.

The minute he released his bomb, you could see the bomb taking a different trajectory from the aircraft itself, generally falling short because their dive wasn't quite as steep as it should have been for good dive-bombing, and you knew that that particular bomb wasn't going to hit you. It might hit the side of the ship. I watched this a number of times. I was fascinated to watch the bomb leave the airplane and realize then that it was probably going to fall short.

The torpedo planes came in about the same time--a fine, nicely coordinated attack--and launched their torpedoes at about, I'd say, 1,000 yards. They were down to flight deck level when they dropped the torpedoes. And, of course, they were successful in having excellent dive bombers. I believe they got three hits on the Lexington. We got, I believe, four torpedo hits. I might add that in the account that was finally sent out later, only two torpedo hits were recorded officially. I personally believe this is wrong. I think the Lexington probably took four.

Q: What part of the ship?

Admiral Stroop: I believe all the torpedo hits were on the port side and pretty well distributed along the length of the ship, because immediately after the attack we took a port list, and I watched some of the torpedo planes passing from port to starboard. It was pretty discouraging to see these Japanese at it. They'd launch their torpedoes, and then some of them would fly very close to the ship, you know, to get a look at us. They were curious and sort of thumbed their noses at us. We were shooting at them with our new 20-millimeters and not hitting them at all. The tracers of the 20-millimeters were falling

---

* The Aichi Type 99 carrier dive-bomber was known to the Allies by the code name "Val."

astern of the torpedo planes. It was very discouraging to see enemy planes pass within range of your guns and not be able to knock them down.

Q: It must have been a sickening experience.

Admiral Stroop: We . . .

Q: Did it seem real, or somehow could you . . . ?

Admiral Stroop: Oh, yes.

Q: No question but what it was really happening to you?

Admiral Stroop: Very, very realistic, but you were fascinated by what was going on. You had some personal interest in what they were doing and scared--all at the same time.

Q: And not able to do a thing about it.

Admiral Stroop: No. Oh, at this point in time--as far as the senior people were concerned-- you were completely helpless. You were depending on the training that had been given to the fighter pilots in the air, and you were dependent on the training and practice the gunners had had. The commanding officer of the ship, Captain Sherman, was very busy twisting his ship, trying to avoid torpedoes. I think he was successful in some cases, but he wasn't successful completely.

Q: You had no planes to defend you at this point?

Admiral Stroop: We had fighters overhead.

Q: Oh, did you?

Admiral Stroop: We had fighters overhead, and they were credited with knocking down some Japanese planes. As a matter of fact, we saw one or two come tumbling down. We'd also taken some of the dive-bombers and put them on close-in patrols as defense against the torpedo planes, figuring that they could overtake them possibly and disrupt the torpedo plane attack. They were not successful, and the torpedo planes pretty much got through.

The <u>Lexington</u> took, I think, three bomb hits. One of the most spectacular ones was on the port gun gallery. A bomb exploded and immediately killed and burned gun crews in that area. I remember walking down there when the attack was over, and here were the Marine gunners, and they were burned right at their stations on the guns. That particular bomb started a fire down in the officers' country, the next deck below. The flag officer's living quarters were set on fire, and it killed a couple of stewards who were down in the pantry in that area. I remember that particular situation, because I considered going down later and getting into the stateroom and taking some gear out of the safe. It couldn't be done. We had another bomb in the after part of the island or stack and another one pretty well aft. I think it was in the boat pocket where the captain's gig was stored.

All these bombs, of course, started fires, which we figured that we could control and put out. We learned a lot, of course, from this action--that ships of that kind were tinder, they had too much inflammable stuff aboard. The furniture in the admiral's cabin, for example, was wood and fabric, and that burned. Paint all over the ship had an oil base, and wherever we got a fire, why, the paint on the bulkhead burned. That was something that had to be corrected. We learned that our fire-fighting equipment was not adequate, that we needed to redesign our hoses and hose nozzles so as to have fog instead of solid water. These were lessons, of course, that came out of the war and which were quickly used to improve situations on other ships.

Q: But the carrier can sustain a bomb hit better than it can sustain torpedoes.

Admiral Stroop: Well, I guess that's probably true. We took, I think, three bombs and four torpedoes, and we were still able to make, I believe, 27 knots, and we had the ship under control. An hour after the attack, we had the ship back on an even keel by counter-flooding. I remember the damage control officer came up to the bridge; his name was Pop Healy.* I saw him discussing things with the captain after he had gotten the ship on an even keel. His station was down in central station, where he took charge of the damage control parties, and counter-flooding and all of that.

After the attack we were able to steam into the wind. We landed some aircraft aboard. Bob Dixon was the last one. He'd been out there still scouting. He came aboard late in the afternoon. The Yorktown, of course, was also suffering the same kind of attack. She took one bomb that I recall went down about four decks and exploded and killed, oh, 20 or 30 people. But she was in much better shape than the Lexington and, of course, was able to have her damage repaired and go on to the Battle of Midway, where she was lost.

We kept under way, making about 27 knots. After we got our planes back aboard, the decision was made to head for Australia. I laid out a course for Brisbane, where we could get our battle damage repaired. The other ships formed up--the cruisers and destroyers and the Yorktown--and we were headed for Brisbane. Along about 2:00 o'clock or 2:30 in the afternoon we heard a rather loud submerged explosion. My first reaction was that a Japanese submarine had sighted us and fired a torpedo which probably had an influence fuze and had gone off under the hull. It seemed like that kind of an explosion, right under, deep down, and probably under the ship.

However, when this explosion occurred, we found out later it was not an enemy torpedo at all; it was the gasoline fuel. Leaking fuel had been caused by the bomb hits. Leaking fuel had collected in the elevator well, and some spark had set off the fumes. The immediate effects were quite disastrous. As soon as this explosion occurred, the communication between the bridge and central station was lost. Later testimony showed that Pop Healy and his crew down in central station were wiped out at that time. Fires throughout the ship were accelerated by the effect of this explosion, and also another fire

---

* Lieutenant Commander Howard R. Healy, USN, first lieutenant and damage control officer.

developed underneath the number-two elevator. The elevator was up flush with the flight deck, but you could see flames coming out.

Word came almost immediately that the engineering spaces were untenable and had to be abandoned, so the engineering crews on the afternoon watch shut down the main engines. Here was the ship dead in the water and, worst of all, there was no fire-fighting capability for the ship. All power was lost. This was about 2:00 in the afternoon. From then on, the case was hopeless. No power to fight the fire. We actually had a destroyer come along to try and get hoses over, but this was absolutely hopeless, completely unpracticable. The fires began increasing in size, and by 3:00 o'clock or 3:30 the decision was made to get the wounded off the ship and to get the air group personnel off. These people were not needed in the fighting of fires, and they could be useful, of course, if the ship was lost, which we began to feel would happen. These people could be used again in other action, so they were gotten off about 3:30. They brought destroyers alongside and got these people off.

Q: Where did the air group go, to the Yorktown?

Admiral Stroop: Well, in a case like this, the survivors are taken aboard many ships.

Q: I meant the planes.

Admiral Stroop: A good many of our planes had landed on board, you see, while we were still under way, before this . . .

Q: Then what happened when you decided to abandon ship?

Admiral Stroop: Well, we couldn't do anything about the planes. We were dead in the water, and we couldn't launch the planes.

Q: Oh, of course.

Admiral Stroop: The planes were all left on deck. Many of them were still loaded with ammunition. Rather spectacular fireworks occurred later on. I'll come to that later.

Q: But once the ship has no headway, the planes absolutely can't take off. No catapult?

Admiral Stroop: Well, we'd lost all power, you see.

Q: Of course.

Admiral Stroop: There was just no way at all that you could launch aircraft. Some of our planes had landed on the Yorktown, but the majority were still on the Lexington. They, of course, were left there and lost with the ship. All we hoped to do was save personnel, without belongings. So we started a very orderly abandonment of the ship, the wounded and the air group personnel going off first, along about 3:00 or 3:30 in the afternoon.

We continued trying to fight the fires, but it became increasingly evident that the ship not only couldn't be saved, but that it was very dangerous to stay aboard much longer. Fires had gotten increasingly violent on the hangar deck, and we were beginning to get explosions. On the hangar deck, apparently torpedo warheads were going off from the storage back aft. You could hear an explosion towards the fantail on the hangar deck, and it sounded like a freight train rumbling up the hangar deck. Actually, it was a rushing wall of flame, you see, which would erupt around the perimeter of the elevator. These flames would shoot up two or three feet, and these were occurring with increasing frequency.

Finally, Admiral Fitch, in order, I think, to ease the captain's problems and to ease him into making the proper decision, said, "Well, Fred, it's about time to get the men off." This was around 5:00 o'clock in the afternoon. So the order was given to abandon ship. Everybody sensed this was the proper thing to do, and they ought to do it in a hurry. We had lines over the side, the sea was calm, the water was warm, and it was still daylight, so it was a pretty good situation.

Q: If you had to do it, it was . . .

Admiral Stroop: That's right. And there were destroyers and cruisers in the vicinity of the ship, so that we had places to go. The men started going down over the side of these lines and being picked up by boats.

Q: From the other ships?

Admiral Stroop: From the other ships. We didn't have any of our own boats in the water. We had a destroyer alongside almost continuously, first taking off the wounded and people from the air group. Later on they were taking off other people when this order was finally given.

Q: It sounds like such an enormous job--with how many thousand people on the carrier?-- to get off.

Admiral Stroop: We had a total of, I'd say, about 2,500 or 3,000 on there. Strangely enough, loss of life was rather minor. We lost about 150 people in this total action, many of whom, of course, were killed in the initial attacks. Practically all those killed were in the initial attacks, and then from the internal explosion down deep in the ship, where it wiped out all the crew of the central station. I'm sure others were lost throughout the ship--smoke and fighting fires--and there may have been a few lost in abandoning ship. This, of course, we don't know.

    I remained on the bridge with Admiral Fitch and his orderly, his chief of staff, the communications officer, and the flag lieutenant. We were probably the last to abandon ship, except for the captain. We all left the bridge area about the same time. By this time it was quite noticeable that everybody else had gone. The captain of the ship, Captain Sherman, went down on the flight deck. According to his story, he made a trip aft and inspected the ship to see that everybody was off, intending, of course, to carry out the tradition to be the last man off the ship.

The admiral and the few of us on the staff who were left, left the bridge and selected port side, forward, as the place where we would go over the side. I remember going across the flight deck and realizing it was pretty hot, and pretty soon the whole thing was going to be in flames. Of course, port side forward we had what little breeze there was that made that the coolest part of the ship. So we got up to the port side of the flight deck, and there were these lines all led over the side, large mooring line types of hawser that made it very easy to haul yourself down into the water. Boats from the other ships were close aboard, ready to pick up survivors.

Q: You had to be awfully strong to hold on to them.

Admiral Stroop: Well, you find you're awfully strong in those situations.

Q: What were you wearing?

Admiral Stroop: Just khaki shirt and trousers, shoes, helmet, which I took off. I thought maybe I was going to have to jump from the flight deck. I didn't want to have the helmet on with a strap under my chin, so I took it off, I remember.

Q: Why did you think you would have to jump?

Admiral Stroop: Well, I didn't realize that these lines were all still available.

Q: I see.

Admiral Stroop: And we also had to cross the flight deck. We weren't sure that we had enough time. If the ship erupted in flames, why, you're going to want to get into the water in a hurry.

Q: Weren't you glad at that point that you were a good athlete?

Admiral Stroop: Actually, we had plenty of time. We had about half an hour. I remember one rather interesting incident as we crossed the flight deck. The admiral's Marine orderly was still with him, and he walked across the flight deck with the orderly in an absolutely correct position, one step to the left and one to the rear, carrying the admiral's coat over his arm. The admiral was the only officer who arrived on the rescue ship with a jacket, just because the Marine orderly had taken it with him.

The Marine orderly also had kept all of the dispatches that were handed to the admiral during the action. When the admiral would read a dispatch, he'd hand it to his orderly, and the orderly put these in his pocket. This was to be important later on. My job as flag secretary had been, among other things, to keep the war diary, which I was keeping in longhand on the bridge. Just before I left the bridge, I tore all the pertinent pages out of the war diary and folded them up in a square and stuffed them in my pocket. Of course, this, too, was useful in writing a battle report later.

Well, we arrived up at the forward port edge of the flight deck, and it was getting dark. The sun was just going down. The boats that had been in the water picking up survivors were all heavily loaded and headed back to their ships. There was no boat immediately available for the admiral and the rest of us. So I silhouetted myself against the edge of the flight deck and began trying to attract attention from the nearest cruiser. Pretty soon I got an acknowledgement by searchlight, and they saw that I was trying to semaphore them. You know, this was 1942, and I hadn't semaphored a message in 15 years, but it all came back.

Q: Isn't that incredible?

Admiral Stroop: At the Naval Academy we had to learn to semaphore on cruises, and it came back. I sent a message in semaphore, "Send boat for admiral." Well, they got the message through, and right away a motor launch came round from the bow of the cruiser and headed right for our spot. When the boat was quite close, we started getting ready to go down the lines and get into the boat. I remember the admiral's orderly trying to insist that the admiral go first. He was still very proper, and finally the admiral got a little annoyed, and he ordered the orderly to go down. The admiral, of course, wanted to be the last one to leave the flight deck. The communications officer, Lieutenant Bowen, and I had selected the same line to go down, and we didn't argue over protocol. I got on the line first and started lowering away. I'd been a rope climber at the Naval Academy. Never felt stronger in my life. So I started down the line, and I got down to the water.

Q: That's what, 40 feet?

Admiral Stroop: Yes, at least. I got down to the water, and I didn't want to get wet. The boat wasn't quite there yet. I'd timed my descent so that I'd get there about the time the boat came. So I stopped with my feet just short of the water, and I felt Lieutenant Bowen's feet on my shoulders. He was much heavier and longer and, I guess, didn't have the force and arm strength. But he couldn't hold on any longer, and he said, "Pardon me, sir, while I pass you."

Q: Oh, isn't that incredible at a time like that.

Admiral Stroop: So he went clear down into the water, dropped off the line and went in the water. When I felt the pressure on my shoulders, I lowered myself a little bit and got my feet wet. Actually, the waves wet the lower part of my body, and I remember worrying about my electric razor, which was still in my pocket. I didn't want to get that wet. Before I left the bridge, I'd taken some cellulose tape and wound it around my watch. I still have that watch. I figured it was going to get wet, and this resulted in protecting the watch. As a matter of fact, it never did get immersed.

So Bowen went in the water. The admiral and the orderly were still arguing about who should go down first, I think. The boat got under their line and picked the admiral and his orderly up dry shod. So they got off the ship dry, and the orderly still had the admiral's coat and still had the dispatches, a whole sheaf of flimsies which we used later on. I hung on the line till the boat came over and picked me up. Then we cruised along the side of the ship, picking up a few individuals that had come down and were still in the water--hadn't been picked up by the other rescue craft.

Q: Did they have life preservers on?

Admiral Stroop: Yes, I think most of them did. I had an inflatable life preserver on; I hadn't inflated it yet. I didn't think I was going to need it and didn't. The rescue craft did a very fine job, picking everybody up. But, of course, this was because they had a lot of time. The weather was good, the water was warm, and there was still daylight. As far as I know, they searched up and down the side of the ship, and nobody was lost from not being able to be found in the water. After we picked up all the survivors on board, we left, got the admiral aboard and his orderly.

Q: Was Captain Sherman with you?

Admiral Stroop: Captain Sherman came off aft, as far as I know. He went aft. The admiral went forward. Captain Sherman was rescued by another boat and put aboard another ship, as a matter of fact. We were taken over to the Minneapolis, Admiral Kinkaid's flagship. As soon as we got aboard the flagship, we went right up to the bridge. It was getting quite dark. Just about the time we got to the bridge of the cruiser, there was a tremendous explosion on the Lexington. The whole number-two elevator, right abeam of the island, lifted out of the ship. There was a sheet or solid mass of flame just the size of that elevator that came up and went as high as the mast of the ship. The whole mass of the bridge area broke out in flames. It was quite spectacular, silhouetted against the night sky.

Q: I'm sure it was, but that was what you'd been afraid of.

Admiral Stroop: Yes, and if the decision hadn't been made when it was to get the men off, there'd have been a lot more people lost, because, of course, anybody who was in that bridge area would have been enveloped in that flame.

Q: Was it an awfully difficult decision to make, to abandon ship at that time?

Admiral Stroop: Well, it seemed to be. Here was a very valuable ship. She had a very brave and stubborn captain, and he just didn't want to make the decision to leave the ship. As a matter of fact, I think finally the admiral recognized this and encouraged that decision by making it himself. In other words, he said, "Well, Fred, it's about time to get the men off." We there on the staff, who were also professional naval officers, had been advising the admiral for about half an hour or an hour that this was the thing to do. The ship was dead in the water; there was no power; the fires were increasing; and the explosions were increasing throughout the ship. To remain aboard--keep people aboard--make no sense at all.

Q: But still that was really then an exercise of awfully good judgment because of timing, wasn't it?

Admiral Stroop: Yes. The only thing that I could fault was that the decision wasn't made earlier. It could have been made an hour earlier and would have left even more time. Whether or not we lost anybody due to just the very end confusion of the last half an hour, I don't know.

Q: You mean after the deep ship explosion?

Admiral Stroop: Yes. Well, you see, that occurred around 1:30 or 2:00 in the afternoon, so we could evaluate that within one hour, 3:30. That's when, of course, we made the decision to get off the air group and the wounded. When that decision was made, at the same time it would have been just as well to have said, "Get everybody off." The process would have been a little more orderly, though it wasn't bad. There was no panic, no confusion. Everybody did what he was supposed to do, and it was done, I think, in a quite creditable manner.

Well, to continue, after our rescue by Admiral Kinkaid's flagship, we proceeded to the bridge, met the admiral and his staff. Of course, all eyes were turned on the Lexington. They'd heard this tremendous explosion which I spoke of earlier, and following that the whole topside of the ship was in flames. We had probably 50 aircraft parked, tied down in the launching area of the flight deck. Many of these aircraft, of course, were loaded with ammunition in their fixed guns, and with fuel in their tanks they made a most spectacular fire. As the aircraft began to burn, the ammunition cooked off, and the night sky was filled with tracers coming up off the after deck of the Lexington, as well as this fire which was still engulfing, outlining the entire bridge area clear up to the top of the mast. It was a spectacular sight. The task force then was ordered to steam away, and one destroyer, the Phelps, was left behind with orders to sink the Lexington.

Q: How did that make you feel?

Admiral Stroop: Well, the Lexington was already dead. We hated to see it happen, but, of course, the decision, plus the aftereffects, had already occurred. So the decision to go ahead and sink her was the right decision to make.

Q: To see it in flames, what was your emotional reaction?

Admiral Stroop: We felt very sorry, of course. We felt very badly about the whole business and wondered what could have been done to have prevented it. I guess the ship I was on, Admiral Kinkaid's flagship, was about ten miles away when the Phelps fired her torpedoes. I was down in the ship, actually in one of the officers' staterooms, getting cleaned up and, incidentally, drying out my electric razor. I washed it out with fresh water and put it under a lamp. I dried it out, and it worked perfectly. As a matter of fact, it served as a razor for about 20 people for the next two or three days.

We arrived down in the stateroom, and we felt the effect of a tremendous underwater explosion. I felt at the time that this must have occurred after the Lexington had gone down. To this day I don't know really what caused that explosion, but I read, of course, later that the Phelps, which was closest to the ship, felt the same thing. As a matter of fact, the captain of the Phelps reported that he thought he had been torpedoed. He himself had launched four torpedoes against the Lexington. This, of course, had occurred earlier, and the ship sank from the effect of those torpedoes. But what caused this tremendous underwater explosion when the Lexington might have been down several hundred feet below the surface, I don't know.

The task force then took a course to Noumea. Some of the personnel were redistributed by highline during this period. The general idea, of course, was to reassemble the survivors and get them on designated ships and eventually return them to the United States. We went to Noumea and I, with members of the staff who had been on Admiral Kinkaid's flagship, transferred to the flagship of Admiral W. W. Smith, who was the other cruiser division commander in the group.* We had some more consolidation of survivors in Noumea Harbor. Then the survivors were all taken in various ships to Tongatabu in the Friendly Islands.

When they arrived in Tongatabu, they found the Yorktown there, and at that time our whole staff, Admiral Fitch's staff, reassembled in the Yorktown. It was here that I organized and wrote up the battle report for the Coral Sea action--or at least the carrier part of the battle report.

I forgot to mention earlier that on the day of the battle, the morning of the eighth of May, Admiral Fitch received a message from Admiral Fletcher, who was senior and who was in command, directing Admiral Fitch to take tactical command of the fleet. Well, this, of course, was another admission or recognition that an admiral with aviation experience and a staff with aviation competence and background should be in charge of these kinds of combat operations. So for the rest of the day, until after the action, Admiral Fitch was in tactical command. I believe that Admiral Fletcher, who was still in the Yorktown, directed

---

* Rear Admiral William W. Smith, USN, Commander Task Unit 17.2.2, embarked in the cruiser Astoria (CA-34).

Admiral Kinkaid to take charge of the rescue operations. Of course, when the Lexington sank, Admiral Fitch and his staff were off the ship, and they had no official responsibilities. We were survivors.

We spent several days in Tongatabu. There was an airfield there. Some of the air group had been flown off the Yorktown on the way in and were based ashore. I remember during part of this time I went over and borrowed an airplane and did some flying around the island after I'd gotten the battle report organized.

Q: How long did it take you to write the report?

Admiral Stroop: I suppose it took two or three days. And it had to be written in a rush. It wasn't very comprehensive. It was based on my own personal observations largely, the ones that I've given here, plus some inputs from the commanding officer of the ship and some of the other staff officers. And we also had that sheaf of messages the orderly had brought off, and we had the rough war diary that I had written on the Lexington up until 11:20. I don't think I put any entries in it after that.

Q: What happened to the war diary? Did it become part of the official record?

Admiral Stroop: I suppose I forwarded that. I don't know. I think probably I forwarded it along with a smooth copy of the battle report to CinCPacFlt, Admiral Nimitz's headquarters, and it's probably in the archives in Washington now.

In writing up the battle report, I ran into some rather interesting observations. I had an argument with Captain Sherman about the number of torpedo hits that he'd taken. Captain Sherman said he'd counted two, and I counted four. Naturally, I still think I'm right, but the official report, which was signed by Admiral Fitch, says the Lexington took two torpedo hits. In all the history books that you'll read, you'll find that she took two torpedo hits.

Q: I'm sure it was four.

Admiral Stroop: I don't know.

Q: Did the ship lurch?

Admiral Stroop: No, no. The ship was too heavy for that?

Q: How do you feel [unclear]?

Admiral Stroop: Well, first, of course, you see the plane coming in, and you see him drop his torpedoes in the water and see the splash. Then you can see the wake of the torpedo directed toward the ship, and finally you lose sight of it as--of course, most of these torpedoes were fired from the port side, and we were on the bridge on the starboard side of the ship. So you lost sight of it probably 100 yards out, before it hit the ship. And you don't know really whether it's going to hit the ship or going to pass ahead or astern or go underneath. And then you wait for the explosion. You hear an explosion and you see some water come up in that general vicinity and . . .

Q: You can hear their noise?

Admiral Stroop: Oh, yes. You can hear the noise and feel the explosion.

Q: So if it hit there wouldn't be really any doubt in your mind that if you heard it, it had hit.

Admiral Stroop: No, no question about it. As a matter of fact, if you're in the general vicinity of a hit, you can be hurt. The shock to the deck you're standing on is enough to break people's legs if a torpedo hit in that general vicinity.

Q: I would think so.

Admiral Stroop: So there's no doubt about it that, even as remotely situated as we were up on the 06 level on the bridge of the Lexington, we could feel those torpedoes. Of course, there were other things going on at the same time. We were watching enemy airplanes fly by, we were watching dive-bombers coming in, so it's a little difficult to be accurate in accounting for all of this. As I say, my impression was three bomb hits and four torpedo hits. But I think the official records of the battle will show only two torpedo hits and three bomb hits.

We stayed in Tongatabu about four days, I guess, and completed the battle report. I remember the occasion when the admiral signed it. He wanted to be particularly sure that his signature was good, and he had signed about four final pages before he was completely satisfied. That report was short, didn't have any lessons learned in it or anything like that. It was just a chronological account of the action, as clearly as we could put it together.

Q: But that really was the official report on which everything else has been based?

Admiral Stroop: I suppose so. Now, I'm sure that other staffs--for instance, Admiral Fletcher's staff--put in a report also. This was actually the account of the carrier action, as observed by Admiral Fitch, who was in tactical command of the two carriers at that time. While we were in Tongatabu Harbor, we joined up with two large transports. These transports had brought Marine garrison troops to several of the South Pacific islands, including, I think, Samoa, and emptied their Marine troops. They were available to collect the survivors of the Lexington and take them directly back to San Diego.

Q: Whether they were injured or not?

Admiral Stroop: Well, I think most of the injured came back, too, in the various sick bays. Actually, the group coming back consisted of the crew from the Chester and these two transports.* All the ships' officers and enlisted men and air groups were put on the two transports. The admiral and all of his staff were assembled and put in the Chester. We rode back in company with the two transports, and I don't think any other survivors except the admiral's staff were on the Chester. We had an uneventful trip across the Pacific from Tongatabu to San Diego.

I recall the morning of the day we were scheduled to enter port. We decided we'd send a couple of planes on in ahead. Those cruisers carried four scout planes and, being an aviator with some cruiser experience, I was selected to fly one of the planes in. That was a great privilege, because I would arrive home about 8:00 o'clock in the morning instead of 5:00 o'clock in the afternoon. We had two planes, one of which had Captain Sherman, commanding officer of the ship, as a passenger, and one of the ship's pilots. I piloted the other plane, and I've forgotten who rode in with me. I landed here off North Island about 8:30 or 9:00 in the morning.

Q: Before we leave the Coral Sea action, were you aware of the importance of the battle at the time, or of the effect it had on the Japanese advance in that part of the Pacific?

Admiral Stroop: Yes, I think we were. As I probably mentioned earlier, Admiral Crace's summation of the situation and the importance of the Coral Sea also brought it home.

Q: But did you realize you had actually stopped the Japanese at that point, even though you did not sink the two carriers of the striking force?

Admiral Stroop: Yes, we knew that, because, you see, the invasion force was intercepted on the seventh of May, after that initial report from this Army Air Corps aviator--29 boats proceeding in all directions.

Q: And did you know it had turned back?

---

* The Chester (CA-27) was a heavy cruiser that had been in Admiral Smith's task unit and did not have a flag officer embarked.

Admiral Stroop: Oh, yes. That attack, which really lost the show for the Japanese, when I believe they also lost another combat ship besides the Shoho--I think the report showed a cruiser was lost.* This discouraged the Japanese, and the invasion of Port Moresby was canceled, and they turned around and went back to land on the north coast of New Guinea.

Q: I wondered if you knew that at the time, however.

Admiral Stroop: Oh, yes. We knew.

Q: So you were aware of what you'd accomplished?

Admiral Stroop: We were aware. Now, we didn't realize how long this was gong to stay that way. We didn't realize that it was a major turning point of the war, and we didn't know what was going to happen next.

Actually, of course, the Japanese then came down and landed on Guadalcanal after that. I remember quite distinctly a day or two before the battle, I was on the bridge of the Lexington with one of our very capable intelligence people, Lieutenant Commander Steve Jurika, who was a Japanese-language officer.† We were looking over charts, and he pointed to Guadalcanal. Here was a very large island, a lot of land area, and he said, "This is going to be important in the immediate future." Now, just what information he had, whether this was just conjecture on his part or whether as a very special intelligence officer he had knowledge of some Japanese plans, I don't know. But I'd never heard of Guadalcanal before. Here we saw this large island, and, of course, almost immediately after this action it became important.

---

* The light carrier Shoho was the only Japanese ship sunk in this battle.
† Admiral Stroop's usually reliable memory apparently betrayed him on this point. Lieutenant Stephen Jurika, Jr., USN, was indeed a Japanese-language specialist. However, he was assigned to the carrier Hornet (CV-8) at the time of the Battle of the Coral Sea. The oral history of Jurika, who retired as a captain, is in the Naval Institute collection.

Q: But you wouldn't have felt so bad about losing the Lexington if you had known the accomplishments of the battle.

Admiral Stroop: That's right. That's right. And history, of course, proved that it was right. It was a major turning point in the war.

Q: Definitely.

Admiral Stroop: The Japanese were headed for Port Moresby and presumably were going to land even in Australia, which was probably . . .

Q: It was the first time they'd been turned back on any attempt they'd made so far in the war.

Admiral Stroop: That's correct.

Q: You didn't stay in San Diego very long, I presume.

Admiral Stroop: No. I landed with these two scout planes in the mid-morning. I had in my possession numerous letters from the staff who had written to their wives, and I delivered them very soon. The news of the Lexington, of course, had not reached the public back here in the United States. It was interesting to watch the reactions of these wives as they read their letters. Their husbands in no case, of course, told them that their ship had been lost, but the letter carried instructions about going to the ship's service and going to the tailor's and starting a new outfit of clothing. So it was quite obvious from the wifely eye that the husband was arriving home just with the clothes he had on his back. They knew immediately that they'd been through some sort of a disaster where they'd lost their clothes.

Q: Could you say that your wife was glad to see you?

Admiral Stroop: Yes. I was fortunate, of course, being the first one on the staff to be in contact with my wife. We then proceeded on personal business, to buy some clothes and so forth. That evening, about 5:00 o'clock, the Chester pulled in to the Broadway Pier. All the other wives were on hand, and so was I, to greet the ship and meet the admiral. We disembarked the staff who came back and had the evening with our families. We had the next day to complete our arrangements for clothes purchases and knew then that the Chester was to be ordered back to Pearl Harbor--back to the war zone--immediately.

On the second day, after just 40 hours in port, the Chester sailed with us on board. We had intelligence, of course, of the upcoming Battle of Midway, and the reason for our hurried departure was to get the Chester in position to participate in the Battle of Midway if it drew out for a long enough period.* Actually, we made 27 knots out. When we were about halfway across between San Diego and Honolulu, it was obvious that we were not going to be able to get into the Battle of Midway before it was over. We put into Pearl Harbor, the first ship to enter after the Battle of Midway and found, of course, that Pearl Harbor was completely empty. All the ships had gone, and we created quite a bit of interest, because the people on the shore, not realizing where the Chester had come from, thought we were probably the first ship in after the Midway battle. Actually, we were not.

Immediately upon arriving at Pearl Harbor, Admiral Fitch was assigned the task of taking charge of all Pacific Fleet air operations in what we would now call a type commander: Commander Air Force Pacific Fleet. It has another title now.

Q: U.S. Naval Air Forces Pacific Fleet, I think it was called.

Admiral Stroop: That's about right. We set up headquarters again on Ford Island, this time in the administration building. We had about two-thirds of Admiral Halsey's staff. Here

---

* The battle took place from 4 to 6 June 1942 and resulted in a major victory for U.S. forces.

again, I repeat that this was a job that really was assigned to Admiral Halsey and his staff, but he had taken his staff and gone to sea to fight.

Q: On the Saratoga, wasn't he?

Admiral Stroop: No, he was on the Enterprise at this time, and he left his old friend Jake Fitch sitting on the beach there to handle the nuts and bolts and training and that sort of thing, supporting aviation activities in the Pacific Fleet.* We stayed there until later on in the summer, when we were all ordered down to the South Pacific. I think probably this might be a good place to stop this.

Q: Yes, I do too.

Admiral Stroop: I have just examined my logbooks, aviation flight logs. I find an entry here which indicates that the flight from the cruiser with the commanding officer of the Lexington was made on the second of June. I did not have Captain Sherman with me; he was a passenger in the other plane. My passenger was Lieutenant (junior grade) Whiteside, who was one of the aviators from the ship.† He was, of course, to take charge of the plane and get it back to the cruiser after the Chester docked at the Broadway Pier in San Diego.

We returned to Pearl Harbor on the Chester, trying to get in on the end of the Battle of Midway, but obviously it soon became apparent that this was impossible. We sailed, I think, on the fourth of June from San Diego, and the Battle of Midway was already under way at that time.

We stayed in Pearl Harbor until September of 1942, and during this period I had one interesting trip with the admiral. He was asked to come back to Washington, and he picked

---

* Vice Admiral William F. Halsey, Jr., USN, had been in the carrier Enterprise (CV-6) during the early months of the war in the Pacific. In late May 1942, prior to the Battle of Midway, he had gone ashore because of a case of dermatitis and spent the summer recovering.
† Lieutenant (junior grade) George A. Whiteside, USN, was one of the pilots in the Chester's aviation detachment.

me to go along with him. We flew up to San Francisco on a Pan American flight, were picked up by Navy planes, and brought down to San Diego. We joined our wives and flew back with them commercially to Washington. We spent a few days in Washington, then back out again and on to Pearl Harbor.

Q: What was the purpose of the trip?

Admiral Stroop: Admiral Fitch had to make some reports in Washington, and I went along as his acting aide. I had nothing officially to do, except take care of the admiral.

Q: In September the Under Secretary of the Navy, Secretary Forrestal, came out on an inspection trip to the South Pacific.[*] The operation had gotten under way down there. The Japanese had landed on Guadalcanal. We had set up a base at Espiritu Santo and another base at Noumea in New Caledonia. Admiral Fitch was asked by Secretary Forrestal to accompany him on this trip to the South Pacific. They were to see, of course, down there the senior naval commander, who was Admiral J. S. McCain, who was a naval aviator and had the title of Commander Aircraft South Pacific.[†]

When Secretary Forrestal made his inspection trip down in the South Pacific, it was obvious that he felt that the two senior naval commanders down there should be relieved. He made a decision right on the spot to leave Admiral Fitch down and relieve Admiral McCain. Admiral McCain's staff and Admiral McCain himself had been working hard. They had gone through the Guadalcanal invasion and the fighting there, and it was decided that Admiral Fitch would remain and relieve Admiral McCain at that time.[‡]

At the same time, Secretary Forrestal decided to recommend to the Secretary of the Navy that Admiral Halsey be sent down to become Commander South Pacific Force, which occurred later on. This made a very interesting situation for those of us on Admiral Fitch's

---

[*] James V. Forrestal served as Under Secretary of the Navy from 21 August 1940 until the spring of 1944, when Secretary of the Navy Frank Knox died. Forrestal became Secretary of the Navy on 19 May 1944.
[†] Rear Admiral John S. McCain, USN.
[‡] This change took place in October 1942.

staff. Here the admiral had gone down on a short inspection trip, and he didn't come back. Admiral Jack Towers was ordered out from Washington; he was Chief of the Bureau of Aeronautics at the time.[*] He was ordered out to take the job that Admiral Fitch vacated, and Admiral McCain was ordered back to Washington to relieve Admiral Jack Towers.[†]

Q: What did you think of Forrestal in those days?

Admiral Stroop: I thought a great deal of him. Forrestal was a fine man. He was a fighter, and he worked well with people in uniform in the Navy. He was a very, very wonderful Navy Secretary. At this particular time, he was Under Secretary, but he was later to become Secretary of the Navy, a great wartime Secretary. He finished the war as Secretary of the Navy. He was a fine man.

Admiral Towers arrived in Pearl Harbor, and he was an old friend of mine. I'd worked for him in the Bureau of Aeronautics earlier and was awfully glad to see him. He made me part of his official household. We were situated in Quarters K on Ford Island, where I'd been previously with Admiral Fitch. Admiral Fitch decided after he was ordered to remain in the South Pacific that he wanted a few of his staff officers to come on down there with him. He asked for his flag lieutenant, who at that time was Lieutenant Pace; he asked for his chief steward Rettig, who had been sunk with us on the Lexington; and for Stroop. I always put them in that general order, indicating that the flag lieutenant and the chief steward were more important than Stroop. But I was ordered to the South Pacific, and we got all the admiral's clothes and gear . . .

Q: What were you ordered to be, planning officer?

---

[*] Rear Admiral John H. Towers, USN, served as Chief of the Bureau of Aeronautics from 1 June 1939 to 6 October 1942. As a vice admiral, Towers served as Commander Air Force Pacific Fleet from 14 October 1942 to 28 February 1944.
[†] McCain served as Chief of the Bureau of Aeronautics from 9 October 1942 to 7 August 1943.

Admiral Stroop: I was ordered down as plans officer for his staff. I didn't know when I went down just what job I was going to get, but I . . .

Q: He must have had that Marine orderly come too.

Admiral Stroop: You know, I'm sorry, but I can't tell you what happened to that Marine orderly in the Lexington. No, I'm afraid not. The Marine orderly and all the Lexington crew remained back here on a well-justified leave period and were redistributed to other organizations, all except the admiral's staff. We got all the admiral's gear together, and our own gear, and flew from Pearl Harbor down to Noumea in a PBM-3 with, oddly enough, a Pan American crew.[*] My flight log here shows that we left Pearl Harbor on the 21st of September 1942, landed at Palmyra Island, and I hadn't been there since the war started. There I saw my old friend Jim Dudley, who was in command at Palmyra, spent the night, and then on to Canton Island the next day, Suva the next day.[†] I remember at Suva we remained overnight and passed Admiral McCain and his staff, who were coming north. I had a chance just during the night to have a little conversation with some of my old friends on the staff who were coming out with Admiral McCain.

Q: Was he glad to be relieved?

Admiral Stroop: I think not. I think not. But this was a very logical thing. He had . . .

Q: No reflection on his performance, was it?

---

[*] The Martin PBM Mariner was a two-engine flying boat that first entered fleet patrol squadrons in 1941. The PBM-3C was 80 feet long, had a wing span of 118 feet, a gross weight of 58,000 pounds, and a top speed of 198 miles per hour.

[†] Commander James R. Dudley, USN, had been the navigator in the Lexington prior to the ship's sinking.

Admiral Stroop: Not at all. He had done a fine job down there, and he had a fine spirit, and he'd been through a touch series of actions. You recall that Admiral Halsey, at this time, was in the hospital in Richmond, Virginia. He'd missed the Battle of Midway.

Q: Oh, I thought he was in the hospital at Pearl.

Admiral Stroop: No, Richmond, Virginia. Apparently Admiral Halsey had some sort of skin disorder, and they had some experts there, and that's where he went.

Q: I see.

Admiral Stroop: And Admiral Spruance had Admiral Halsey's staff at the Battle of Midway, whereas Admiral Halsey was in the hospital.* When he left the hospital and recovered, then he was ordered to the South Pacific as Commander South Pacific Force.

Q: To relieve Admiral Ghormley, wasn't it?

Admiral Stroop: To relieve Admiral Ghormley down there.† Admiral Ghormley was affected by the decision of Secretary Forrestal--his recommendation to make two changes. Now, Admiral Ghormley, of course, was an older man than McCain, and he never came back to active combat command, whereas McCain did.‡ McCain came back to Washington and did a very fine job in the latter part of the war, getting these large airplane programs going. Then, as soon as he could, he got to sea again and, of course, became Admiral Marc Mitscher's counterpart in the fast carriers in the war.§ He was one of the very fine, effective

---

* Rear Admiral Raymond A. Spruance, was serving as Commander Cruiser Division Five when he was ordered to take command of Task Force 16. He embarked in the carrier Enterprise (CV-6) and used Admiral Halsey's staff.
† Vice Admiral Robert L. Ghormley, USN, served as Commander South Pacific Force from June 1942 until his relief by Vice Admiral Halsey in October of that year.
‡ Ghormley, born 15 October 1883, was then 59; McCain, born 9 August 1884, was 58.
§ In 1944-45, Vice Admiral Marc A. Mitscher, USN, served as Commander Task Force 38/58, the fast carrier task force.

commanders. There was no reflection on Admiral McCain in being relieved by Admiral Fitch.

Q: What about the Ghormley relief? There's some reference to it.

Admiral Stroop: Well, of course, Admiral Ghormley was an older man, and he'd been through a great deal of strain. He was very close to retirement, so, here again, probably without reflection on his performance, it was decided to put a younger, more vigorous man in this particular theater where we were going to have some very tough fighting.[*] Admiral Ghormley, as I recall, did not get any more combat assignments after that one, whereas, of course, Halsey, McCain, and Fitch all did.

Q: What ship were you on when you went down, and was Admiral Fitch in?

Admiral Stroop: Well, I finally made contact with the admiral in Espiritu Santo. We landed in this big seaplane with a Pan American crew finally at Noumea. We had a nonstop flight from Suva, where we had met several members of McCain's staff, and on into Noumea. Then I caught a ride in a Marine Corps Douglas transport, a DC-3, and flew up with a lot of cargo to Espiritu Santo.[†] We landed on the new strip that had been made there by the Seabees and made contact with the staff on the USS Curtiss.[‡]

The Curtiss was a large seaplane tender, and she was based there in Segundo Channel, which is the main harbor in Espiritu Santo.[§] They had based there also two squadrons of PBY Catalina seaplanes, as well as the staff of Commander Aircraft South

---

[*] Halsey was born 30 October 1882, making him about a year older than Ghormley.
[†] R4D Skytrain was the Navy/Marine Corps designation for the Douglas DC-3 commerical airliner and transport.
[‡] Seabees is the name universally applied to members of the Navy's mobile construction battalions (CBs).
[§] USS Curtiss (AV-4) was commissioned 15 November 1940. She was 527 feet long, 69 feet in the beam, had a draft of 22 feet, and a displacement of 8,671 tons. Her top speed was 20 knots, and she was armed with four 5-inch guns. She had been damaged by the Japanese attack on Pearl Harbor in December 1941.

Pacific.* I had a very interesting period of duty during this stage of my career. I was planning officer and also did some intelligence work for the staff of Admiral Fitch. This, of course, included a number of trips up to Guadalcanal, where the fighting was quite heavy.

I was on Guadalcanal numerous times during this period and witnessed from the beach some of the night actions off Guadalcanal and saw some of the attacks by the Japanese. I also conferred with the Marine aviation general, Geiger, up there on the use of our Navy squadrons that were shore-based due to the loss of carriers.† We had remnants from the Wasp and remnants from the Saratoga.‡ When the Saratoga had to leave the area, she left her squadrons down there in the South Pacific. These small squadron remnants were operating under Marine command on Guadalcanal, and that was my particular concern, along with the Marine squadrons and along with a New Zealand squadron and U.S. Air Corps aircraft.

Q: Were you involved either with the Battle of Savo Island or Santa Cruz?

Admiral Stroop: Only to the extent of being in the area at the same time. I watched one of these from the beach, saw the action from the beach, and the next day saw some of the damaged cruisers that had been taken in to Tulagi, where they were hastily repaired enough so they could get out of the area and down to Australia, which I think was their next stop. But I was not directly involved personally in any of those actions. However, I was on Guadalcanal several times under quite heavy attack from the sea and went through several of those.

Q: Can you expand on them?

---

* The PBY Catalina was a twin-engine flying boat that performed extensive service before and during World War II. Built by Consolidated, it first entered fleet squadrons in 1936. The PBY-2 model had a wing span of 104 feet, length of 65 feet, gross weight of 28,400 pounds, and top speed of 178 miles per hour. Cruising speed was 103 mph.
† Major General Roy S. Geiger, USMC, Commander Aircraft Guadalcanal.
‡ The carrier Wasp (CV-7) was torpedoed and sunk by the Japanese submarine I-19 on 15 September 1942. On 31 August 1942, the Japanese submarine I-26 torpedoed and damaged the aircraft carrier Sartaoga (CV-3) while she was operating in the Solomons.

Admiral Stroop: Well, I think probably the most interesting night I spent there was with then Captain Gardner, who was chief of staff for Admiral Fitch.[*] He had been chief of staff to McCain and had been retained in the area along with the rest of that staff. Admiral Gardner and I had flown up first to Tulagi and looked at the little seaplane base which the Japanese had established over on Florida Island. We were then using it as a temporary base for cruiser-type airplanes that weren't operating from a cruiser. They were doing some patrol work there, and they were using this base.

We then went over to Guadalcanal and landed on the rather short strip there--3,500-foot strip--where they operated B-17s as well as all the Navy carrier planes and Marine Corps planes and New Zealand aircraft.[†] During our first night, we were under quite heavy attack. The Japanese brought down battleships--the Hiei, I think it was--and gave Guadalcanal the heaviest bombardment they had during this period.[‡] We were in a pretty good spot to get the effect of this. We were located at a Seabee camp down on the beach, and this was the beach over which the shells were coming. Fortunately for us, at least, the Japanese were trying to reach the airfields behind us.

Q: Henderson Field?

Admiral Stroop: Henderson Field--and their big guns, 14-inch shells--were going through the palm trees right over our heads. It was a pretty interesting experience.

Q: I'm always astonished at your use of the word "interesting," because I would think it would be a horribly frightening experience.

---

[*] Captain Matthias B. Gardner, USN, who later became a vice admiral and served as Commander Sixth Fleet, 1951-52.
[†] The Boeing B-17 Flying Fortress was a four-engine bomber used widely by the U.S. Army Air Forces in World War II.
[‡] This bombardment began at 1::00 A.M. on 14 October 1942. The Japanese battleships involved were the Kongo and Haruna, sisters of the Hiei.

Admiral Stroop: We spent most of that particular night in a foxhole during the bombardment.

Q: Was that the only protection you had?

Admiral Stroop: That's right. These foxholes weren't covered. They were just slit trenches, really. That was quite an experience. One of the sad things that happened that night--a Marine squadron which I had briefed just two days earlier in Espiritu Santo had arrived, a dive-bombing squadron. One of these shells hit right in the middle of their bivouac area and killed five of the pilots: the squadron commander, the executive officer, the operations officers, and two more pilots.[*] They hadn't even had a chance to get in the air to do anything. They'd arrived that day, and they were killed that night by an unfortunate hit. I saw the bodies being taken away the next day.

Q: They had no protection either?

Admiral Stroop: They were in slit trenches like we were.

Q: I see.

Admiral Stroop: As a matter of fact, though, as the story goes, they had taken cover in a slit trench, and the salvos were landing uncomfortable near where they were. So they decided to change their location, and they were actually out in the open, running, when this next salvo landed and wiped them all out.

Q: Had they stayed in the trench, presumably, they would have . . .

---

[*] These pilots were from VMSB-141. For a list of the names of those killed from the squadron that night, see Robert F. Sherrod, History of Marine Corps Aviation in World War II (San Rafael, California: Presidio Press, 1980) page 100.

Admiral Stroop: Could have been. We don't know. Well, this period was . . .

Q: How long did that bombardment last--hours?

Admiral Stroop: Yes. A bombardment would probably last two hours. It seemed longer.

Q: Sure.

Admiral Stroop: It seemed longer, and there'd be various ships coming in--destroyers, cruisers. Of course, we never knew exactly, and, of course, this particular night a battleship came in. She, incidentally, was finally lost there. She was incapacitated--I've forgotten how they stopped her, but she was floating around out there the next morning.[*]

Q: Oh, that was the night she was sunk?

Admiral Stroop: Well, besides visiting Guadalcanal--here, again, referring to the log, I notice that I got down to the island of Efate and made an occasional trip back to Admiral Halsey's headquarters at Noumea.

Q: How well did you know Admiral Halsey?

Admiral Stroop: I got to know him pretty well. I have a picture which he autographed for me after the war, and a very friendly autograph. But he and Admiral Fitch were very good friends, and our staffs worked together. I remember an amusing incident that I knew about because when Admiral Fitch and Admiral Halsey really got together, they would go ashore together on liberty, and I would hear the details the next morning of their expedition ashore. So we got to be quite good friends.

---

[*] The battleship Hiei sank a month later, early on the morning of 13 November 1942, after a bombardment mission that was thwarted by U.S. cruisers and destroyers.

Paul D. Stroop #3 - 133

Q: At the Battle of Santa Cruz Islands, I read that he extended his calculated risk policy by sending both the <u>Hornet</u> and the <u>Enterprise</u> to attack the Japanese Combined Fleet, and lost the <u>Hornet</u>, the <u>Enterprise</u> being heavily damaged.[*] Do you have any feeling of criticism about him for that action?

Admiral Stroop: No, I don't think so. I think this was the obvious decision for a commander to make. I must admit that Admiral Halsey was the kind of a man who would take a calculated risk, and he encouraged his staff people to do it. Most of the time he got away with the calculated risks. He didn't here in this case, and you remember later on in the Philippine Sea action he failed to avoid some heavy hurricanes, and he lost three destroyers there. And, of course, he's been criticized for taking the attack carriers north, you know, and chasing the Japanese, hoping he would get a fleet action, when in this particular case he probably should have stayed down round the San Bernardino Straits. But I don't fault him for this.

Q: It's easy in retrospect, I'm sure, for armchair historians to criticize.

Admiral Stroop: That's right. Well, we're getting far afield from the South Pacific action.

Q: I remained with Admiral Fitch down there, operating chiefly out of Espiritu Santo and based on the seaplane tender <u>Curtiss</u> for about one year. Toward the end of the tour, I remember, it was decided to release the <u>Curtiss</u> from the difficulty of handling the staff, and I guess she was probably ready to leave the South Pacific anyway. So we set up headquarters ashore, on the north shore of Segundo Channel. Had a very fine camp built by the Seabees: a nice mess hall, and Dallas huts for the senior people on the staff, two people to a Dallas hut. This was quite a comfortable situation, although I didn't enjoy it very long. I was ordered to my first command at this time.

---

[*] This battle was on 26 October 1942.

I had a rather interesting little experience just before we left the Curtiss. Admiral McCain came out from Washington to make an inspection tour. He was then Chief of the Bureau of Aeronautics, and due to my previous experience in the Bureau of Aeronautics and in aviation planning, where I'd been relieved by George Anderson, Admiral McCain got me ordered back to the same job, for me to relieve Anderson. This was early in '43. The job had been expanded greatly, and it was essentially a captain's job. It was a fine job, except I didn't want to go back. My orders were out in the mail, and I protested to Admiral Fitch about it. He knew, of course, that Admiral McCain was coming. He, in turn, protested to Admiral Halsey. Well, Admiral Halsey and Admiral McCain met on the quarterdeck of the Curtiss. I was there with them, and the first thing that Admiral Halsey did was to start berating Admiral McCain for ordering me to be out of the war zone. I have a wonderful picture. The photographers began hearing a noise about this . . .

Q: They heard the noise and came to take a picture of you?

Admiral Stroop: They took a picture, and it shows Admiral Halsey talking to Admiral McCain. I'm standing in the middle, because it's obvious that Admiral Halsey's going to have his way and get the orders rescinded, which he did. Well, I had been told that if I stayed down there, I'd get command of a small seaplane tender. But when Admiral Halsey made his protest to Admiral McCain, it didn't seem like quite the appropriate time for me to ask for a different set of orders. So I was left attached to Admiral Fitch's staff for another month or two. Right after the Halsey-McCain confrontation on the deck of the Curtiss, we did then move ashore. I was ashore, I guess, with Admiral Fitch for another month, and then I very quietly got orders to the seaplane tender Mackinac.* It looks like "Mackinack," pronounced "Mackinaw."

---

* The USS Mackinac (AVP-13) was commissioned 24 January 1942. She had a standard displacement of 2,592 tons, was 312 feet long and 41 feet in the beam. Her top speed was 18.2 knots. She was armed with one 5-inch gun, eight 40-mm., and six 20-mm.

Q: Before we leave this area of your tours of duty, I'd like to read here the citation that you received in your commission. The Legion of Merit which was awarded you for "exceptionally meritorious conduct as flag secretary for Commander Task Force 11 during the Coral Sea action on May 7 and 8 and as planning officer for Commander Aircraft, South Pacific Force, during the period from September 26, 1942 to April 4, 1943. Frequently called upon to make numerous recommendations affecting military decisions of great importance, he displayed unerring judgment and excellent foresight in planning. His calm deliberation while under fire by Japanese aerial forces was an inspiration to his subordinates."

That ends that particular quote. The next award is a letter of commendation from Commander in Chief, U.S. Pacific Fleet, "for distinguished service in the line of his profession as intelligence and planning officer on the staff of the Air Task Group Command in preparation for, during, and after the successful engagement with the enemy in the Battle of the Coral Sea on May 7-8, 1942. He assisted in planning the air attack, maintaining an excellent system of reporting intelligence information received, and gave valuable assistance to the task group commander."

I can somehow feel that you would have had the same calm deliberation then that you have now, and you've made a graphic description of this particular period of duty, which I think is very, very exciting. And now we come to your first command after all of this period. Let's see, from 1926 to 1943, that's 17 years after you graduated.

Admiral Stroop: That's right. I got dispatch orders to command the Mackinac, and this, of course, pleased me very much. It sort of complicated my personal life.

I had a friend back in Washington, Captain Whitey Blick, who was a detail officer in the Bureau of Aeronautics.[*] He had quietly told Mrs. Stroop that I was being ordered back to Washington and that she should start getting ready to move. She had a lease on a very nice little home over here in Coronado at a prewar price. So she gave up the lease and announced her intention to leave. She started packing boxes and was ready to move, just

---

[*] Captain Robert E. Blick, Jr., USN.

like a good Navy wife. Then, all of a sudden, it was found that I wasn't coming back at all. My orders had been changed to remain in the South Pacific. This caused a little flurry in the domestic household, but we managed to live that down all right. I spent another year out there and enjoyed this new duty.

Well, the log book here shows that on the fifth of April, 1943, I flew from Espiritu Santo in a Catalina PBY-5 on a long-range patrol up toward Ocean and Nauru islands, and then doubled back to Vanikoro Island. This was where the seaplane tender Mackinac was anchored. The Mackinac's mission there was to act as a forward support base for our seaplane patrols in that area. The planes themselves were based most of the time at Espiritu Santo, which was quite a safe area. They didn't have enough range to leave Espiritu to go to the full extent of the patrol that was assigned and come back. So they would come back only as far as Vanikoro Island, which was 300 or 400 miles farther north. They would remain overnight there and then take off before dawn the next day and reverse their patrol. They would wind up at Espiritu, where the Curtiss was located, their permanent base, or as permanent as anything could be under those situations.

Well, I landed at Vanikoro and was taken on board the tender. I met an old friend of mine, Horace Butterfield, who had been an instructor at Pensacola.[*] He was in command, and I had orders to relieve him. I remember this part of my career very well, because getting a first command is the most unusual highlight in your life. It occurs not too frequently.

Q: There's nothing else like it, is there?

Admiral Stroop: That's right. I'll never forget--I was given one of the senior staterooms on the ship to spend the night. I'd gotten there about dark and talked a little bit with the commanding officer. The ceremony--change of command--was to take place the next day. The captain's steward came down to wake me up in the morning. I had by this time made the rank of commander. He knocked on the door, woke me up, and said, "Captain, how

---

[*] Commander Horace B. Butterfield, USN, commanded the Mackinac from 2 September 1942 to 6 April 1943, when Stroop relieved him.

will you have your eggs?" He was the first person to call me "Captain," you see, and I've never forgotten that experience.

Q: What did your insides do with that?

Admiral Stroop: Felt pretty good. So we had breakfast, and during the course of the morning we went through a few of the general drills and fired the forward gun, the only gun we had on the ship, a 5-inch. Then we went through the change-of-command ceremony, and Captain Butterfield left--I think that day. He flew down to Espiritu Santo, and I had the ship.

Q: How many people were under your command?

Admiral Stroop: We had about 230 on the seaplane tender itself, and we would have as many as six airplane crews stationed on board, in addition to these. Each crew would be about, oh, eight people per crew. So it would be about 48 or 50 people in addition who would be spending the night there. Our job was to provide a base for the crews to fuel the aircraft, service the aircraft, and . . .

Q: And repair?

Admiral Stroop: We could do minor repairs, which we had to do on occasion. We'd check engines and change cylinders and that sort of thing. We even changed an engine one day, which was quite a big chore. We had to do that on the beach. We also patched a hole in the hull of a seaplane one day. Even though we didn't have a crane to lift the seaplane, we managed to steady it in the water and plug it from the inside.

This was a fine independent command, an interesting experience, and you felt like you were accomplishing something. When the first commanding officer put the ship in commission, he had gotten a little SOC assigned to us, a little single-engine seaplane, and this was very unusual.* This type ship normally wouldn't carry a seaplane, but they had done some work earlier in the South Pacific where they needed it. The seaplane was still on board, and I had the great pleasure of having my own private airplane to fly around, which I used. We knew that if we were going to be observed by the Japanese, this would probably occur around noon, so I would take the seaplane up and get to a level of about 12,000 feet over the harbor with my two little .30-caliber guns loaded. I figured if a Japanese patrol plane came over, I could at least make one pass at him.

Q: Why did this happen at noon?

Admiral Stroop: Well, we figured they were patrolling on about the same schedule as we were.

Q: I see, and the same distances?

Admiral Stroop: And the same distances, so they would be overhead around noon. So I'd get airborne about 10:30 or 11:00 o'clock, and I was the only pilot on board the ship, by the way. All the rest were deck officers. I'd go up and stay overhead, and I had a plan to make one pass at the Japanese patrol plane. I figured I could never make more than one, because they were really faster than I was. I'd surprise them, and then I'd go down right close to the ship. If he came down low, why, the guns would shoot him down. Well, it never worked out. We never were observed there. The Japanese for some reason--maybe their patrols weren't coming out as far as we gave them credit for--did not ever find us at Espiritu Santo. We operated on a very pleasant, profitable, worthwhile existence.

Q: Maybe here is a good time to ask you some questions about your ideas. Did you have any personnel problems?

---

* Commander Norman R. Hitchcock, USN, was commanding officer of the Mackinac from her commissioning on 24 January 1942 to 2 September 1942.

Admiral Stroop: No, none to speak of. I think we were extremely fortunate that way. We had a good staff of officers. I was a little shocked when I took the ship over to find that there was only one other regular officer on board. All the rest at this time of the war were reserves, but they were outstanding men in general. I had the finest group of chief petty officers you'd ever want to find. They were mostly fleet reserve people that had come back in. They'd been trained in destroyers. I had four or five of these old-time chiefs that had 20 years in the Navy, had retired, and come back at the beginning of the war. They had been assigned to this ship just as she was being commissioned right at the beginning of the war up in Bremerton, and these people were the backbone of the organization. They had a lot of experience that the reserve officers didn't have, and they were able to handle the inexperienced men in the crew very well. I really had an outstanding organization that way and absolutely no problems on that ship at all. I inherited a fine operation, and it continued to be quite effective, I thought, during the ten months I had command.

We would base at Vanikoro, which incidentally is the name used in Michener's <u>Tales of the South Pacific</u>.* Most of those glamorous things that he found on Vanikoro or people on Vanikoro didn't happen on my watch, I can tell you. There were a few people ashore on the island there. An Australian administrator, who had responsibility for all those islands in that general area, and Vanikoro had been the headquarters for a large lumbering operation. They had exotic hardwoods growing on this island. It was a volcanic island with a high peak in the middle and some ridges and a good stand of timber. The man and his wife who had been there before the war and were still there, with one other Australian and a crew of natives who were taking care of the machinery, keeping it oiled and preserved. So we had sort of a tight little group: the British administrator and the caretaker for the lumber company and his wife and myself. So we had a little bit of social life.

I was invited ashore for dinner, I think every Tuesday, to the administrator's house, and the following day I'd have him to dinner out on the ship. Set up a little pattern of that kind. We had recreation ashore. No place to swim, but we had a baseball diamond and set up a little rifle range. We'd go over and learn to shoot rifles and pistols. We were allowed

---

* James A. Michener's popular novel <u>Tales of the South Pacific</u> (New York: Macmillan Company, 1947), was later transformed into a Broadway musical and a motion picture.

in those days to carry beer on the ship, not to consume it on board, so each day I would send a couple of cold cases of beer over for the crew and for the officers. The crew would have it for the baseball game and after the game. The officers had taken over one of the residences there left vacant by the lumber company, and we had a little officers' club. We'd gather there in the evening, then go back to the ship just before dinner, have dinner on the ship, and remain on the ship all night.

Q: The ship, of course, didn't tie up?

Admiral Stroop: No, the ship was anchored out right in the vicinity where all the planes were anchored.

Q: Oh, sure.

Admiral Stroop: One other interesting recreation was fishing. Probably the finest fishing in the world around these islands. I used to go out in the morning after the patrols were off and things had quieted down and take a spin around the reef and across the entrances and come back with fresh fish.

Q: What kind of fish?

Admiral Stroop: Oh, various kinds of jack fish and barracuda, which weren't good to eat, of course. Fish of that nature--also, small tarpon.

Q: But you would bring it and then have it for the mess?

Admiral Stroop: Bring it back, yes. I had a regular routine. I'd go out before breakfast and come back to the ship with three fish. These would be sent up to the galley as soon as I landed. I'd go back and take my bath and shower and shave, and there'd be fresh fish for breakfast.

Q: Delicious.

Admiral Stroop: Almost ideal. And, of course, you'd frequently catch enough for all the messes, including the officers' mess too. I'd take some of the ship's officers out, and occasionally one of the aviators would come up and stay over after his patrol. He would stay until his next patrol and go fishing with me. It was a . . .

Q: It sounds almost ideal.

Admiral Stroop: It was a pretty ideal existence. It didn't stay that way forever, though.

We had about three weeks' endurance there. We were limited in our stay at Vanikoro Island by the amount of aviation fuel we carried. That determined our cycle. We carried 80,000 gallons of avgas, and that would last these patrol planes about three weeks, at which time we would have to go back to Espiritu Santo and replenish.[*] I'd be relieved then by a converted destroyer called an AVD, and they were limited to about nine or ten days' operation. So I had just enough time to leave Vanikoro, go back to Espiritu Santo, refuel, get other supplies aboard, go alongside a tanker and get oil--diesel for the ship--and return to Vanikoro, where I would stay for another three weeks. This went on for about three or four months, I guess.

Finally, a new ship of the same class came down to relieve me. It was Commander Ira Hobbs, who had been a friend of mine at the Naval Academy, in the Chincoteague.[†] Ira had a brand-new crew, a brand-new ship, and was a very, very methodical, conscientious man. He brought his ship in there. We were carrying on our job with really a rather pleasant and effective way. I thought we were quite efficient, and actually few worries on the captain's part because we had such a fine crew and fine officers. I'll never forget when Ira came in, I told him about all the advantages of the place and how to do the job, and

---

[*] Avgas--aviation gasoline.
[†] Commander Ira E. Hobbs, USN, was the first commanding officer when the USS Chincoteague (AVP-24) was commissioned 12 April 1943.

there was really no difficulty. I said, "You're going to enjoy it here very much. I think you're making a contribution to the war."

But I also told him that there was a plan later on, a few days later, to carry on an attack using six PBYs against Ocean and Nauru islands, Japanese islands about 600 miles north of us. And, of course, he would be supporting this attack. I stayed overnight there. We remained at anchor all night, showed Ira the facilities on the beach, and sailed the next day for Espiritu. I was then to go on up to San Francisco. The ship had been gone about 15 months and had suffered some battle damage before I took command. It needed some overhaul work, which was to be done at Mare Island Shipyard.*

I remember as we steamed out the harbor, one of our PBYs landed and made the mistake of taxiing up on a reef. So here was Ira Hobbs, with his new crew, faced immediately with an unusual difficulty, getting this plane off the reef and probably fixing up the bottom. Then, as we went on down toward Espiritu Santo, I, of course, was listening on the airplane search circuits and found that one of our PBYs had gone down in the sea. So Ira had to set up some temporary facilities on the beach, take his ship out of the harbor, and go down and try to pick up this airplane and tow it in. So right away, right at the beginning of his tour, he had two things to do that I'd never had to do.

But the real test--the real trouble--came when this attack group came through to go up to Ocean and Nauru islands. Of course, these were extra airplanes. I think there were six or seven in the attack group, and Ira had to put them up as well as the regular patrol crews. He got them off on their attack, which was made, I believe, at night. The Japanese, of course, didn't like this attack, and so they followed the planes back to Vanikoro and found out where they were based, and mounted their own attack on Ira Hobbs's Chincoteague. She took some close misses at the anchorage, and he decided to get his ship under way. He went out to sea and out there got a direct hit in one of his engine rooms, which put that engine out of commission.†

I don't know what happened after that, but I think they probably overspeeded the diesels on the other shaft. They overspeeded and finally caught fire, and so he lost all of his

---
* Mare Island Navy Yard, Vallejo, California.
† The Japanese attacks on the Chincoteague were on 16 July 1943.

power. Here he was, off Vanikoro Island with a ship that was damaged enough to sink, and he had no power aboard. Of course, here I was--I'd left Espiritu Santo and was on my way to San Francisco and expecting any minute to get orders to turn around and go back and relieve Ira. But they found another ship to take his place, so I did not get turned around. They finally got a destroyer alongside, one of the converted destroyer seaplane tenders, and helped Ira out. Then a fleet tug came alongside and put some pumps aboard. They saved the ship, of course, took it under tow, and he finally arrived in Espiritu Santo.[*]

Q: He probably believe the stories you told him of how calm and good the duty was were all made up.

Admiral Stroop: Well, I finally heard from him in person about two months later. Ira was under fairly frequent attack during this towing operation. The Japanese would come over in their Bettys and would make very deliberate passes over the ship.[†] If they didn't like a pass, they wouldn't drop a bomb. They'd circle back, make another run, and finally let the bomb go. He was too far away to get fighter cover during the early part of this. Finally, the last day out, they sent some F4Us, fighters just arrived in the South Pacific, to cover him.[‡] They'd been over him most of the day and were just leaving to go back to Espiritu when the Japanese Bettys showed up. The F4Us had enough fuel left, enough time left, so they came in and sawed off these four Japanese. So Ira finally had the satisfaction of seeing his tormentors dumped in the ocean. He came into Espiritu Santo, where they patched up his holes. His engines were gone, and they couldn't repair them at all, so he had to come back to San Francisco on the end of a towline, which is a long, long tow.

---

[*] Towed by the Thornton (AVD-11) and then the Sonoma (AT-12), the Chincoteague reached Espiritu Santo on 21 July for emergency repairs and then was towed to San Francisco.
[†] The G4M (known by the Allied code name Betty) was a Mitsubishi Type 1 two-engine, land-based torpedo bomber.
[‡] The Vought F4U Corsair was in production longer than any other U.S. fighter plane of World War II. It first entered fleet squadrons in 1942. The F4U-1 was 33 feet, 4 inches long; wing span of 41 feet; gross weight of 14,000 pounds; and top speed of 417 miles per hour.

Q: Oh, terrible.

Admiral Stroop: And no ability to make fresh water, and these little ships carried no fresh water supply to speak of at all. They had to cut the crew down to a minimum and get towed all the way back to San Francisco.

Q: Miserable. It took what--weeks?

Admiral Stroop: Yes, I guess it must have taken about five weeks, because I continued on to Mare Island, of course, and had gone into the shipyard there. Mrs. Stroop had been warned that it would be a good idea to take a trip to San Francisco for her health, so she arrived the night before I got in, and we had a wonderful reunion there in San Francisco. I went into the yard, and we had about six weeks' overhaul. Just at the end of the overhaul, when I was all freshly painted and ready to go to sea again, to go out to the war zone, and here came the poor old Chincoteague on the end of a towline. She was moored just across the dock from me.

Ira was one class senior to me, so I went over to pay my respects. The first thing he said to me was, "I thought you said it was quiet at Vanikoro." Then he smiled, and we've been good friends ever since. That little action which his ship went through was so important, so tough, that they gave the ship a battle star for it.

Interview Number 4 with Vice Admiral Paul D. Stroop, U.S. Navy (Retired)

Place: Admiral Stroop's home in San Diego, California

Date: Saturday, 1 November 1969

Interviewer: Commander Etta-Belle Kitchen, U.S. Navy (Retired)

Admiral Stroop: In February 1944 I was ordered to shore duty in the Navy Department. I turned over command of the <u>Mackinac</u> to my relief at Makin Island in the Central Pacific and proceeded by air to Pearl Harbor and San Diego.[*] My wife and I went to Washington first, leaving our three children behind at Coronado until we could find a place to live.

I was originally ordered back to Washington to take the same job that Admiral McCain had wanted me for over a year earlier. However, on the way back and before I arrived, my orders had been changed. I was directed to report to the staff of Admiral E. J. King, who was then not only Chief of Naval Operations but also the Commander in Chief of the United States Fleet.[†] I was attached to the planning section of his staff and worked directly with Captain A. K. Doyle, later to be Admiral Doyle; Rear Admiral Bieri; and Rear Admiral Duncan.[‡]

In this position I had frequent contact with Admiral King, particularly in the area of aviation planning. I found this job to be quite interesting, because we had all kinds of advance information on planning. We had theater reports on the progress of the war and participated in studies which were soon implemented in the form of operations. In addition,

---

[*] On 27 January 1944 Commander Gerald R. Dyson, USN, relieved Stroop as commanding officer.
[†] Admiral Ernest J. King, USN, served as Chief of Naval Operations from 26 March 1942 to 15 December 1945 and as Commander in Chief U.S. Fleet from 20 December 1941 to 2 September 1945; he was promoted to the rank of fleet admiral in December 1944.
[‡] Captain Austin K. Doyle, USN; Rear Admiral Bernhard H. Bieri, USN, whose oral history is in the Naval Institute collection; Rear Admiral Donald B. Duncan, USN, whose oral history is in the Columbia University collection.

I was detailed to accompany Admiral King and other members of his staff to the various international staff conferences at Quebec, Yalta, and Potsdam.

Q: In Malta also?

Admiral Stroop: Malta was a minor conference between the British and the U.S. just prior to Yalta. In a way, it might have been considered a teaming-up of the English-speaking people, and quite possibly resented by the Russians.

Q: Did they know about it?

Admiral Stroop: Oh, yes. The Russians knew about it, of course. But that, of course, is getting ahead of the story.

Q: Yes, it is.

Admiral Stroop: The Quebec conference was my first experience of this kind.*

Q: Before we get to that, can you tell me how much preliminary planning is done for this kind of a conference?

Admiral Stroop: In Yalta we were quartered in Livadia Palace, which had belonged to the Tsar. As a matter of fact, I felt that probably President Roosevelt, because of his physical condition, was given the best, most adequate quarters that the Russians had.† This

---

* Quebec was the site of two major Allied conferences during the war: Quadrant, which met 14-24 August 1943, and Octagon, which met 12-16 September 1944. The first reaffirmed the plan to invade continental Europe in the spring of 1944; the second dealt with plans for the postwar treatment of Germany. Stroop was still in command of the Mackinac during the first of the Quebec conferences.
† Franklin D. Roosevelt was President of the United States from March 1933 to April 1945. In the early 1920s had suffered an attack of polio that left his legs paralyzed.

happened, of course, to be the place where the tripartite meetings were to be held, in the Livadia Palace. In other words, the British principals and the Russian principals came to the Livadia for all the meetings.

Q: I read someplace that all the furniture for that palace, for that meeting, was brought down from Moscow specially.

Admiral Stroop: I suspect that this was largely true. I recall when we were getting ready for the Yalta Conference our staff officers in Moscow were very much concerned that they were not permitted by the Russians to participate in making arrangements for the conference. They felt that the Russian resources would be inadequate, they would not have proper furniture or proper staffing and all that sort of thing. But the Russians were obviously not about to have any assistance or advice from any other nationals.

As a matter of fact, we were so much concerned about this that we loaded up a command ship, the Catoctin, in the Mediterranean with all sorts of office equipment, typewriters, a language team, other furniture, and medical and PX supplies--to have them accessible for our delegation at Yalta if they were needed.[*] The commanding officer was an old Naval Academy friend of mine, Captain Owen Comp.[†] And they were available and did help us out to some small degree. They had to come about 50 miles from Sevastopol to Yalta to give us what services they were required to provide.

Q: Did you stay in the palace?

Admiral Stroop: Yes.

Q: Was it quite lavish?

---

[*] PX--post exchange.
[†] Captain Charles Owen Comp, USN.

Admiral Stroop: As a matter of fact, the palace was fairly well equipped for the conference. It certainly wasn't furnished in the manner in which the tsars had it furnished, simply because they were required to house a lot more people than the palace normally expected to house. The room that I was assigned, for example, would probably have been a small sitting room. In this room we had, I think, 12 or 14 officers in single beds, with the rank of captain, U.S. Navy; colonel, U.S. Army Air Forces; and some brigadier generals. The principals, of course, had single rooms. One of the big problems we had was the question of bathrooms. Obviously, the Tsar's palace was not equipped with very adequate bathing facilities for this number of people, and everybody was assigned by card to certain bathing facilities. I might add that the hand bathing facilities were separate from the regular bath facilities, which consisted of very large, old-fashioned bathtubs. The other facilities were also separate.

Q: What did your card say, the time you could go or . . . ?

Admiral Stroop: The card simply gave you the number of the room to which you were assigned for bathing. It did not give you the hours; you would just check up and see if it was available. I recall that in our particular bedroom, or dormitory, we soon found out that we had one problem, and that was bedbugs. The beds were Russian-provided, as were the mattresses and bedding. So we sent out a hurry-up call to the Catoctin, and the next day they provided a DDT squadron.* They gave an application of DDT to all the beds, which conquered that particular problem.

Q: Did the Russians have any comment on it?

Admiral Stroop: The Russians didn't comment, as far as I know, one way or the other. Or, really, they may not even have observed what we were doing. I think one of the outstanding features of the Yalta Conference was the way the Russians were able to provide

---

* DDT was a powerful insect spray of the period.

food at this stage of the war. I was told that the cooks and the waiters and the food and all the silver and furniture were brought down on a special train from Moscow, and a very fine, elaborate dining facility was established. That part of Russia had been famous before the war and still was, I guess, for raising grapes. There was an ample supply of wine at each table, and, of course, vodka was always present.

Q: Beautiful spot, don't you think?

Admiral Stroop: Yes, that coast of the Black Sea is quite beautiful. The Crimea is a high plateau with a rather abrupt descent to the Black Sea. The hillsides are covered with pines. The coast is a little rocky and very picturesque. Also, strangely enough, you find snow and blizzardy conditions up on the Crimea plain, and when you descend down into the Yalta area you find it's quite mild, much like our own Gulf Coast. Some days were quite pleasant and not freezing.

Q: That was the middle of winter when you were there?

Admiral Stroop: That was February of 1945. We found except for a few small details that the Russians had done an outstanding job of fixing up the facilities. I recall one rather amusing incident. The President apparently liked to have an old-fashioned every afternoon, and some complaint was made by members of his personal staff that there were no oranges around for old-fashioneds. The next day I happened upon a large Army truck right outside the President's quarters unloading a full-grown orange tree with oranges on it. It was moved into his living room, so he did finally have oranges for his old-fashioneds.

Q: A whole tree?

Admiral Stroop: Whole tree.

Q: I'll be darned.

Admiral Stroop: The military staff conferences at Yalta were, to my mind, not very important. Certainly I could tell from the attitude of the people who attended that they felt they were accomplishing nothing and that the conference should be adjourned, simply because the war was going favorably for the Allies. The strategy had been established. General Bedell Smith brought down the latest reports of operations, and it was obvious that the business at hand could only be in the area of political decisions. So the military staffs were ordered home after about four or five days.

The President, Stalin, and Churchill stayed on and went through the process of making political decisions, some of which were, as we all know now, unfavorable to the United States. My last act at Yalta was to ride down the coast 50 miles to Sevastapol and to inspect the Catoctin and to make sure that it was ready to take care of the President if he decided to return that way, which, in fact, he did. He left Sevastapol on the Catoctin, and he went over for a short conference in Saudi Arabia.

Q: Who was that with? I don't remember that.

Admiral Stroop: He met with King Ibn Saud. I'm a little hazy on that, but I'm sure there was some sort of a short two-way conference at that time.

I think the most important impression I have of the Yalta Conference occurred just before the military conference broke up. All the principals were asked to assemble the last afternoon for a formal picture. This was to include President Roosevelt, Mr. Churchill, Stalin, their civilian secretaries of state, foreign office, and their three principal military superiors, that is, the heads of the three armies, navies, and air forces. I wanted to witness this picture-taking and first tried to get out on a balcony overlooking the enclosed patio area where the principals were assembling. Here I ran into Russian armed guards, which were very heavily posted all around the place, and was not permitted to get out on the balcony. I then went down below to the patio area and walked around behind the cameras, where I had a good observation point to see the grouping for the pictures.

Probably the most interesting and certainly shocking thing that I noticed was the physical condition of our President. I had not seen him personally for some time, and it was quite obvious that he was in very, very bad physical shape. As a matter of fact, I think his immediate staff and family had anticipated some difficulty because, you recall, his daughter, Mrs. Boettiger, went along on the trip. The pictures were rather hurriedly taken, and it was a little bit chilly there; everybody was dressed up in greatcoats and capes. The President had on the Navy boat cloak that he liked so much.

I recall one little incident that further shocked me. One or two of the photographers began taking pictures before our President felt that he was ready to have his picture taken. I think he realized that he was quite sick, and he wasn't going to make a very good appearance, which he realized that he didn't. He became very annoyed with the photographers who were taking pictures before he gave them permission, and he began talking to them in a very loud voice, making them stop. Rather embarrassing to see this great man who obviously was not mentally himself. I noted that Churchill and Stalin both tried to look the other way and not observe this little bit of outburst.

Q: Not only was he physically ill, but he was mentally less than . . . ?

Admiral Stroop: Mentally upset--let's put it that way.

Q: Mentally upset--maybe that would explain some of the decisions made at Yalta.

Admiral Stroop: I think it probably did, because it was in just the following two or three days that these decisions and agreements were reached which were unsatisfactory from the U.S. point of view.

Q: I really think that's an interesting footnote to history.

Admiral Stroop: When the pictures were all completed and the photographers were gathering up their gear, everybody left the scene, with the exception of the President. Of course, he was crippled and was unable to move from the chair in which he was seated. It seemed a little symbolical to me that he was sitting out there for a few moments all alone--all by himself, nobody there at all, just a couple of observers and the photographers. At this point, of course, an attendant came out--a Navy chief steward came out with a very small wheelchair without arms on it. This wheelchair was pushed up next to the President's chair, which was, I believe, a dining room type chair without arms. The President, who had great strength in his arms, lifted himself across unaided, from out of the dining room chair, where he had been seated during the picture-taking, into this very small wheelchair. He was then wheeled down on into his room in the palace. In the meantime, of course, everybody else had departed. The patio was deserted. That's the last time I ever saw the President.*

Q: It must have been a sad thing to see this.

Admiral Stroop: It was very sad, and you were embarrassed for him. You knew that he was embarrassed; he realized his condition. I think all the people who were close to him did. It was obvious that he shouldn't have been at the conference. I don't think he was in any condition to make the right kind of decisions or to argue or reach agreements with the other principals.

Q: And yet he was making world-affecting promises, decisions.

Admiral Stroop: Yes, this is true, and I think it probably explains some of the difficulties that resulted for the United States out of this conference. I might say that my personal observation of the staff work for the President at that conference made me feel that his staff was not well coordinated or well organized.

Q: Is that so?

---

* He died about two months later, on 12 April 1945.

Admiral Stroop: It seemed to me that they did not have a staff system the way we think of it in the military--that is, a chief of staff who controls and coordinates all the actions of the staff. There were individuals who reported personally to the President. They were responsible to nobody else and didn't talk to each other. So there was a great lack of coordination.

Q: That's an awful responsibility on him to try to tie all the ends together.

Admiral Stroop: Yes, that's correct. On the other hand, my observation of the British staff indicated that these people were really well organized. That is, the transmission of information from one staff member to the other, the teamwork involved, and the responsiveness to their chief, Churchill, left little to be desired.

Q: Interesting, isn't it?

Admiral Stroop: We found out actually that some of our opposite numbers on the British staff could be very helpful in transmitting information and decisions that had been reached at the highest level and which hadn't been passed on down to us. For this reason, we tried very much to have good relationships with our opposite numbers on the British staff.

Q: Did you observe any staff work on the part of the Russians?

Admiral Stroop: We had no contact with the Russian staff at all, and I don't think anybody on our staff did. The only time we seemed to meet was at the summit conferences, and then only a few staff members were permitted to sit in with our President or with the other principals. I was not one of those. I did not sit in on those main conferences.

Q: But you must have realized that you were at the heart of where history was being made.

Admiral Stroop: Yes, this is quite true. We didn't realize when we left, however, that some very far-reaching political decisions were about to be made.

Our return from Yalta was rather interesting. We left Livadia Palace in the evening and drove to a railway junction, a little town called Simferopol. It's a small town in the southern part of the Crimea. There we found a railroad train made up of sleeping cars to accommodate us for the night and to take us the remaining distance to the airfield at Saki, which is up in the northwest corner of the Crimea.

Q: When you say "us," does that include Admiral King?

Admiral Stroop: That included Admiral King and all of his staff.

Q: On this particular train that we were on, we were being entertained by a Russian admiral and his staff. The sleeping cars were quite old, European-style sleeping cars in rather poor condition, with the exception of one. The last car on the train was a Finnish diner, which had probably been liberated from Finland and brought down for this particular purpose. It was extremely well appointed, new, and clean. This is where we had our dinner that evening. The train didn't have very far to go, maybe 50 or 60 miles from Simferopol to Saki, so we traveled slowly during the night and stopped early in the morning at the point where we were picked up by cars and taken to the airfield.

The airfield at Saki was covered with snow, and we had a small amount of precipitation apparently during the night which left ice on the wings of the airplanes. So we had to delay our departure until there was enough sun. Some artificial heating was made available to get the ice off the wings before we could take off. The return to the U.S. was accomplished without incident. We refueled in North Africa and then came back.

Q: I wanted to ask you about Quebec, as I read some of the material that indicated that the Quebec Conference was where the decisions, or the timetable, was set up for the invasion of the Philippines, and that Halsey got word to it, via Admiral Nimitz, that we should bypass some of the islands that were in the timetable and go ahead and go directly to the Philippines, two months ahead of time.*

Admiral Stroop: Yes, that's right. That was probably the most important event of the Quebec Conference. I recall during the process of going over the strategy for the Pacific when this rather long message came in from Admiral Halsey, proposing an advance in the timetable and that the next big operation be made in the Philippines. This, of course, turned out to be excellent strategy, and the U.S. and the British saw the wisdom of this, agreed with it, and authorized Admiral Halsey to go ahead.

Q: Do you know what he based his recommendation on?†

Admiral Stroop: Well, I think he based his recommendation on the success he had in the previous operations and the fact that he hadn't been required to use up all of his resources or commit his reserves. I know, for example, that immediately after Kwajalein we went into Eniwetok on very much the same principle. Of course, this was a much smaller operation. Eniwetok was taken because he had not committed all his reserves at Kwajalein and had these forces to go ahead.‡ On a rather minor scale, this proved the wisdom of this course of action.

With MacArthur's forces coming up from the Southwest Pacific and Halsey's forces converging from the Central Pacific and both of these with uncommitted reserves, it was possible to advance the timetables. It was pretty obvious that we had overwhelming power, that the Japanese resources were inadequate, and that we could go ahead with an

---

* Admiral William F. Halsey, Jr., USN, Commander Third Fleet from March 1943 to November 1945. Admiral Chester W. Nimitz, USN, Commander in Chief Pacific Fleet and Pacific Ocean Areas, 1941-45. He was promoted to five-star rank in December 1944.
† For the perspective from Halsey's flagship, written by one of his staff officers, see Carl Solberg, Decision and Dissent: With Halsey at Leyte Gulf (Annapolis: Naval Institute Press, 1995).
‡ U.S. forces captured Kwajalein and Eniwetok in the Marshall Islands in February 1944. However, the commander for those operations was Vice Admiral Raymond A., Spruance, USN, Commander Central Pacific Force, not Halsey.

accelerated timetable. This turned out to be exactly the right decision. It was made and, of course, shortened the war. That was the most important development at the Quebec Conference.

Q: Did you stay there at the Chateau Frontenac?

Admiral Stroop: Yes, we were all based at the Chateau Frontenac. I remember they had a hard time, I heard, getting some of the old residents out of the place.

Q: Did you take over the whole thing?

Admiral Stroop: Yes, took over the whole hotel. I think maybe one or two were permitted to remain. It was an ideal location for a conference. There was adequate space for all members of the two delegations in the hotel, and you simply proceeded from one conference to another by elevators in the hotel. They had floors assigned to the various delegations and various sections of delegations. It was by far the best physical arrangement for any of the conferences we attended.

Q: Aren't you impressed when you think back on your experiences that you had the opportunity to meet all of the top people of our time?

Admiral Stroop: Well, this, of course, was the opportunity, and I felt that I was fortunate just to be there, particularly with my rather junior rank, that of a brand-new captain, and rather a junior job in the delegation.

Q: Yes.

Admiral Stroop: I enjoyed the designation of deputy planner. I was deputy to Admiral Duncan in the first two conferences and deputy to Admiral Gardner in the last conference. Since they sat in most of the meetings, I merely backed them up; I was there to sit in if they needed me. It was only in some of the minor meetings that I actually personally participated.

The third conference, the Potsdam Conference, was in many ways the most interesting. I don't think from the decisions that were made there--because, here again, the European war was over and the Japanese war pretty well along--that the physical conditions, that we were having this kind of a conference in enemy territory, and, of course, were very curious about the situation in Berlin. We found it very interesting to go sightseeing, see the physical condition of the country.

Q: How did you react to seeing the devastation?

Admiral Stroop: Well, I think it was probably about what we expected. I recall that we were based in a town called Babelsburg, which is near Potsdam and on the outskirts of Berlin. Babelsburg is a very nice residential community which is reported to have been the Hollywood of Germany before the war. The quarters were all quite nice. Admiral King had a very large house--as did Mr. Churchill and Stalin--which served as a mess for his staff. The various staff members, more junior staff members, were quartered in, billeted in, smaller houses in the general vicinity.

The Soviets had gone in there just a few days ahead of us and had removed all the civilians with great dispatch and with some cruelty. I remember one house where they had a very large dining room and a lot of banquet facilities and was used as an officers' club. In the back yard in the garden was a new grave. We were told that an old couple lived in this house, and they were given a couple of hours to take all of their things and leave. They had done this, but at the last minute the old lady who lived there decided that she'd forgotten something. She went back to the house and started entering. She was shot, killed, and buried there, right on the premises.

We found that these houses were in good shape. There was no evidence of war damage anyplace in this area. Services were good, and we were quite comfortably situated.

Q: It was President Truman now, wasn't it?*

Admiral Stroop: Yes. Here again, this conference at my level in the delegation--I did not sit in at the principal conferences; however, I did have two interesting personal experiences. Just before the conference adjourned, the Soviets asked for a two-way conference with the U.S. delegation--that is, without the British. This was to be held in a small palace that was rather isolated in a nearby forest. We had about half an hour to get ready and go to this conference.

I arrived there along with the rest of the delegation and found, among other things, that the U.S. did not have any photographers, whereas the place was heavily manned with Soviet photographers. I happened to have a camera with six exposures left in it, and I took six good pictures in a conference as the principals were filing in. These pictures turned out quite well and were later published in the Naval Institute Proceedings. Probably the most important contribution I've made to the Proceedings.

Here again, though, when they actually got down to conferring I was invited outside, along with some of the other junior people. The Russians were apparently talking with the U.S. delegation about the division of ships from the captured German Navy and other naval matters. They wanted to find out what the attitude of the U.S. would be regarding the Lend-Lease items which we had furnished the Soviet Navy in large quantity.† What they were trying to do, of course, was to retain all or as much of this equipment as they could at no cost.

The other incident which I enjoyed very much at the Potsdam Conference occurred on a free Sunday when Admiral King got all of us and took us over to Bremerhaven. On the trip over we saw some of the countryside. The most impressive sight there at Bremerhaven was this very large, well-equipped shipyard which had been building

---

* Harry S Truman became President of the United States following the death on 12 April 1945 of President Franklin D. Roosevelt.
† The Lend-Lease Act, passed by the U.S. Congress on 11 March 1941, was a device that enabled the United States to provide military aid--war materials--to Great Britain without intervening directly in the Eureopean war then in progress. The program was later expanded to include material for the Soviet Union, once it joined the war on the Allied side.

submarines. A large part of the operation was underground, covered with very heavy slabs of concrete--about 12 inches of reinforced concrete--and submarines were assembled there very quickly. As a matter of fact, I believe the production rate was estimated to be one every other day.

Q: Some of the parts had come from other places?

Admiral Stroop: That's right. This was the assembling point. The submarine hulls had been articulated in large sections and brought in with large cranes and put together. All the necessary equipment was in underground warehouses. We went through many of these and saw sonars, torpedo tubes, torpedoes, engines, all in large quantities and ready to be moved into where the submarines were assembled.

Q: Was there damage above ground?

Admiral Stroop: No. Strangely enough, we saw very little damage. The shipyard itself had supplies all over the place. It was quite crowded, and it was obvious that if the war hadn't ended, if the Russians had been able to continue the war, that the Germans would have continued to mount quite a good submarine effort, even though we were having quite a bit of success at sea in killing them. They were able to build plenty of them. I think probably the problem wouldn't have been material as much as providing crews for the submarines. We had no way of evaluating what success they were having there, but certainly from the material point of view in this particular line of effort, they were well equipped when the war ended. I was quite surprised.

Another impressive feature of that visit was the damage that we saw in Berlin. As you drove into Berlin from Babelsburg, which is on the edge of Potsdam, you noticed as you got closer to Berlin there was more damage, until you got into the center of the city and every building was knocked down.

Q: I've seen pictures of that and . . .

Admiral Stroop: The Russians had done an amazing job, however, of clearing the streets. Apparently they'd mobilized thousands and thousands of Germans into a labor force. They had shoveled the streets clear and even swept them--big, broad streets--and patched up the holes. The big, broad avenues were swept clean, and you really were going down a street with just piles of rubble on either side; they'd be as high as a two-story house. It was quite a sight.

Q: That was in July of '45. The war had been over, what, a month?

Admiral Stroop: Two months.

Q: May '45.[*]

Admiral Stroop: Two months, I guess. The most interesting point, the place where all of us wanted to go, of course, was the Reich Chancellery, Hitler's headquarters. We did visit it and found that it had been already visited by the Russians and pretty well torn up, and minor souvenir-taking occurred. I recall visiting a room where they apparently had kept records of all war decorations, and they had a great supply of medals on hand. There was a big pile of medals just on the floor in the middle of the room. They'd emptied out drawers of these. I picked up a dozen or so and brought them back two secretaries and officers back in Washington. I still have one or two around.

After Potsdam I did receive a very important assignment. An Army officer, two Air Force officers, and one naval officer were selected from the three U.S. staffs to proceed around the world and stop at the various headquarters and inform the commanders of what had gone on at the Potsdam Conference. We were assigned to an Air Corps C-54 for the trip.

---

[*] V-E Day--Victory in Europe Day--was 8 May 1945, when the German surrender was ratified in Berlin.

The three of us left Berlin and did proceed on around the world. We stopped first at Naples, Italy, and visited with General McNarney, four-star Army Air Corps general who had charge in that theater.* From there we went on down to--I guess we landed at Wheelus Air Force Base and then at Abadan just for fueling stops, and in India at New Delhi and on to Calcutta. At Calcutta we saw General Wedemeyer and then flew over the Hump and up into China.† The Army and Air Force representatives did that. We flew from the interior of China.

Q: Where did you stop in China--Chungking?

Admiral Stroop: We stopped at Kunming, and the Army colonel and the two Air Force generals then proceeded on up to Chungking for their briefing duties.

Q: I read someplace that Chiang Kai-shek was at the Potsdam Conference.‡ Do you recall that?

Admiral Stroop: I don't think so. I think that's wrong. I certainly would have remembered it. Truman and Churchill. But a rather interesting thing happened there. Churchill failed for reelection during the Potsdam Conference, and Attlee relieved him.§ Attlee actually had come to the early part of the conference and sat as an observer behind Churchill. The elections were held in England, and Attlee won. Churchill went back to England on election day, and Churchill never returned.

Going back to this trip around the world in the Army Air Corps C-54, after Chungking and Kunming we flew down to Manila and, here again, we separated. The

---

* General Joseph T. McNarney, USA, succeeded General Eisenhower as commander of the European Theater of Operations shortly after V-E Day.
† Lieutenant General Albert C. Wedemeyer, USA, chief of staff to Chiang Kai-shek and commander of U.S. forces in China.
‡ Chiang Kai-shek was President of China and Allied Supreme Commander of the China Theater of Operations. He attended the Cairo conference with Roosevelt and Churchill in 1943 but not Potsdam.
§ Clement R. Attlee became British Prime Minister in July 1945.

Army and Air Force representatives reported to General MacArthur, who was in Manila at the time, and I reported to the senior Navy amphibious commander there, who was going to participate in the next operation. Then from Manila, we went up to Okinawa, and I saw General [Unclear] in Okinawa, over to Iwo Jima for a refueling stop, and then on down to Guam.

Guam, of course, was headquarters of Admiral Nimitz, and I had the honor of being quartered in his guest house with his chief of staff, who was Admiral Forrest Sherman, an old friend of mine.[*] I recall my appointment with Admiral Nimitz occurred about 11:00 o'clock on the day that the first atomic bomb was to be dropped on Hiroshima.[†] I noticed Admiral Nimitz looking at his watch, and he asked me if I'd been briefed on this, which I had not, because we were flying over enemy territory. My official responsibilities had not included any briefings or any clearances on the Manhattan Project. So I was completely unaware of this. Admiral Nimitz said, "Well, there's a special event going to occur at 11:00 o'clock." Of course, by afternoon, after I'd talked to Admiral Nimitz, why, the whole world knew what had happened. The first atomic bomb had been dropped on Hiroshima, and there was quite widespread publicity.

Q: Can you amplify a little bit about Nimitz and how he looked and how he acted?

Admiral Stroop: Well, Nimitz hadn't changed any since I saw him, except that I thought he talked with a little more authority and certainly had more assurance, and he had more confidence in the outcome. He was the same wonderful, courteous, understanding individual that I had seen at Pearl Harbor in December of '41.

Q: Was he nervous about what was going to happen or what?

---

[*] Rear Admiral Forrest P. Sherman, USN, deputy chief of staff (plans).
[†] B-29 bombers of the U.S. Army Air Forces dropped atomic bombs on Hiroshima, Japan, on 6 August 1945 and on Nagasaki, Japan, on 9 August 1945. The Japanese surrendered shortly afterward.

Admiral Stroop: No, not at all. I don't think Nimitz was ever nervous. I think he was interested; he was following the event quite closely. He was waiting for news.

Q: Deeply concerned, I presume.

Admiral Stroop: Deeply concerned, but certainly he wasn't nervous.

Q: Did he give you any indication as to whether he thought it was good, bad, or . . . ?

Admiral Stroop: No, he did not. He did not express an opinion at all, of any kind, and I didn't see him after the bomb was dropped. I only saw him this one time in his office.

Q: The morning, before 11:00 o'clock, of that day?

Admiral Stroop: Yes. I think I was probably sitting in the chair talking to him when the event occurred.

Q: That, again, is a moment in history, isn't it?

Admiral Stroop: Yes. Well, the next day after the bomb was dropped, we were off for the U.S. Just before I left, Admiral Sherman, gave me a very large package of top-secret documents which I was to take back to Washington. He told me they were the plans for the occupation of Japan.

Q: Did you feel weighted down with that?

Admiral Stroop: Well, I never carried that volume of that highly classified paper before, and, believe me, it is a chore. You live with it and sleep with it.

Q: Have to practically tie it to your wrist, don't you?

Admiral Stroop: Take it right along with you every place you go.

Q: How big a package was it?

Admiral Stroop: Oh, they were larger than legal-size envelopes. There were two of them, and each one was about three inches thick. Quite a heavy package.

Q: Well, not easy to put in your pocket.

Admiral Stroop: No. They were tied together, and you carried it under your arm. Pretty obvious that you had something of importance with you. We left Guam, refueled at Johnston Island, and then came on into Pearl Harbor. I remember we stayed a couple of days at Pearl Harbor, and I was able to get the documents locked up there. Had a little freedom. Admiral Hoover was the senior officer present there.* He was in charge of the rear headquarters, rear echelon, of Admiral Nimitz's headquarters.

I recall rather painfully one incident. I attended a morning staff conference as a guest. At the end of the staff conference, Admiral Hoover acknowledged my presence. I think I'd had breakfast with him earlier and told him about some of the things that had happened. He asked me to get up and talk to the attendees at the conference about what had happened at Potsdam and about some of my impressions. Well, one of the impressions I carried away from the Potsdam Conference--and this came out of a joint meeting with the British--was that the British were extremely anxious to keep military aid and Lend-Lease coming. Even though the war had ended in Europe, and after it was ended in Japan, they wanted to keep a lot of these resources. I didn't realize that on the staff there, there was a British representative. I spoke rather freely and had rather a harsh opinion of the British attitude. I felt that Admiral Hoover probably shouldn't have called on me . . .

---

* Vice Admiral John H. Hoover, USN, Deputy Commander in Chief Pacific Fleet and Pacific Ocean Areas.

Q: He knew who was there, whereas you didn't.

Admiral Stroop: . . . under those circumstances.

Q: Of course, he didn't know what you were going to say.

Admiral Stroop: No. At any rate, this passed all right. We came on to the U.S., landed at Long Beach and refueled, and then came on to Washington. I remember we landed at Washington . . .

Q: I forgot to ask you if you delivered your package safely, because otherwise I'm going to think about it staying in that safe in Pearl Harbor.

Admiral Stroop: Well, I still had the albatross around my neck when we landed in Washington about 3:00 o'clock in the morning. I had a decision to make and decided to go home and take the package with me, which I did. I put it under my pillow and went to sleep, thinking that I would get it down to the Navy Department in plenty of time at the beginning of working hours. I slept in a little bit late that morning, and I recall my wife coming upstairs to wake me up and telling me that the war was over, that Japan had capitulated.* I said, "My God, here I am with the plans for the occupation of Japan under my pillow."

Q: Everybody was looking for them, huh?

Admiral Stroop: So I hurried down to the Navy Department and checked these plans in very quickly, and apparently no damage had been done.

Q: That's an interesting anecdote.

---

* Japan ceased hostilities on 15 August 1945 in the Far East, 14 August in Washington, D.C.

Admiral Stroop: Just before going to Potsdam, I had received orders for sea duty, and I had been ordered to command a small carrier in the Pacific. As a matter of fact, I had been held over in order to go to Potsdam, because the man I was assisting, Admiral Gardner, had not been to one of these conferences, and I'd been to two previous ones. It was felt that I could be of some assistance to him. My relief, who happened to be George Anderson, had reported before we left for Potsdam, and he was able to hold down my job in the Navy Department while I was gone.

I arrived back in Washington, and with the end of the Japanese war it was decided that I would no longer get my command in the Pacific. They would let me have command of a small carrier in the Atlantic, and I was ordered to take command of a small carrier, a CVE, it was called in those days, the Croatan.* It was a small, single-engined C-3 merchant ship converted to a carrier. This carrier had been engaged in antisubmarine work in the Atlantic until the war was over and was now assigned to training duty based at Quonset Point, Rhode Island. This tour of duty, of course, was not what I had anticipated.

Q: How did you feel, of course, besides getting rid of your papers, when war--I asked you originally how you felt when war was declared. What was your reaction--a letdown, a relief?

Admiral Stroop: Well, it was a sort of a relief and a realization that the pressures we'd been working under would probably be lighter, and that we could look forward to a more pleasant way of life. And, hopefully, the Navy would settle back down into peacetime routine, better family life, pleasanter life all the way round. And, in general, that's, of course, what occurred. The tour of duty on the Croatan was very short-lived. I didn't regret this very much, because we were only doing training duty, and we were . . .

---

* The USS Croatan (CVE-25) was commissioned 28 April 1943 as ACV-25. She was reclassified CVE-25 in July 1943. She had a displacement of 9,800 tons, was 496 feet long, 70 feet in the beam, an extreme width of 112 feet on the flight deck, and had a draft of 26 feet. She had a top speed of 17 knots and could accommodate approximately 28 aircraft.

Q: Training for aviators?

Admiral Stroop: We were training aviators in their final phase of training before they were ordered to combat squadrons, and it was obvious that this kind of activity would be ordered stopped almost immediately. As a matter of fact, it was hard to understand why it was still going on.

Q: They just hadn't . . .

Admiral Stroop: Just hadn't gotten around to issuing their orders. We had rather routine work there off Quonset Point for about three months. Then I was ordered to deliver the ship to the naval shipyard at Norfolk, where it was to be converted into a troop transport and assigned to what was called "The Magic Carpet"--bringing the troops back from . . .

Q: I didn't realize they actually converted ships to do that.

Admiral Stroop: Well, the carriers were particularly well adapted, because they could just install thousands of bunks on the hangar decks--deck spaces--and that's what they did. Of course, it was uncomfortable and crowded, but it was a way to get these troops back. That's what happened to the Croatan. However, I delivered her in the Navy yard, and my relief had been ordered. I had other orders, and my relief was then-Captain Don Griffin, who later on became four-star Admiral Griffin, class of 1927.[*]

I was ordered at that time to join the staff of Admiral Jack Towers, whom I'd worked for twice before, out in Japan.[†] I was to participate, oddly enough, in the occupation of Japan, carrying out the orders that I'd carried back from Guam. I was

---

[*] Captain Charles Donald Griffin, USN. Griffin's Naval Institute oral history discussed his command of the Croatan, along with many other tours of duty.
[†] On 8 November 1945, on board the battleship New Jersey (BB-62) at Yokosuka, Japan, Admiral John H. Towers, USN, relieved Admiral Raymond H. Spruance, USN, as Commander Fifth Fleet.

relieved in Norfolk by Captain Griffin and proceeded home. I had about five days' leave, which I spent with my family, then flew across the continent and across the Pacific. I joined Admiral Towers in Yokosuka Harbor, Japan, where he was commander of the Fifth Fleet, and I was to become his fleet aviation officer. I joined him, I believe, in late November or early December.

Q: I have November '45.

Admiral Stroop: I remained attached to that staff the remainder of the time that Admiral Towers was there, which was, oh, early January. He was relieved by Admiral Sherman.[*] I remained on with Admiral Sherman until my relief reported on board, who was then-Captain Allen Shinn.[†] In the meantime, I had fleeted up from fleet aviation officer to assistant chief of staff for operations. I was relieved, I guess, in February of 1946 and reported back again to Pearl Harbor, where Admiral Towers had already taken over as commander in chief in the Pacific and the Pacific Fleet--CinCPac/CinCPacFlt.[‡] I became fleet aviation officer on his staff with our headquarters at Makalapa, if I remember.

Q: What was the state of the Navy at that point?

Admiral Stroop: Well, the Navy, of course, along with the other armed services, was being reduced in size. A great many of the ships were being converted and put into the "Magic Carpet" service, along with converted liners like the Lurline, and bringing troops back from Japan and from Europe.

---

[*] On 18 January 1946, Vice Admiral Frederick C. Sherman, USN, who had been commanding officer of the carrier Lexington when Stroop was on board in 1942, relieved Admiral Towers as Commander Fifth Fleet.
[†] Captain Allen M. Shinn, USN.
[‡] Admiral Towers served in the billet from 1 February 1946 to 28 February 1947. On 1 January 1947, his title changed from Commander in Chief U.S. Pacific Fleet and Pacific Ocean Areas to Commander in Chief Pacific and U.S. Pacific Fleet

Q: How long did that go on?

Admiral Stroop: I would guess it went on for about three months. There was a constant stream of people coming back by ship. I remember the B-29s were coming through from Guam and Saipan and Tinian. They were being ferried into bases in the U.S. And, of course, a lot of the material was being abandoned in the Pacific. One of the big jobs that our headquarters carried on--the service force--was the disposition of material.

The time at Pearl Harbor--two and a half years, I guess, I spent there--as aviation officer and later on assistant chief of staff, operations, was extremely pleasant. I was quite busy, had a nice set of quarters, and a very pleasant reunion with my family. Had three growing children at home, and this, of course, was where our last child was born in 1947. It was a very, very pleasant tour of duty and a great pleasure, of course, to work for my old friend Admiral Towers. He was relieved by Admiral Louis Denfeld, who later went back to be CNO, and he was relieved by Admiral Duke Ramsey.*

I think that about wraps up the war effort.

Q: Yes, I think so too.

Admiral Stroop: The next tour of duty was at Monterey, California.

Q: Sort of funny, you know. It's easy to read history up to this point. Then it's easy to pick it up for Korea--not easy, but at least there are things written on it. But the interim and then afterwards, it's difficult to find books written on what actually happened. It has to be your putting in on the record, the things that happened then, in the interim.

---

* Admiral Louis E. Denfeld, USN, served as CinCPac/CinCPacFlt from 28 February 1947 to 3 December 1947. Admiral Dewitt C. Ramsey, USN, held the billet from 12 January 1948 to 30 April 1949.

Paul D. Stroop #4 - 170

Admiral Stroop: As time drew near for me to be transferred from Pearl Harbor as the assistant chief of staff for operations, CinCPacFlt, I received warning orders that I'd been slated for a job in Washington, to work for Admiral Denfeld as his administrative assistant.

Q: He was then CNO?

Admiral Stroop: Admiral Denfeld had become CNO, and I was to get the job of handling his Joint Chiefs of Staff papers.[*] I also was offered the opportunity of becoming the executive officer of the Line School at Monterey, California, and I felt that although from a career point of view this would not be a particularly important job, it was the kind of job I felt that I would like to have at this stage of my career. It entailed very pleasant living. I'd never been mixed up in education before, and I had no particular desire to return to Washington. As a matter of fact, I'd always gone back to Washington under protest. This was one tour I'd just as soon get out of, and I think I was rather fortunate that I did. Admiral Denfeld released me, and I did then receive orders to go to Monterey as the executive officer of the General Line School.

Q: Had you gone back there, would that have put you in the middle, do you think, of this Air Force interservice problem?

Admiral Stroop: Yes, there's no doubt about it. Of course, we all recall the controversy that the Navy had with the Air Force over the B-36s and the carriers.[†] Admiral Denfeld finally was relieved as Chief of Naval Operations as a result of all this. I undoubtedly would have been mixed up in it.

---

[*] Admiral Louis E. Denfeld, USN, served as Chief of Naval Operations from 15 December 1947 to 2 November 1949.
[†] For details on this inter-service squabble, see Captain Paul R. Schratz, USN (Ret.), "The Admirals' Revolt," U.S. Naval Institute Proceedings, February 1986, pages 64-71.

Q: So although it sounded interesting to begin with, you probably were better off not being involved.

Admiral Stroop: This is very likely.

Q: Did you foresee that, or did it just . . . ?

Admiral Stroop: No, no.

Q: Just good fortune on your part?

Admiral Stroop: Just good fortune. It was just a personal desire on my part not to go to Washington, but to take the alternative and go to Monterey for duty. I had an opportunity to move my family by air from Pearl Harbor to Monterey, and this is a very fine way to travel. We took one of the big flag planes that I'd been responsible for. They were coming up empty to bring the type commanders back for a conference in Pearl Harbor, so I loaded my family, which consisted then of four children and two dogs and my wife and mother-in-law.

We all flew overnight from Honolulu airport to Monterey, California. Landed right there on the small naval air station at Monterey and moved in immediately to quarters. It was the most expeditious and pleasant move I had ever made in my naval career. Our commanding officer, my commanding officer, Captain Watkins and his wife, were close personal friends.[*] I found that they had made sure that the house was all in running order, the beds were made, there was food in the icebox, flowers in the vases around the house. I had visited the quarters before and knew exactly the layout, so the children had already been assigned rooms. They picked up their suitcases and went to their rooms. Then we sat down in the living room with the commanding officer and had a drink to celebrate the new duty.

---

[*] Captain Frank T. Watkins, USN.

Q: Wasn't that lovely? One of the first times, too, that you had moved with Mrs. Stroop. Usually you went away, and she had to do the moving.

Admiral Stroop: That's right. I happened many, many times that we hadn't gone together, and this was extremely fine that I could be with them this time.

Well, this began probably the most pleasant tour of duty I ever had in the Navy. The Navy had just bought the property at Monterey. It had been leased all during the war-- the old Del Monte Hotel--and used as a training station or a training base for prospective naval aviators, the aviation cadets. This was their first assignment, where they were physically conditioned and given some classroom training. They accumulated there until they were ready to be sent to Pensacola for their first flying. This had occurred all during the war under a lease arrangement with Del Monte Properties. At the end of the war, the Navy decided that they would move the PG School out of Annapolis, and a committee went around looking for the most suitable location in the country, and Monterey had been settled upon.[*] As a result, the Navy did then buy the Del Monte Properties, which they had been leasing all during the war. We found that we had a very good physical plant and plenty of real estate otherwise to put housing on. We had made a very fine acquisition.

The first school that was set up there was the General Line School, which was not a postgraduate school per se. It was to be the forerunner of the Naval Postgraduate School. The General Line School concept was an educational process that took former reserve naval officers who had accepted commissions in the regular Navy and who needed to be brought up to the level of their Naval Academy contemporaries in the way of a general education. That was really the function of the General Line School--to round out these former reserves who had spent the war just in one phase of Navy operations.

Q: It was a good idea.

---

[*] Originally established at Annapolis, Maryland, on 9 June 1909, the Naval Postgraduate School was moved to the grounds of the former Hotel Del Monte in June 1951.

Admiral Stroop: It was an excellent idea, and actually it was sort of a promise that Mr. Forrestal had made to these people. He had told them when they took their regular commissions that he would set up an educational process that would bring them up to the same educational level with their contemporaries in the Navy.

Q: Put them on an even basis as long as they were in it as a career.

Admiral Stroop: The classes that were accumulated there--and I saw three of them during the next two years--numbered about 500 to 800, and there wasn't, of course, a single Naval Academy graduate in any of the classes. They were all former reserve officers.

Q: What was your observation of their competence?

Admiral Stroop: Well, this was quite a singular educational process, because we found that each one of these individuals had been a specialist during the war, and in his specialty he probably had more knowledge and was better equipped to teach some of the courses than the instructors were. But in the other specialties, of course, he was woefully lacking.

Q: Had no knowledge at all, probably.

Admiral Stroop: Had no knowledge at all. Looking back on it, I think we probably made a mistake in not giving some sort of academic credits, just to keep these very competent individuals out of the classes where they were well equipped and let them spend some of their time on subjects they didn't know. However, their presence in the classes quite frequently added a lot to the class, so at least we can rationalize it that this was a good thing. We found, I think, that the course there pretty well accomplished what we set out to do. It wasn't ideal, of course, and some of the reserves had rather mediocre education. They had a hard time getting through. On the other hand, we did bring up the general level of their education, and we managed to teach them some of the Navy lore that they had missed and I think, in general, helped them to understand the Navy better and want to continue as professional naval officers.

Q: I'm sure they were eager to learn.

Admiral Stroop: I found it a very satisfying job, and I found that as time went on--in later years, I mean--I made a great number of friends. All through the rest of my career in the Navy, these young men would come up and say, "I worked for you at Monterey, California."

Q: Well, you have many friends in the Navy I'm sure you know anyway.

Admiral Stroop: Well, this was a fine tour. I also enjoyed very much working for my friend Frank Watkins; he was a submarine officer. He had a very fine wife, Peg, and we got along beautifully.

One of the extracurricular activities we both had--we were told by our seniors in the Bureau of Personnel that we were to spend a lot of time on community relations. The establishment of a naval school at Monterey had been opposed by some of the community. They felt that their very pleasant little towns of Monterey, Carmel, and Pacific Grove would be ruined by the influx of a large number of students and also that instructors would come along and supporting staff, and then finally the Postgraduate School. As a matter of fact, it was roughly estimated that we would increase the total population by about 10,000 people when the process was completed, and the people there had some concern about it. So Frank Watkins and I worked very hard at establishing good community relations, and I think we were quite successful. We joined the civic clubs, and we attended all sorts of civic functions.

Q: That was a new thing for you, too, of course. You'd never had a chance to do it, whether you wanted to or not.

Admiral Stroop: That's right. This was a new experience. We did lay the groundwork for the establishment of the Postgraduate School. Just as I was leaving Monterey, two years later in 1950, the first move was made to bring out sections of the Postgraduate School, and the plans for the improvement of the physical plant were laid out. This, of course, has resulted in a very fine, capable institution.

The line school a few years back was discontinued and a complete postgraduate curriculum established. They have, I think, several thousand students; I'm not sure.* They have a very large group of postgraduate students and do a lot of fine work. I've gone through the plant with very knowledgeable people, and they say that it's probably the finest plant of its kind in the country, so we can be very proud of that. The two years at Monterey were pleasant. I had a chance to take up golf and enjoy it, made a lot of civilian friends that have remained friends for the rest of my life. I left there with some regret, really.

I was ordered from Monterey to the National War College, which is a one-year course, and did take me back to Washington.

Q: Had you wanted that?

Admiral Stroop: Yes, I was happy to go there. The National War College was a new experience, and actually it was new to the services. I think it was either the second class or the third class at the National War College. It was quite an honor to be selected. We were told that the Navy captains and the Army and Air Force colonels that were selected were of the highest caliber and were certainly candidates for flag rank. That was why they were being sent to the National War College. The class at the war college numbered about 120,

---

* For a status report on the school from the period of this interview, see Rear Admiral Robert W. McNitt, USN, "The Naval Postgraduate School: Sixty Years Young," U.S. Naval Institute Proceedings, June 1970, pages 68-93. It reported a population of 1,600 officer students for the 1969-70 academic year.

and it had students from the Army, Navy, and Air Force. The Navy, of course, included three or four Marine officers, and the State Department had a large group in there.

Q: Is that so? What were they there for?

Admiral Stroop: Well, the State Department people, of course, in the overseas assignments, foreign assignments, work quite closely with the armed services. You might really say that the Department of Defense is an extension of diplomacy. So it was considered important that we have some sort of a common medium of education, and I think that's turned out to be a very wise . . .

Q: It is an intelligent approach.

Admiral Stroop: Very fine institution. I made many lasting friendships there. As a matter of fact, you might say that one of the most beneficial results of the tour at the National War College are these fine acquaintances that you make with different people in other services and with the State Department people.

Q: If you go on to become flag rank, you're going to be working with them.

Admiral Stroop: That's right. Then, of course, I associated with a number of these people later. Most of the State Department people later became ambassadors, and the majority of the military people went on to flag rank in the various services. Later I worked closely with several of those people, to our mutual benefit.

After the war college I was ordered to command the Princeton.*

---

* The USS Princeton (CV-37) was commissioned 18 November 1945 She had a standard displacement of 33,300 tons, was 888 feet long, 93 feet in the beam, an extreme width of 148 feet on the flight deck, and had a draft of 29 feet. She had a top speed of 33.5 knots and could accommodate approximately 90 aircraft.

Paul D. Stroop #4 - 177

Q: Now we get into a really different phase of your career again, don't we?

Admiral Stroop: This was my first big command and probably the finest experience you have in your life--command of your first big ship. I moved my family to Coronado, California, and got them established, and then went on out to the Sea of Japan to take over the Princeton. I relieved Captain Bill Gallery in the Sea of Japan, just at the end of a very long and eventful tour in the Korean War.[*] The Princeton was one of the early carriers out there and had done quite a fine job in supporting our forces ashore. I relieved Bill Gallery just the day that the Princeton left the line in Korea for the last time.

We took the ship into Yokosuka for a couple of days, where we prepared for our long voyage back across the Pacific. We came back through Pearl Harbor and finally docked in San Diego. When the Princeton returned to San Diego, I found that the crew had decided that they would have a homecoming queen, and they would also, of course, have a big ship's dance the night after they got back and this queen was named. This was rather common in those days, and usually the queen selected would be a Hollywood starlet or the sweetheart of one of the sailors.

In this particular case, for some reason or other, the crew decided they would pick a handicapped girl to be the queen, and they did pick a little crippled girl. They sent an advance crew back, led by one of the young ship's officers, and they picked a little girl called Janie. She was about 16, and she was a victim of muscular dystrophy. However, she was able to be moved around in a wheelchair and to sit up and participate in all of the events. She was waiting on the dock in her wheelchair with her four little princesses, one of each race, and with a couple of smart-looking Marines attending them. She was carried aboard the ship soon after we docked and was surrounded on the hangar deck by a large number of sailors . . .

Q: That's a touching thing, isn't it?

---

[*] Captain William O. Gallery, USN, commanded the Princeton from her recommissioning on 28 August 1950 until relieved by Captain Stroop on 11 August 1951.

Admiral Stroop: . . . and I'm sure that she thoroughly enjoyed and appreciated all the attention she got. She was crowned queen the next night at the ship's ball, and she also was invited up to Hollywood for an audition and an appearance on a television show. In addition to all of this, the sailors had collected $5,000, which they made available in the form of a trust fund for her.

Q: How perfectly lovely.

Admiral Stroop: And this was the beginning of a very happy association for this girl. Every time the ship returned, she was homecoming queen, and she would meet the ship on the dock. On her birthday and holidays, a delegation of sailors would go out to see her.

Q: I'm sure it gave her a reason for living that she'd never had before.

Admiral Stroop: Yes. Janie still lives here in San Diego. I hear from her occasionally. She honored me by coming down to my retirement, and at this time she was not in a wheelchair. She was able to get out and walk a little. She came down the receiving line and had a little gift for me when I retired. The ship continued to collect money for the cause of muscular dystrophy, and today there's a little hospital or training center out in the Miramar area called the Princeton Center for Muscular Dystrophy. I've visited down there. The last time I went there, I went with Captain Tazewell Shepard, who was then the commanding officer of the Princeton, showing that the ship still has an interest in this institution.[*]

Q: Who was responsible for this? Was it yourself or . . . ?

Admiral Stroop: Oh, no. No. It was a committee of crew members who decided that this was what they wanted to do, and they sent back a delegation to San Diego by air to select the princess, and . . .

---

[*] Captain Tazewell T. Shepard, Jr., USN, commanded the Princeton, by then redesignated LPH-5, from June 1966 to May 1967.

Q: Nice things like this don't get too much publicity, do they?

Admiral Stroop: Well, there was a good bit of publicity at the time in the local papers, certainly, and three distinguished local citizens became trustees for her little estate which was set up, so it was well known.

After the ship docked here in San Diego, we had about six weeks of leave and liberty, and a large number of the crew were discharged. The ship then was sent up to Bremerton for overhaul. I left my family here in San Diego and took the ship to Bremerton. This was, I guess, November or December of 1951. We had four months of overhaul then at the Bremerton Navy Yard, got the ship back in condition and ready to proceed again to training and finally deploy again to Korea.[*] We went through normal refresher training in San Diego. I had a small swipe with a tanker which apparently didn't hurt my career too much.

Q: You're brushing over that lightly.

Admiral Stroop: Yes. We were refueling for the first time, and this was part of the training operation. We'd broken away from the tanker, I had the conn, and the base course was 260.[†] I was supposed to sheer off to the left two degrees. Actually, I gave the wrong order to the helm, 262, and we came in close to the tanker and touched her.

Q: Didn't do any damage, did it?

Admiral Stroop: Oh, yes. It did some damage. We had to go to the yard and get fixed up, but nobody was hurt. The subsequent board of investigation, which had to he held, recommended me for a letter of caution, I think, which I got. It's in the record.

---

[*] Puget Sound Naval Shipyard, Bremerton, Washington.
[†] The individual with the conn--normally an officer--directs the ship's movements in course and speed.

Q: Apparently didn't do you any harm.

Admiral Stroop: No, but it didn't help any!

Q: I know. I was in officer performance section at . . .

Admiral Stroop: I say it didn't help any, because the following year I came up for selection to flag rank, and there was one officer selected below me. So I always felt that I might have been selected that year if it hadn't been for this, although I was selected the following year.

Q: It's possible, but Admiral King even when he was a youngster got a letter of admonition or something.

Admiral Stroop: I'd be very surprised if he hadn't.

Q: Why do you say that?

Admiral Stroop: Well, a lot of people who get places also speak up and get in trouble.

Q: True, and if you sit back and do nothing, nothing's going to happen.

Admiral Stroop: We hurried through refresher training. We had a short period in a shipyard to repair the damage caused by the brush with the oiler and went on out to the Western Pacific again and into the Sea of Japan. I had a very wonderful air group--Air Group 19--which consisted of a squadron of Grumman F9F jet fighters, the first jets in the fleet; two squadrons of F4Us, single-engined World War II Vought fighters that were serving as dive-bombers; and a squadron of ADs, which was to be the workhorse of that war and the workhorse of the Vietnamese War later on.

Q: Excuse me, what day did you reach Korea?

Admiral Stroop: Well, let's see. We had gone into 1952 then, so this would be along about April of 1952. We established a regular routine of operations, which consisted of about three weeks on the line in the Sea of Japan off the coast of Korea, and about ten days back in for R&R and upkeep on the coast of Japan.*

Q: What group were you a part of?

Admiral Stroop: There were a total of about four or five carriers operating out there during the period that I was there. We would have two as a minimum, sometimes three, and even one time four carriers on the line. These would not be any fixed group, but they would be rotated in and out, one carrier at a time. There were two flag officers kept in the area, division commanders, and they rotated in and out.

Q: This was 77?

Admiral Stroop: This was Task Force 77. I served during that period under about six different flag officers, and it was a very odd situation in that either I was changing or the flag officers were changing quite frequently. Each time, of course, it meant a new fitness report. I was getting a fitness report every two or three weeks during this period.

Q: Wasn't that miserable?

Admiral Stroop: It was miserable in a way, but it also served to create a pretty good record back in the Bureau of Personnel during a critical period in my career. I was coming up for selection, you see--very serious selection the following year. So the operations off Korea were, I think, very fine operations. They were well conceived, and I think we were doing

---

* R&R--rest and recreation.

an excellent job of supporting the troops ashore, and we were cutting lines of communications of the North Koreans. We suffered to some extent from the same limitations that occurred later in Vietnam, as the target systems were limited. I'll never forget, we had some very juicy targets in North Korea, consisting of power plants with long flumes leading down from rivers or dams high up in the valley. These were very lucrative targets, and we felt for a long time that we should be hitting them. I remember the day--it was the 26th of June--when we were finally permitted to make a coordinated attack against all of these in North Korea. It was a most exciting day. We did a very splendid job and damaged all these plants, put them out of operation. It was just a fine operation. I was glad that I was still a part of the task force and had been able to take part in it.

Q: I know, of course, of all the restrictions in Vietnam, but my mind doesn't go back to picturing the same kind of restrictions in North Korea.

Admiral Stroop: The restrictions weren't quite as severe. I remember this particular day, the 26th of June, one of my squadrons had a target just on the edge of the Yalu River.[*] When they went in to hit this target, they could see right across the Yalu River a Red Chinese airfield covered with fighters. Here these fighters were on the ground, could have been easily destroyed, and we were not permitted to cross the Yalu to hit them. In other words, the fighters were permitted to take off at their leisure and come up and hit our people. Fortunately, we got in and out before they could get at us.

As I recall, on that day, the 26th of June, we did not lose any people of the Princeton air group. We did, however, during the course of the seven months that I was out there on the line, lose about 18 pilots, and we had at least 30 pilots downed. I never failed to get a pilot back who had a chance to get back. We had some very spectacular rescues that we accomplished, but as far as I can determine, we got every living pilot back that went down, either in the water or even behind enemy lines.

---

[*] The Yalu River separated North Korea from Communist China. The rules of engagement prevented offensive action across the Yalu, because President Harry S Truman did not want to risk setting off a still wider war.

Q: You speak of spectacular rescues. Could you enlarge on them?

Admiral Stroop: Well, there were two. They were both behind enemy lines and both picked up by helicopters.

Q: Attached to the Princeton?

Admiral Stroop: Both of these young officers were attached to the Princeton.

Q: I mean the helicopters were also?

Admiral Stroop: The helicopters, no. One was attached to the battleship Iowa, and I've forgotten the other one. I think there was a special detachment operating from--probably off an LST close in to the beach. I've forgotten the name of the first boy. He was from Eugene, Oregon, I remember, and this was quite a story. I really should get his name, because it's worth remembering. This youngster was in an F4U and, as he told the story later when I went down in the sick bay to see him, he realized he was hit. His plane began to smoke, and his teammate, who still had radio communication, said, "My God, you'd better get out of there. You're on fire." So he did. He jumped out and landed behind enemy lines.

Q: Can you pinpoint the location?

Admiral Stroop: Well, of course, it was north of the 38th parallel.[*] I don't know the exact location. His teammates saw him go down. They remained circling overhead. When he landed, he immediately picked up his parachute and tried to hide it. He gathered what gear he could get, ran away from the location, and hid in a ditch alongside a rice paddy. He'd no

---

[*] North and South Korea were separated by the 38th parallel of latitude.

sooner gotten in the ditch and was covering his face with mud than three North Korean soldiers came up. They stood around his parachute and the gear that he'd left behind.

Quoting him to tell the story, he had a .38 pistol with him, and his teammates were circling overhead. He decided that his only way to get away from there was to shoot these people while he had the opportunity. So he waited till one of the planes came down and started zooming the area, making a lot of noise, and he'd taken very careful aim with his pistol. His right hand had been burned a little bit, so he had to hold the pistol with both hands. Then he remembered the pistol kicked a little bit, so he lowered his point of aim a few inches and fired just as the airplane zoomed. He shot this soldier in the back and killed him. The other two soldiers looked at this one, and he moved his gun over and covered the next one and waited for the proper time to kill the next one. The third one took off with that. So he had a little freedom there. His teammates . . .

Q: Did the noise cover where the shot was coming from?

Admiral Stroop: That's right. That's why he wasn't discovered. Just a farm boy, too, from Eugene, Oregon. With his friends circling overhead, sort of watching out for him, keeping the area sanitized, he said he remained in hiding until a helicopter started in. Then he got out of the ditch and across the rice paddy and up into a field, and he said it was a potato field. He looked at me with a twinkle in his eye and said, "Captain, they weren't very good potatoes." But he hid down between the potato rows, and the helicopter pilot discovered him. In the meantime, he had noticed that there was some firing from the woods around the edge of this open area, and the helicopter came down, let the hoist down, and picked him up. He began pointing out to the pilot where all the firing was coming from. The pilot handed him a carbine, so he began suppressing the fire on the way out.

Q: He really had a cool head, didn't he?

Admiral Stroop: He certainly did. In the meantime, one of his own planes that had been circling overhead had a forced landing while trying to get back to the ship; the engine had quit. He was down in the water with a great circle of dye marking the spot. So this same helicopter, which by this time had used up enough fuel so he could take on another passenger, went down to rescue his buddy. So they all arrived back on the ship.

Q: That's a wonderful story, isn't it?

Admiral Stroop: And the next day--I've forgotten just how they were transferred, but the next day he came aboard the Princeton. He was sent to the sick bay, where I saw him and got the story that I just gave you.

The other incident occurred a little bit later in the cruise, when we were a little farther north up in North Korea, and one of the pilots was shot down and parachuted down. I remember this boy's name was Red Riedl, and, here again, his teammates remained overhead until the last possible minute, and a helicopter from the battleship Iowa was sent in.[*] She was doing some bombardment work on the coast, and they could reach in. It was late in the afternoon, and there was some fog setting in, so the helicopter pilot could not, or would not, go down through the overcast to pick up Riedl, although he knew exactly where he was. He was in sight in an open area, so he was left there to spend the night.

His teammates--there were six of them, as I recall--remained overhead until the last possible moment. As a matter of fact, I can remember the fact that they remained so long that they didn't have enough fuel to get back to the Princeton. I remember the carrier division commander and I had a little argument over the TBS over this, and he suggested that maybe I hadn't been exercising enough command in getting these planes back in time.[†] However, the planes, although they didn't get back to the ship, did land on an emergency strip that had just recently been established on an island. It was just, I think, 2,200 feet long, a very short strip. They landed there, they had to spend the night on the island, they had to refuel from drums, which they did. They took off early next morning and got back

---

[*] The pilot was Lieutenant (junior grade) Harold A. Riedl, USN, and the incident was on 15-16 July 1952. For more details on this rescue, see Malcolm W. Cagle and Frank A. Manson, The Sea War in Korea (Annapolis: U.S. Naval Institute, 1957), pages 429-430.
[†] TBS--voice radio.

to the ship with no damage, so I got off the hook on that one. In the meantime, we set up the machinery to rescue Riedl, if we could find him.

Q: That's one question. You say they stayed with their teammate too long. Was it their decision as to when to start back?

Admiral Stroop: Yes. Actually, I had very little control of them. The squadron commander was there.

Q: That would be the way I pictured it, rather than you being . . .

Admiral Stroop: He was a very capable man, Nils Boe, knew what he was doing.[*] He had made the decision to remain in the air as long as he could. He knew what his fuel situation was. I didn't know what it was. He started back, and they passed over this emergency field, and he decided to land there rather than stretch out for the ship.

Q: That's the way I would think, rather than your being in a position to say, "You've stayed there long enough. Come home."

Q: Well, the admiral just had to be mad at somebody, and he was mad at me. Part of the argument was as to whether we would try to rescue the man the next day. Well, we did set up the rescue for the next day, and it turned out all right. We sent the squadron commander back in again. He insisted on going back; he wanted to lead the rescue group. We got a helicopter pilot from the Iowa again, sent him in, and we sanitized the area with rockets and machine gun fire. Riedl came out in the open and was picked up and brought back. I went down in the wardroom and celebrated his return the next night at dinner.

Riedl had quite a story. He said after the planes left, things quieted down. He could hear people looking for him, and he got down in a ditch underneath some trees and bushes.

---

[*] Lieutenant Commander Nils W. Boe, USN, commanding officer of Fighter Squadron 193, which was flying F4U Corsairs.

These people were going up and down and around. He was tempted to give himself up, because he felt that the chances for rescue the next day were minimum. He thought if he gave himself up peacefully, at least he'd be alive, whereas if he waited till daylight, he might be shot or something like that. But he didn't. He stayed down there, and mosquitoes bit him and bugs ran all over him, but he stayed quiet. It must have been a long night for him. The next day at daylight his pals were over there, and the helicopter pilot had enough fortitude to come down and pick him up. He said one of the things that impressed him the most about this being down on the ground was the noise the 5-inch rockets made when they were fired from those protective planes. He said, "Boy, that was enough to scare people."

Q: Just the noise.

Admiral Stroop: Just the noise. He said it was really impressive. So we got Riedl back, and those are the two big rescues we had.

I had a number of people who went into the water in carrier landings or carrier takeoffs, or couldn't quite get back to the ship, but we got every one of them back. We had some 32 incidents, I think, and lost about 18 pilots.

Q: All by helicopter.

Admiral Stroop: I think so.

Q: The helicopter actually came into its own in Korea. Can you expand on that?

Admiral Stroop: Well, by the time the Korean War came along, it was a fixed part of the air group and was quite useful. It was common practice, at the beginning of air operations, that the helicopter was launched, except at night, and took station usually right off the island on the starboard side so as to be out of the flight pattern, and they'd maintain that station. Of course, the helicopter came along late in World War II, but its full usefulness hadn't been realized, and it didn't have the performance. But they developed a technique, even then in late '45. I used them, but by the time the Korean War came along, they were a regular part of operations.

Q: Were your squadrons Marine or Navy?

Admiral Stroop: All Navy. All Navy. That's rather interesting. I'm glad you brought that up. Two of the squadrons were manned by reserve officers and two by regulars. You remember after World War II they established a very fine reserve training program.

Q: Yes. Weekend warriors, weren't they?

Admiral Stroop: That's right, with headquarters at Glenview.[*] My friend, Admiral Eddie Ewen, started this up and was in command of it.[†] When Korea came along, these people still were young enough to be brought back in the service as organized squadrons. I had two of these squadrons operating on the Princeton, and I couldn't tell the difference. There was no difference. Of course, they'd been out once before, but these people were veterans, they were smart, they were well led, they were effective. They were a fine testimonial. Of course, they had the benefit, most of them, of World War II experience, and a lot of them, of course . . .

Q: They weren't new into the program of the reserve?

Admiral Stroop: No, no, no, no, these were mostly World War II aviators. They were people who at the end of World War II had just gotten into it, were ensigns--well, some of them were lieutenants, lieutenant commanders. Some of the squadron commanders were, of course, highly decorated. They were World War II pilots. These people performed excellently. They were outstanding.

---

[*] Naval Air Station Glenview, Illinois, near Chicago.
[†] Rear Admiral Edward C. Ewen, USN, served as Chief of Naval Air Reserve Training from December 1945 to February 1948.

It was just a fortunate circumstance that the Korean War was close enough to World War II to have these kinds of people still active. I don't think that normally we could expect this kind of a reservoir of talent. And I don't think, even today, that the reserve squadrons are as closely comparable to the active duty squadrons, for a couple of reasons. One, they haven't had the recent combat experience. Two, the equipment has gotten so much more complicated. You see, in the case of these reserve squadrons in Korea, they were not only fairly recently experienced, but they were flying the identical aircraft. Two of my squadrons had F4Us; one of my reserve squadrons had F4Us in World War II, so they were right at home. They were real experts, real professionals.

Well, we had about six or seven months off Korea and had four tours, I think, on the line in the Princeton. Finally, my relief caught up with me, and he was a classmate named Hollingsworth.* As a matter of fact, he arrived on the day that we had a very amusing little incident. One night in Yokosuka our pilots were talking about attacks on Korea and said we had thrown everything at Korea but the kitchen sink. Well, these people decided that they'd throw the kitchen sink, so they liberated a kitchen sink someplace in Yokosuka and brought it back to the ship late one night. We went to sea the next day, and, sure enough, the squadron was in possession of a kitchen sink.

Q: How would they carry it along in a place?

Admiral Stroop: Well, they actually wired or bolted this kitchen sink on a bomb. I've got a picture of it in my archives here of a kitchen sink attached to a bomb. The picture shows me down there by it and my relief, Captain Hollingsworth, looking at the kitchen sink. The first day on the line we were assigned to make the first attack that was made on the city of Pyongyang. So the squadrons took off with this special load, and the kitchen sink was dumped on Pyongyang, along with a lot of bombs. This incident, of course, made publicity. When the ship returned under my relief to Alameda, it was met by a delegation from the plumbers' union, who gave him a special award for dropping a kitchen sink on Pyongyang.

---

* Captain William R. Hollingsworth, USN, commanded the Princeton from August 1952 to June 1953. On 1 October 1952 the ship was redesignated CVA-37.

I was just about to return to the U.S. As a matter of fact, I had orders to command China Lake, the naval ordnance station at Inyokern, California. The day before the change of command ceremony, I was down in my in-port cabin, which I got to visit every other day while we were operating on the line, and the chief yeoman came running through the cabin with a message. In those days, messages came in on teletype tape, and the tape was then transcribed or pasted on a message blank. He had this tape all just in his hands, and he had been reading it as it came off the teletype. It was a change of orders, and he said, "You have been ordered to command the Essex," which was another ship in the task force.

It turned out the commanding officer of the Essex had an emergency family situation back here in Coronado and had to return, so he had been given orders to come back, and they had orders to catch me wherever I was. They thought I might have left and would catch me in Japan or in Pearl Harbor. I was to return and take command of the Essex. Fortunately, I hadn't left the area. The Essex was right there in the same task force. Admiral Soucek, who was the division commander out on the station at the time, CTF 77, asked how soon I could go over to the Essex.[*] I said, "Well, it'll take about an hour."

Of course, we had done all the paperwork, the ship had been inspected, and Hollingsworth was ready to take command. So Admiral Soucek turned the formation downwind so we had a nice quiet flight deck. We had the crew mustered and had a ceremony up on the flight deck.[†] For the occasion, I recall that I presented six Purple Hearts as the commanding officer. I had authority to award Purple Hearts to people who rated them, and we had the change of command.

In a few minutes I was in a helicopter going over to the Essex. I got over there and found that Captain Rodee was not quite ready to be relieved.[‡] He had fitness reports to make out, and he wanted two days, which was fine with me. I was very happy to just relax for two days, which I did. I said I wanted to have two drills. I wanted to inspect the steering gear, because I'd had trouble on the Princeton with the steering gear, and I wanted

---

[*] Rear Admiral Apollo Soucek, USN, Commander Carrier Division Three, was then serving as Commander Task Force 77.
[†] The change of command was on 31 August 1952.
[‡] Captain Walter F. Rodee, USN.

to have a fire drill. I went through the Boxer after her fire, and I wanted to make sure that these people understood about fires on carriers.* Other than that, I was quite happy and went down and slept for 12 hours each day. I finally relieved Captain Rodee right in the midst of flight operations. In between launches we gathered around the microphone up on the bridge and read our orders.† That was it, and he took off and went back to San Diego.

Q: You said you were in a fire on the Boxer. We haven't mentioned that.

Admiral Stroop: That statement was a little bit wrong. I was on the board of investigation of the fire on the Boxer. During one of the in-port periods on the Princeton I was made a part of this investigation, and I was very sensitive to fires on carriers. I came back to the Princeton and instituted certain procedures which I thought were beneficial, and that was what I wanted to do on the Essex when I went over there. Fire on a carrier's a horrible thing.

Well, the six weeks on the Essex were really wonderful. I had left the Princeton after 13 months of very hard operations, and I thought that I was quite a competent carrier commander, so I went to the Essex with a great deal of confidence.

Q: Isn't it wonderful to go to a job that you know that you know how to do?

Admiral Stroop: That's right, and it's just unfortunate that your tours were so short. I noticed this later on as an admiral in AirPac. Just as the carrier skippers got to be good, they had to be relieved to make room for other skippers. If you wanted to run your Navy as efficiently as possible, you'd have longer tours of duty for these people.

---

* On 6 August 1952, while the Boxer (CV-21) was operating off the east coast of Korea, a gasoline tank in a parked plane exploded, causing fires to spread throughout the ship's hangar deck and a 500-pound bomb to explode. All told, eight men were killed and two severely burned.
† This ceremony was on 2 September 1952.

Q: I always felt, of course, as a WAVE in the Navy you never did have any background of experience, but whenever I left a job, I thought, "If only I'd known when I came what I do now." I was always learning a new job without ever thinking I was being very competent at it. Why did you stay only six weeks on the Essex?

Admiral Stroop: Well, I'd had my command tour, and I just stayed there long enough for them to get another commanding officer out from the States.

Q: Rodee's actual relief.

Admiral Stroop: Rodee's actual relief, who happened to be another classmate named Benny Lovett.[*] I finished the Essex's tour on the line. I took her into Yokosuka Harbor, and here I was able to demonstrate my ship-handling ability. I had to turn the ship around in the inner harbor at Yokosuka and bring it into the dock stern first, which I did without tugs. I'd done this to the Princeton.

Q: That's hard to do anytime, isn't it?

Admiral Stroop: Well, we had a technique called "pinwheel," where we took about eight planes and placed them with their tails outboard at each corner of the flight deck. You actually twisted the ship, or turned it, or moved it sideways by using these planes in place of tugs.

Q: As a spot of reference, you mean?

Admiral Stroop: No, no. They would have their engines running, and they would actually push the ship. It was a technique that we don't use anymore, because now you have jets. We did it only with the prop planes.

---

[*] Captain Benjamin B. C. Lovett, USN.

Q: But they aren't touching--you mean they did it with the force of their engines?

Admiral Stroop: That's right. They were tied down on the flight deck.

Q: And their engines--one moving or the other . . . ?

Admiral Stroop: All eight of them at one time, in one sport, or eight in another spot.

Q: And they gave you enough force to . . . ?

Admiral Stroop: Either to twist the ship or push it sideways.

Q: Did you think of that?

Admiral Stroop: No, no. This technique was used prior to World War II, but we developed it to a high point. If you've ever been to the inner harbor of Yokosuka, it's a tight little place for a big carrier. I brought her in there, and I had a pilot on board, but he never gave an order. We turned the ship around, back it in between two piers, and then moved her sideways into the dock. Well, this was the result of 13 months of operating experience.

We had ten days' R&R there in Yokosuka, then back out again on the line. This is where my second relief found me, Admiral Lovett. He came aboard, and we went through the ceremony again, relieving in between flights. I took off and flew over to the Princeton again. She was just leaving the line to return to the States. My old friend Jocko Clark was on board making some combat awards to the crew, and he thought it would be proper that I should be present.* So we were there together, and I was honored with the award of a

---

* Vice Admiral Joseph J. Clark, USN, served as Commander Seventh Fleet from 10 May 1952 to 1 December 1953.

second Legion of Merit under combat conditions. Then Jocko and I took off in a helicopter, went over into Korea, landed, and got in a plane and flew up to Japan.

Q: I wanted to read the award that you received that day. You were awarded a gold star in lieu of a second Legion of Merit, and the citation says that, " . . . a capable and resourceful leader, he organized a group of recalled reserves, inexperienced recruits, and members of the regular Navy into a highly efficient fighting team, thereby overcoming numerous obstacles presented by increasing shortages of trained personnel and deficiencies of material, and enabling him to apply the striking power essential against an enemy with maximum effectiveness." And it says you are also entitled to the ribbon for and a facsimile of the Navy Unit Commendation of the Princeton.

Admiral Stroop: Yes, she was recommended for a Navy Commendation at the same time as I got this award.

Q: Did Admiral Clark give you the award?

Admiral Stroop: Yes, old Jocko. And then I flew back with him to Japan in his plane, and we had dinner together at the Sanno Hotel in Tokyo that night.

Q: Which hotel?

Admiral Stroop: Sanno. It's still a sort of a U.S. service billet.

Q: And then you began going into a completely different line of Navy duty, didn't you?

Admiral Stroop: Yes. I had been under orders for a good many months to go to the Naval Ordnance Test Station at China Lake, California, near the city of Inyokern, California, and that's where I proceeded. My wife had gone through the same situation she had once before of giving up her house, thinking I was coming home when I didn't, but this time she was a little more fortunate. They knew I would ultimately wind up at Inyokern, so she went on up to Inyokern. She was driven up there with our family and given a set of quarters. So she was actually ensconced at Inyokern and arrived there in advance of me.

Q: How did you happen to get those orders? Do you know?

Admiral Stroop: Well, it goes clear back to the time when I was associated with ordnance and the Norden bombsight.*

Q: Have you told me about that?

Admiral Stroop: Yes, I think so. At any rate, as a young officer I'd introduced the Norden bombsight into the fleet, and I'd had some spectacular luck doing some test bombing with it.

Q: What year was that? At the risk of being repetitive, I don't recall it.

Admiral Stroop: This was in 1931. At any rate, this had drawn me to the attention of Admiral Schoeffel, who had been interested in Navy ordnance all of his life.† At this particular time, when I was in command of the Princeton and later in command of the Essex, he was the Chief of the Bureau of Ordnance. So he offered me the job to become commanding officer at Inyokern. And I think they had special requirements for that job, and they wanted an officer who was an aviator, because it was concerned with aviation ordnance. They wanted an officer who had been associated with ordnance, because it was aviation ordnance, and I had had both experiences. So that's why I was ordered to that particular job.

---

* The Norden bombsight was a precision optical device developed in the early 1930s by Carl L. Norden, a civilian consultant employed by the Navy, together with Lieutenant Frederick L. Entwistle, USN. Its gyrostabilized automatic pilot kept the bomber straight and level during bomb runs. It was used in both Navy and Army bombers in the 1930s and 1940s.
† Rear Admiral Malcolm F. Schoeffel, USN, served as Chief of the Bureau of Ordnance, 1950-54. His oral history is in the Naval Institute collection.

Q: Were you pleased with it?

Admiral Stroop: Yes. It was a large command.

Q: I've been there, so I can picture what it was.

Admiral Stroop: There were 11,000 people in the community. There were 4,000 people in the government employ there. It was a place where research was carried into development and into actual service use as weapons. It was a place where the best the Navy had in scientific talent was gathered together, and it was a place where very competent operating naval aviators were ordered. You brought these two skills together and the scientists and the engineers, very competent and intelligent operators, and as a result you developed weapons that were practical, simple, and useful. It was probably one of the finest scientific-technical arrangements the Navy's ever had. I didn't know all of this when I was ordered there. I knew in general what they did, but you asked me if I was happy to go, and the answer is yes, I was very happy to go there.

Q: What were the developments when you were there?

Admiral Stroop: Well, the most significant and important development was the Sidewinder missile, air-to-air missile which became world famous. It was in the process of being tested and brought along while I was there. There were other developments. We were having acceptance tests of the Terrier missile. We had an underwater branch down at Pasadena. We were developing torpedoes down there. A broad scope of activities. We had some highly classified atomic weapons programs going on also.

Q: What was that thing that went on the sled?

Admiral Stroop: Well, many weapons were tried out on the sleds. This was a fine way to get data. A missile in flight could be simulated and be instrumented to see how it was performing. We had several tracks there and several types of sleds, the longest being the Snark track, where you could actually fly whole parts of airplanes down the track at the speed that they would be flying in the air and test them.

Q: I'm sure that was the part that would be exciting.

Admiral Stroop: Well, this tour of duty at China Lake at Inyokern was very, very interesting. It was almost inspiring to be associated with these people.

Q: What was the name of the man who's now down here who was the . . . ?

Admiral Stroop: Dr. William B. McLean. He was head of the aviation ordnance department at the time. He was very busy with the Sidewinder missile at that time. It was my good fortune to be associated with him and watch this weapon being developed and tested. One of our pilots was a young man named Wally Schirra.[*]

Q: Really?

Admiral Stroop: He was a lieutenant, and he was in the Sidewinder program. The administration and command of a station like that is not easy. It's very much different from an ordinary military command. It's very much different from a ship. The scientific community--they're all individuals, and they do not respond to military-type discipline at all. There must be a reason for everything.

Q: They don't want to be regimented.

---

[*] Lieutenant Walter M. Schirra, Jr., USN, who later became one of the first seven Mercury astronauts in the U.S. space program. His autobiography, written in collaboration with Richard N. Billings, is Schirra's Space (Annapolis: Naval Institute Press, 1995).

Admiral Stroop: They don't want to be regimented, and I think probably one of the reasons I was ordered there was because I seemed to have a facility to get along with people. I had plenty of problems there, but they seemed to be resolved--most of the time, at least.

Q: You had all of them. You had civilians with all their housing problems, which was a terrible problem up there. You had military people, and then you had the scientists, plus your top-flight aviators. So you had the whole gamut of people that you had to have work together.

Admiral Stroop: Well, that is true. One of the fine things about a place like Inyokern is that you're isolated, and people are forced to live and work and play together. Rather purposefully we didn't have any groups isolated in the housing. They were all intermingled, intermixed, so the squadron commander might be living next door to a top-flight scientist. The kids went to school together. They were all members of the officers' club, and a highly intelligent group of people like this who are isolated in that kind of a community find a great number of activities. I guess we had 20 or 30 kinds of clubs of various kinds, social activities and a semi-scientific activities, hobby groups, and that sort of thing. These people were all associated in those. I took great interest in the PTA groups out there. We were all interested in good education for the children.

Q: Was there a school on the station?

Admiral Stroop: We had about four.

Q: Right on the station?

Admiral Stroop: Sure, and they were good schools. They were all well monitored and, as I say, the PTAs were very active. We had all kinds of activities. They had rock hounds, they had jumping clubs, they had little flying clubs, they had skiing clubs, they brought musical stars up there, they started a symphony group. You name it, and we had it at China Lake.

Q: I think it should be pointed out for the record and someone who might not know that Inyokern is out in the desert, what you think of as a Godforsaken spot.

Admiral Stroop: Well, this is right. It started out, you know, and it's rather odd that it was called a test station, the Naval Ordnance Test Station, because it started out as exactly that. It was an extension of the wartime operations at Cal Tech, where rockets were being developed, and they had to have a place to develop, to fire the rockets.

Q: A place where nobody wanted to come.

Admiral Stroop: That's right, and they went up to a little field which is now west of Inyokern called Harvey Field, named after a naval aviator called Sid Harvey.* They would fly in there, and the scientists would be there, and they lived in shacks and tents and tested their rockets in the desert.

Finally it was decided to make it a permanent installation, and they moved eight miles east to what is now China Lake. That's where they built their community, which is eight miles east of Inyokern. This community was laid out generally as it exists today, and it's quite an oasis in the desert. It has a very fine laboratory, the Michelson Laboratory, and a lot of minor laboratory activities and test activities. Probably the finest thing of its kind in the world, and it's very fortunate for the United States and the Free World that we have this, because many of the weapons that are used by not only our Navy but our Air Force and by Army aviators nowadays and by NATO aviators were developed right there at China

---

* Inyokern Airfield was renamed Harvey Field on 10 May 1944 to honor the late Lieutenant Commander Warren W. Harvey, USN, for his contributions to the development of aviation ordnance and fighter tactics.

Lake.* There are at least a half a dozen, and this development is continuing today, recognized as the foremost laboratory and development activities in the world.

Q: How interesting.

Admiral Stroop: I was very fortunate to be there, although that experience lasted only ten months. The selection board met and one day, when I was in the swimming pool, I noticed my wife coming down all excited. It was pretty obvious that she had some pretty important news. The news was that the selection board's report was out, and my name was on the list.

Q: That's a very exciting experience, isn't it?

Admiral Stroop: I was selected for flag rank and very soon ordered back to Washington.

I think maybe this is a good place to stop. I've now become a flag officer and finished a tour of duty.

---

*NATO--North Atlantic Treaty Organization.

Interview Number 5 with Vice Admiral Paul D. Stroop, U.S. Navy (Retired)

Place: Admiral Stroop's home in San Diego, California

Date: Sunday, 11 January 1970

Interviewer: Commander Etta-Belle Kitchen, U.S. Navy (Retired)

Q: Our last interview concluded with your tour of duty at the Naval Ordnance Test Station in Inyokern, Admiral, and from there do you want to pick up this morning?

Admiral Stroop: I'd been at the Naval Ordnance Station at Inyokern, California, for only ten months and had found the duty extremely interesting, very pleasant, and I was also very busy. I regretted very much that I had an early detachment to go back to duty in Washington again.

I believe I may have told you earlier that I was selected for flag rank at this time, and since the Navy Department did not want to have a flag officer in command at China Lake--or, let's put it another way, the spots for flag officers were greater than the number of flag officers in the Navy, and they couldn't spare a flag officer for China Lake. So I was ordered back to the Navy Department and had duty in the Joint Chiefs of Staff section in what is called the Weapons Systems Evaluation Group. The short title for that is WSEG.

This group consisted of officers in uniform of all three services and scientific types, mostly operational analysis types, who had been drawn together to evaluate weapons systems. Actually it was a concept of the first Secretary of Defense, Mr. Forrestal, and I suspect it was an outgrowth of the old Navy-Air Force controversy about B-36s and aircraft carriers.[*] Mr. Forrestal, I think, was trying to establish a group which would be authoritative and which would be able to make early recommendations regarding weapons systems and would avoid controversies of this kind in the future, as well as saving the United States armed forces money.

---

[*] James V. Forrestal served as Secretary of Defense from 17 September 1947 to 27 March 1949.

Personally, I think it was a very fine concept. Actually, in practice, it wasn't working out entirely that way. However, I got back in Washington in the fall of 1953. My detachment occurred so quickly that I didn't have time to move my family but had to precede them. I left my family--consisting at that time of my wife and her mother and our youngest son--in China Lake to pack up and follow me by train. I took off in the car and took our youngest daughter, Barbara, who was going to enter college that year, back with me. I arranged for her on the way back to be entered as a freshman at Hood College.

I arrived in Washington after a five-day transcontinental--oh, one point of human interest. We traveled east over old Highway 40, which went through the town in which I was born, Zanesville, Ohio. I had the pleasure of taking my youngest daughter to see the house where I was born in Zanesville, Ohio. I took some pictures. The house is still standing--a small, modest frame structure. Also on that trip we went through a section of Indiana where my mother, who was still alive, was living in a nursing home. So we stopped and saw her. That was at Peru, Indiana. We arrived in Washington after five days, and a classmate of mine, Admiral Smedberg, and his wife very kindly put us up until the arrival of my family.[*] Having gotten Barbara entered at Hood College, I began house hunting, and we found a house right down the street in northern Virginia, South Arlington, where we lived for several years.

I reported in due time to the Weapons Systems Evaluation Group, where I found that I was the senior naval member of the group. At that time the group was headed by a lieutenant general in the Army. This job rotated and had a flag officer with the rank of major general or rear admiral from each service, and a number of officers of various grades working on the projects. During this period I participated in a number of studies and reviewed all of the work of the various study groups as they became ready for review. I made a number of trips to various operating areas looking over Army, Navy, and Air Force activities. I found it a fine opportunity to get an overview of the activities of the various services in the combat weapons area.

---

[*] Rear Admiral William R. Smedberg III, USN.

It was particularly useful for me for the jobs that I was to get later: Chief of the Bureau of Ordnance and Chief of the Bureau of Naval Weapons and Commander Naval Air Force Pacific Fleet. Actually, it was the only joint staff job that I had ever had in the Navy and the only one that I was to have.

After about a year and a half of this duty, I felt that I was already overdue for sea duty and was extremely anxious to get to sea in any kind of a seagoing command that I could get as a flag officer. I'm sure you realize that it's the ambition of every naval officer, line officer, who's selected for flag rank to go to sea as soon as possible and fly his flag. I'd been anticipating this assignment with a great deal of interest and had been pushing for it.

One day I happened to be walking down the E-ring of the Pentagon, and I bumped into the Chief of the Bureau of Naval Personnel, Vice Admiral Holloway.[*] Apparently he had learned that I was proselyting my case for sea duty. He stopped me abruptly and told me, "Young man, I know you want to go to sea, but you're going to go where you're sent. You've been asked for to be Deputy Chief of the Bureau of Ordnance, and that's where you're going to go."

I didn't particularly like this turn of events, because I did want to go to sea. I knew that if I went over as Deputy Chief of the Bureau of Ordnance that I'd be there probably two more years, and this would really be a handicap to a successful flag career.

However, in accordance with Admiral Holloway's statement and Navy custom, I reported to the Bureau of Naval Ordnance and became deputy to a very wonderful, fine officer, Frederic Withington.[†] Fred Withington had been deputy for only about ten months and was fleeting up to the chief's job on the retirement of Rear Admiral Schoeffel, who had been Chief of the Bureau of Ordnance for four years. So I went over and was assigned the job of Deputy Chief of the Bureau of Ordnance.

---

[*] The Pentagon has lettered corridors, going from A at the innermost to E at the outermost. E-ring offices, which go around the perimeter of the building are considered the most prestigious. Vice Admiral James L. Holloway, Jr., USN, served as Chief of the Bureau of Naval Personnel from 1953 to 1958. His oral history is in the Columbia University collection.
[†] Rear Admiral Frederic S. Withington, USN, served as Chief of the Bureau of Ordnance from 1954 to 1958. His oral history is in the Naval Institute collection.

Q: Excuse me, before we do leave the Secretary of Defense job, did you find conflict between the various services when you were there? Or at your level had that pretty well disappeared?

Admiral Stroop: To a certain extent, yes, there was conflict. There were arguments, naturally. Usually these were informal. They didn't pertain directly to the studies that were in process, so they weren't what you might call official conflicts. They were personal differences of points of view. I can remember a number of unofficial arguments that got quite heated, but so far as the official record went, no, there were no serious conflicts like, for example, the B-36-aircraft carrier conflict.* There were no studies of that kind going on which generated that kind of a conflict. The small arguments that developed were generally differences of opinion and didn't necessarily pertain to any of the studies that were in process. I remember a number of those.

Q: Well, were the final recommendations really made on facts, rather than any of them service oriented?

Admiral Stroop: Generally that was true. As a matter of fact, the technical work of the group was directed by a civilian technical director, and most of the study groups handling the various projects were headed by civilian scientists. It wasn't always true. I know one particular group was headed by a Navy captain, Captain Abhau, now Rear Admiral Abhau.†

I think, to answer your question, during the year or so that I was attached to WSEG, there were no burning issues, and in that connection, I think probably that the group wasn't being managed properly, because there surely were existing at that time--there

---

* In the late 1940s, the Navy and Air Force were competing for scarce defense dollars. Secretary of Defense Louis Johnson accelerated production of the Air Force's B-36 bomber and canceled the aircraft carrier United States (CVA-58) soon after the beginning of construction. The Navy fought back, as detailed in Jeffrey G. Barlow, Revolt of the Admirals (Washington, D.C.: Naval Historical Center, 1994).
† Captain William Conrad Abhau, USN.

always are--issues which ought to be handled by that kind of a group. As a matter of fact, in the present organization of the Department of Defense, there's a group called systems analysis set up in the Office of the Secretary of Defense, which in my opinion is duplicating the work WSEG should be doing. So there is, I think, a need for this sort of thing. Unfortunately, WSEG wasn't directed then and probably isn't today being directed into the area that Secretary Forrestal originally envisaged.

Q: Because the theory of it sounds exactly right.

Admiral Stroop: It sounds exactly right, but the facts weren't working out.

Q: Are you saying that it still isn't, or . . . ?

Admiral Stroop: I don't know about that. I think the effectiveness of WSEG depends on one or two factors. It depends, of course, on the caliber of the people who are there, particularly the director of the group, and they have had some very fine directors. I was not too impressed, I might say, with Lieutenant General Geoffrey Keyes.[*] Later on, WSEG was headed by Vice Admiral Sides, who was an ordnance-trained man, and he was outstanding.[†] The last director of the group, just retired, Vice Admiral Kleber Masterson, had the same type of background as Admiral Sides, and I think under these two directors the group achieved more success and gained more confidence from the services.[‡]

The other factor that determines the usefulness of the group is the confidence and the use the Joint Staff makes of the group--that is, the Joint Chiefs of Staff and the Office of the Secretary of Defense. If they give them the right types of subjects to study and require them to put their time on it, then the group can be useful. If they don't have confidence in

---

[*] Lieutenant General Geoffrey Keyes retired from the Army in 1950 and was recalled for active duty in the Office of the Secretary of Defense from 1951 to 1954.
[†] Vice Admiral John H. Sides, USN, became director of WSEG is 1957.
[‡] Vice Admiral Kleber S. Masterson, USN, served as Director of the Weapons Systems Evaluation Group from August 1966 to August 1969. He retired 1 September 1969. His oral history is in the Naval Institute collection.

them, why, they can't be useful. Now, under Sides I'm sure that the group probably achieved its greatest usefulness, because of the leadership that Sides had and the confidence that the Joint Chiefs of Staff had in his work. He would, fortunately, sit with the Joint Chiefs of Staff and make presentations to them, and during that time he and the group were used. So the usefulness of WSEG has varied throughout the years. Even so, I don't think it's ever attained the stature or the usefulness that Forrestal originally envisaged when it was set up. Does that answer your question?

Q: Yes. Unfortunately, my experience with the joint boards of this type and the Secretary of Defense is that they were pretty nearly useless, and I just wondered what your experience had been.

Admiral Stroop: Well, I would hesitate to put a percentage figure on the useful work they do, but it certainly is not 100%. But, even so, if they do only 50% useful work, they still could be quite useful.

Well, I think we can shift back to the Bureau of Ordnance. I found the work over there to be time-consuming. I had to work fairly hard, but this wasn't unusual. I'd been doing this all of my life. I found Admiral Withington an extremely fine boss. He was the kind of person who gave me all of the authority he thought I could handle and let me run the administration of the bureau, and he was content to establish policy. One habit that I really applauded--he would try to get away from the bureau personally at the end of working hours, which I thought was fine. Admiral Withington was a hard, conscientious worker. He worked fast, he was extremely intelligent, and he provided much fine leadership. I enjoyed my association with him.

One rather unusual aspect of this duty in the Bureau of Ordnance, as my record will show and really supports my biography, I was not a postgraduate student in ordnance. I had had a short course in an ordnance-oriented general line course back in the early '30s, but my postgraduate work was in the field of applied communications. I suspected that I was the first Deputy Chief of Ordnance--and the first Chief of the Bureau of Ordnance later on--who had not had this particular type of advanced education. However, again as the record will show, I have had a considerable amount of experience in ordnance, starting back at the time I was an ensign in my various aviation duties. So that I had a fairly good practical background and have had a life-long interest in it. You will recall I worked on the Norden bombsight early in my career as a naval aviator. So I did have that background and did not feel too inadequate in handling the technical aspects of the job.

The approximately two years that I spent in this job, I managed to do a good bit of traveling. I visited every ordnance installation that the bureau had, I organized a series of conferences with the fleet type commanders in both oceans and tried to get to see them at least once each year. I would lead this safari with a group of officers who were ordnance oriented and who had business in their particular areas of interest. I had the job of administering the ordnance shore establishment, which was quite large, handling the details of that. And, of course, we had a number of interesting projects, important research and development projects, going on all the time. I had close contact with the research and development area and particularly with my former station at China Lake, which I'd just left. I found that, looking back on it, this was one of the most important jobs that I had in my naval career, and it was the kind of a job that led to my subsequent duties, of course, as Chief of the Bureau of Ordnance and Chief of the Bureau of Naval Weapons.

After about two years and with the help of Admiral Withington, I began stirring around and trying to get assigned to a sea job. Admiral Withington himself told me, "If you don't get to sea now, it will just be too late," and I felt that already my career as a flag officer had been made lopsided and maybe even blighted. I was senior enough, at this time, to get a large carrier division, and this is what I was hoping to get. That was the main line kind of a job to get if you were going any higher in the Navy as a flag officer and as a naval aviator. However, my old friend Admiral Holloway was still over in the Bureau of Personnel. He and the Chief of Naval Operations didn't see fit to let me have a carrier division, so I was sent out as Commander of the Taiwan Patrol Force.

Q: You mean you had it all lined up for the other job and then . . . ?

Admiral Stroop: No, it never even got lined up. I just personally asked for it and didn't get it. I felt that I was very well qualified for it. I'd been captain of two attack carriers, but these jobs didn't come up too frequently, and the job with the Taiwan Patrol Force did come up. The Chief of Naval Operations and the Chief of the Bureau of Personnel decided I should go, so out I went to the Western Pacific in about March of 1957.

Here again, we had to split up our family to travel across the continent. I took my young son Patrick and our basset hound and drove across to Coronado. My wife, who by this time had said she'd never make another transcontinental trip by car, went by train with her mother, who was getting pretty well along. We met halfway across the continent in Texas at the home of an old wartime companion, Bill Hughes. This was near Wellington, Texas, and we enjoyed three wonderful days with Bill on his ranch, had a chance to get a little rest and observe some of the ranch operations.

After that interlude, I took off again in the car early in the morning, about 4:00 o'clock, with Patrick and the basset hound. We arrived in San Diego two days later, the same day that my wife had arrived there. We had about ten days, as I recall, in the San Diego area; we lived in a rented place at Coronado. During this period I went on out to Pearl Harbor to have a briefing with Admiral Stump at his headquarters as Commander in Chief Pacific and Commander in Chief of the Pacific Fleet, as it related to my new job.[*]

I had to make this special trip, because we were scheduled for travel by Navy transport right from San Diego to Okinawa, bypassing Pearl. I returned to Coronado after the briefing at CinCPacFlt headquarters, and we embarked on the USS General A. E. Anderson: my wife, her mother Mrs. Halscher, Patrick and I, and the basset hound. I might also add here that our youngest daughter, Barbara, was then in her fourth year of college. We decided to leave her behind to complete college and get her degree before she joined us at Okinawa. The trip out on the transport was a very fine period. There was almost nothing to do except read, which I did a good bit of. As a matter of fact, I had one project--I reviewed a 500-page book for the Naval Institute.

---

[*] Admiral Felix B. Stump, USN, served as Commander in Chief Pacific and Commander in Chief U.S. Pacific Fleet, 10 July 1953-14 January 1958.

Q: Do you remember the book?

Admiral Stroop: I don't remember the name of it, but the record will show that I did write a review, it was published, and I think I got a check for $40.00 for my work on the trip.[*] The other little project I had during this period was making out the year's income tax. I did both of these jobs in a rather leisurely manner. We were fortunate enough to be guests of the captain in his cabin for all of our meals and had excellent accommodations up on the boat deck. I was senior officer present on board and got the best VIP treatment that you could possibly get on a naval transport and found the trip extremely comfortable.

We had very few incidents during the trip. I recall the day a Marine passenger had a family emergency just before we got fairly close to Midway. We diverted our course and one night off-loaded this Marine at Midway. They sent a tug out and picked him up. I might add that the transport was taking Marines out to the Far East. We had about 2,000 Marine troops on board.

Our first real port was Keelung on the island of Taiwan. There I was met by my old friend and squadron mate, Vice Admiral Slim Ingersoll, who took us ashore for a little sightseeing and a luncheon at the Grand Hotel in Taipei.[†] We were there only part of one day and then sailed on up to Okinawa. We docked at the port of Naha, in the southwest corner of the island of Okinawa. This was to be my headquarters and home for the next ten months. On Okinawa I relieved Rear Admiral Dixon, who had been an old-time friend and shipmate, particularly on the old Lexington.[‡]

---

[*] The June 1957 issue of the U.S. Naval Institute Proceedings, pages 668-669, carried Rear Admiral Stroop's review of John Ehrman;s Grand Strategy, volume VI in a series of the same title. The book was published in London by Her Masjesty's Stationery Office. It covered the strategy for the last year of World War II. Stroop was chosen as the reviewer because of his experience as part of the U.S. delegation to the Potsdam Conference in 1945.
[†] Vice Admiral Stuart H. Ingersoll, USN, served as Commander Seventh Fleet from 19 December 1955 to 28 January 1957.
[‡] Rear Admiral Robert E. Dixon, USN.

We occupied a wonderful set of government quarters made out of expanded Quonset huts.* This turned out to be one of the most enjoyable and most interesting periods of my naval career, and I regretted that it lasted only ten months. As a matter of fact, I might make the observation that two tours of duty that I felt that I would personally enjoy the most in the Navy--that is, command of the Naval Ordnance Test Station at China Lake and on the Taiwan Patrol Force--both were to last only ten months. The really top assignments, requiring long working hours and a lot of frustrations, lasted from two to four years.

Q: I think in retrospect you can recognize that they give the jobs to the people who can do them.

Admiral Stroop: Well, be that as it may, at least to people who were willing to work hard at it and are effective. I guess that's saying the same thing. At any rate, this was going to be a very fine job, and I was delighted that I had got it, even though I had been earlier disappointed that I didn't get a carrier division.

The Taiwan Patrol Force had been established by President Truman in the first days of the Korean affair. The mission of the Taiwan Patrol Force was to keep the Taiwan Straits neutral, patrolled, and to keep the Communist Chinese from taking advantage of our preoccupation in Korea and coming across and attacking the Nationalist Chinese on the island of Taiwan. I also felt that it was maybe one of our jobs to keep the Nationalist Chinese from taking advantage of the situation and going the other way. So, really, our job was to neutralize the Taiwan Straits.

To do this we had a force of four destroyers and a destroyer tender. The destroyer tender stayed anchored most of the time in Kaohsiung Harbor on the southern tip of Taiwan. The four destroyers were rotated, a division at a time, and I might point out that, particularly in the wintertime, it was very tough duty, because the weather was quite unpleasant, cold and blowing rough off the coast of China. We kept two destroyers on

---

* A Quonset hut is a semi-cylindrical metal building that can be shipped to an advance base area and erected quickly.

station all the time, operating generally 16 to 20 miles patrolling the Chinese coast opposite Taiwan.

In addition to that, we had daily air patrols. In order to carry out these air patrols, we had a squadron of planes at Iwakuni in Japan, and we had a squadron of P2Vs at Naha in Okinawa, and we had a squadron of seaplanes in Sangley Point.* We had three squadrons for this particular purpose--two seaplane squadrons and one land-plane squadron. In addition, we had a squadron of special-purpose aircraft; it was called VQ-1. This was the outfit that collected special intelligence patrolling the same area.

Q: What kind of planes were they?

Admiral Stroop: At the time we had a large land plane called the P4M. The Navy had only a few of these in inventory, and they were configured solely for this purpose. Later on these P4Ms were to be gradually replaced by twin-engined jet A3Ds, large carrier-type bomber-reconnaissance aircraft.

With squadrons in Japan, Okinawa, and the Philippines, I had rather widespread responsibilities and found it always gave me the opportunities--required me--to do a good bit of traveling. I had a flag plane, an old Grumman amphibian, which I used an awful lot to make inspection trips and visits. I also had a flagship, one of the large seaplane tenders; these rotated on about a four-month basis, all being homeported at San Diego. I used the flag plane and the seaplane tender to make routine visits to the various locations of interest. I would go up to Iwakuni, Japan, and to Yokosuka, for example, to inspect the seaplane squadron and special-purpose forces at Iwakuni. I would check in with the Commander Seventh Fleet, generally at Yokosuka, and this at that time was my old friend Vice Admiral Beakley.†

We would also periodically visit both Keelung and Kaohsiung, and I always arranged for the tender to get at least one, and preferably two, visits in Hong Kong during

---

* Sangley Point was the site of a naval air station in the Philippines.
† Vice Admiral Wallace M. Beakley, USN, served as Commander Seventh Fleet from 28 January 1957 to 30 September 1958.

the time that it was in the Western Pacific. Of course, we went to Manila, Sangley Point, to visit the squadron down there. I also had a second ship of the small seaplane class, which was based normally in Hong Kong as a station ship. Generally, I had just administrative responsibilities with this ship.

However, on one occasion I was able to break it loose from the station ship assignment and took two of the tenders--a big tender and a little tender--down into the Philippines. We had a two-week operation, advanced base type, where we ran patrols from advanced bases. It was probably the last time this kind of an operation was accomplished in the U.S. Navy, and you'll never see it again, because we don't operate seaplanes anymore. It brought back a lot of memories and reminded me of my very early days in aviation, because this was the kind of thing that we did in VP-9 and VP-10 back in the '30s.

With regard to the aircraft patrols, we operated out of the bases I've already mentioned and ran patrols along the coast of China and also the bordering seas: that is, the South China Sea, the Gulf of Tonkin, and the Sea of Japan. We, of course, carried out the primary mission of patrolling the Taiwan Straits and in addition kept track generally of all the shipping in the area. Our patrol aircraft were equipped with cameras, and they got to be very adept at taking pictures and identifying merchant ships. We had a maneuver called rigging, where we would fly down about at masthead height off to one side of the merchant ship and take a picture. This was one of the interesting products of our daily patrols.

There were only two incidents that might have led to more serious affairs during this period. I recall one of our special-purpose planes in VQ-1 was being trailed one night by what he thought were probably Communist night fighters. He had to abandon his patrol and managed to get back to his Japanese base at Atsugi, where he was operating from at that time, without being intercepted. Another incident which was of particular significance was the interception of two Russian destroyers and a tender which were coming around from the east coast of Russia to Siberia. Our intelligence told us that these ships would pass through the Suez Canal, then out through the straits. We trailed these Russian ships from the Suez Canal, through the Red Sea, the Gulf of Aden, and to Ceylon, where they anchored and refueled, then through the Straits of Malacca.

I arranged to intercept them with my flagship in the vicinity of the Bashi Channel, north of Luzon. Our timing worked out perfectly. I'd planned on picking them up about 7:00 o'clock in the morning, on an opposite course. They came over the horizon at exactly the time I expected them, and we passed on opposite courses, starboard to starboard, about 1,000 yards apart. I had photographers up and various competent people making notes, sketching the radars, gun mounts, and so forth.

After we'd passed and exchanged signals, I reversed course and followed them for a while, tried to get some information from the international signal hoists, but this proved to be quite futile. I asked them where they were from, but they would not tell me. I asked them where they were going, and the only answer I ever got back was the signal which, translated in the meaning of the international signal hoist, was, "We are in sailing training." I never did get the name of the officer in charge. The Russians continued on their way, probably to Vladivostok, and I continued on my way to Hong Kong.

This particular tour of duty continued for, as I said, only ten months. I found that I was traveling about half the time, and the other half the time I was able to spend at our headquarters and home port on the island of Okinawa. We had a fine family life during this period. I was one of the three senior military people on the island of Okinawa and, of course, was the senior U.S. Navy representative. However, Commander Seventh Fleet, my good friend Vice Admiral Beakley, dropped in every month or two and would spend a few days with us. During the end of my tour, the Chief of Naval Operations, Admiral Arleigh Burke, and his wife Bobbie flew in and spent a couple of days.[*]

In addition to the regular duties as Taiwan Patrol Force commander, I had a particularly interesting assignment in connection with the Nationalist Chinese Navy. I had the job of cooperating with them and assisting in their training. As a result of this, I had many opportunities to meet many of the senior Chinese, including Generalissimo Chiang Kai-shek and, of course, his wife.[†] Also the senior Chinese Navy people: Admiral Liang,

---

[*] Admiral Arleigh A. Burke, USN, served as Chief of Naval Operations from 17 August 1955 to 1 August 1961

[†] Generalissimo Chiang Kai-shek served as President of Nationalist China on the mainland from 1943 to 1949 and as President of the Republic of China on Taiwan from 1950 until his death in 1975.

who was then their Chief of Naval Operations or Chief of Naval Staff. His deputy was Admiral Ni, who was later to succeed Admiral Liang and become Chief of Naval Operations, and who has been a very close personal friend ever since. I met some of the senior Chinese Air Force people and the senior Chinese Army people at the same time. I might point out that these contacts which I made at that time have been extremely useful in recent years in connection with some of the activities I'm carrying on now.

Q: Oh, since you've been out of the Navy?

Admiral Stroop: That's right. As a matter of fact, I visited Taiwan, I think, five times since retiring four years ago. On each occasion I've seen my old friends over there and have done some business with them.

Q: Isn't it funny that everything you do, even though you can't possibly think it's going to be any value for the future, is invariably a benefit?

Admiral Stroop: Yes, it certainly has worked out in this case. My visits to Taiwan took me generally to Taipei and also to Kaohsiung and the adjacent naval port of Tsoying, which is really the headquarters of the Chinese Navy.

We had one rather significant operation in connection with the Chinese Navy. This was a joint type affair where I used the Taiwan Patrol Force's flagship, the AV seaplane tender, and four destroyers. We had a submarine to give us submarine services, to act as an enemy submarine, and I also had four destroyers from the Chinese Navy. In the initial concept of the operation, I tried to penetrate the Taiwan Straits with the flagship and four U.S. destroyers and had the Chinese destroyers intercepting us, which they did, of course, quite successfully. This was a nighttime operation. Once they'd intercepted us, then I had them join up as a screen for the flagship, and we attempted to continue the penetration of the straits, opposed by the enemy submarine.

I must say that the operation worked out quite successfully from an administrative point of view, but the submarine managed to get through the screen and simulate torpedoing the flagship. We went through this operation twice, and the submarine was successful both times. This was the first time I'd ever attempted to work combined operations with U.S. and Chinese forces, and I was pleased that they were fairly successful.

I had embarked on my flagship a young Chinese admiral who was observing the operation, and also it was rather interesting that we had some German political types--about eight Germans who were paying a courtesy visit to Taiwan--and they had sailed with me out of Kaohsiung and stayed aboard to watch the operation. They were particularly elated when our enemy submarine was successful both times in penetrating the screen and simulating a torpedo firing against the flagship.

I found one unusual communication arrangement. As you probably know, we generally do all of our maneuvering and tactical communications by voice. Of course, the Chinese were bound to have some language difficulty manning our own English-speaking voice circuits. We noted every time a tactical signal would go out, or any instructions would go out over this maneuvering circuit, that the Chinese would come back with a "Wait." I didn't realize it at the time, but they had a parallel circuit on a different frequency and were conferring in Chinese before they would acknowledge the tactical signal. This slowed operations up a little bit, but basically it worked fine with their bootlegged circuit.

This cooperative training was greatly appreciated by the Chinese, and I thought it was also excellent training for our U.S. forces. Had I stayed on longer in that job as Commander Taiwan Patrol Force, we would have had one of these kinds of operation at least once a quarter. Unfortunately, I was to find out in just a few weeks that my tour of duty as Commander Taiwan Patrol Force would terminate after ten months.

I returned to Okinawa about this time and had the visit which I mentioned earlier with Admiral Burke, the Chief of Naval Operations. He and his wife came to Okinawa and spent two days. It just happened that his old destroyer squadron, the Little Beavers, Destroyer Squadron 23, was in Okinawa at the time. This was the outfit that he commanded during World War II in the South Pacific and where he got the name which stuck with him the rest of his life, "31-knot Burke."* Admiral Burke got a big kick out of making a quick visit over to his old flagship.

We had a reception for the Chief of Naval Operations and his wife at our quarters on Okinawa. I had a private late-evening conference with him where I managed to get the thought across that I was enjoying my job very much out there, it was a great relief to be out of Washington, and that I hoped that I could have it for two full years. I thought I particularly deserved it since I hadn't been able to get my big carrier command. In any case, I wanted to stay at sea as long as I could. Admiral Burke gave me very positive personal assurances that this would be the case, and I would remain on as Commander Taiwan Patrol Force until I had to be rotated to shore duty--at least a year from that time.

You can imagine my surprise when, about ten days after Admiral Burke had left Taiwan and gotten back to Washington, I received a personal dispatch from him saying, in effect, that in spite of the fact that he had promised me that I wouldn't be coming back to Washington, and in spite of the fact that he knew that I didn't want to come back, that I was being considered for the job of Chief of the Bureau of Ordnance, to relieve my old friend Admiral Withington, and that this would take place very soon.

In addition, he told me to make arrangements to meet the Assistant Secretary of the Navy for Material, Mr. Fred Bantz, either in Okinawa or in Taiwan.† It turned out that I would not be able to meet the Secretary in Okinawa, because I was sailing the next day for Taiwan. But I could meet him in Taipei, Taiwan, and this I did. I met the Secretary's plane when it landed, and we went immediately to the Grand Hotel, where we had a private conference for about half an hour. This was the first time I had met Mr. Bantz and the first time that he had had a chance to look me over. At the end of our conference, he told me that it was practically certain that I would be going back to Washington very soon.

I went on south to Hong Kong, and Mr. Bantz left in a day or two for Okinawa. Although I wasn't present, Mrs. Stroop gave a reception for him, and they, of course, were

---

* For the origin of the nickname "31-Knot Burke," see E. B. Potter, <u>Admiral Arleigh Burke: A Biography</u> (New York: Randon House, 1990), pages 102-103.
† Fred A. Bantz, who later served as Under Secretary of the Navy at the end of the Eisenhower Administration.

on pins and needles, wondering just what the future held. Mr. Bantz was quite affable but didn't give us any positive information. However, my young son did have a little conversation with him. He just asked him abruptly the question, "Are we going back to Washington?"

And the Secretary said, "What's the matter, Pat, don't you want to go back?"

Pat said, "No." That ended any information we got out of the Secretary.

About a week after this, when I was in Hong Kong, I did get my orders and found out that I was, indeed, going back to be Chief of the Bureau of Ordnance. I had just a couple of more weeks before my relief showed up. It was Rear Admiral Brick Blackburn, a brand-new flag officer.[*] He came out very quickly and caught me still in Hong Kong. We had the change of command ceremony on the flagship in Hong Kong Harbor. It was a very small ceremony. I had a few civilian friends aboard, no other senior Navy people around. Immediately after the ceremony I took off with Admiral Blackburn to stop by Taipei, where we had arranged for a meeting with the senior Chinese, including Generalissimo Chiang Kai-shek. These meetings were very pleasant and productive. That evening a dinner was given in honor of both of us, and I was presented with a Chinese decoration by the Chinese Government. This was the Order of the Cloud and Banner. We spent the night in Taiwan and flew the next morning to Okinawa, where Admiral Blackburn had an opportunity to see our quarters and to meet the rest of the staff, including the personal staff on Okinawa.

Q: You said your quarters were made of Quonset huts?

Admiral Stroop: Yes. These quarters were built right at the end of the war by, I think, Rear Admiral Price, who was the senior naval officer on Okinawa.[†] They consisted of two Quonset huts which had been opened out with additional structures, balconies, large windows, and so forth. There was a very large living room, a large dining room, servants'

---

[*] Rear Admiral Paul P. Blackburn, Jr., USN, who later served briefly as Commander Seventh Fleet from March to October 1965.
[†] Rear Admiral John Dale Price, USN, was Commander Naval Operating Base Okinawa for the final weeks of the Pacific war.

quarters, a large kitchen, and three very large bedrooms with two baths, a two-car garage, and also a guest house.

I might point out, too, that the quarters were quite adequately staffed. As a matter of fact, somewhat unintentionally on our part, they were overstaffed. This happened because when we first came aboard there were no government servants attached to the quarters, because they had not been declared official flag officer quarters. As a result, we had hired three Okinawan maids at about $30.00 a month apiece to take care of the house. We also had a part-time gardener who was the grandfather of two of the girls who were sisters.

Soon after I arrived in Okinawa, these quarters, which had been Army quarters, were declared U.S. Navy flag officer quarters, and two stewards were assigned. I managed to get the two stewards which I had had on the Princeton ordered to Okinawa. One was a very fine colored boy named Boykin, and the other was a Filipino named Florendo.* These two excellent men arrived on Okinawa, and, of course, we still had the three maids, which we felt inadvisable to let go because they needed the work.

At the same time, since the quarters now were government quarters, we were assigned officially a government gardener, an Okinawan, and also an armed guard for the house from 6:00 o'clock in the evening to 6:00 o'clock in the morning. In addition to all of these, I had a Navy driver who was frequently at the quarters during meal hours, and this made quite a large number of people to take care of. But we managed to get along all right. I had the two gardeners plant vegetable plots all around the house, and I could get rice flown in from Taipei at four cents a pound. We brought tea from the ship and, since the Okinawans didn't eat much meat, particularly liked fish, we managed to feed this whole menage at a reasonable rate.

It was obvious, of course, that we were living quite well and enjoying life, and it was with great regret that I finally got my official orders to proceed back to Washington. I was quite disappointed that the orders indicated that I would have to leave ahead of my family, because they wanted to come back again by ship, and I did not have enough time to get

---

* Steward Third Class W. E. Boykin, USN; Steward Third Class T. R. Florendo, USN.

back to Washington. We did fly up together to Japan, where the ship--again the same ship that we came out on, the General Anderson--was leaving from Yokohama. After a couple of days of sightseeing in Japan, which included a visit to Kyoto, I put my family aboard the General Anderson for the return trip to the United States. I took off from Atsugi, Japan, in a Navy patrol plane for Guam, Honolulu, and the West Coast.

I arrived in Washington about two weeks ahead of the family and immediately reported in to the Chief of the Bureau of Ordnance to act as his relief. Admiral Withington, oddly enough, was being sent out as Commander U.S. Naval Forces Japan. He made me a very generous offer to rent his house while he was gone and while I was Chief of the Bureau of Ordnance. This I did and also bought one of his automobiles, and we were all set to begin another tour of duty in Washington. The family arrived in due course, and by this time I'd gotten enough furniture out of storage and had the house ready to live in.

The next two years as Chief of the Bureau of Ordnance were very busy ones. I had the usual responsibilities of a bureau chief, mainly administering the large naval ordnance establishment, running the ordnance programs of the Navy, overseeing the supply of ammunition, missiles, and so forth, and--most importantly of all--preparing and presenting the budget to Congress.

My day would begin about 7:00 o'clock in the morning, when I had the duty officer deliver dispatches to the house. I would read these dispatches during breakfast and on the way to work, being fortunate enough to have a car and driver during most of the period. My first appointment was at 8:00 o'clock in the Pentagon, when I sat in on the Chief of Naval Operations's morning briefing conference. This meant, of course, a trip from where I lived across the Potomac River to the Pentagon. By about 8:45 this briefing was over, and I returned to my office in the Main Navy building on Constitution Avenue. The days were all very busy, and I frequently would be in my office until 6:00 or 7:00 o'clock in the evening.

About a year after I became Chief of the Bureau of Ordnance, a set of government quarters became available in the old gun factory, and we moved down there.* This was of

---

* The Naval Gun Factory, on M Street in southeast Washington, D.C., for many years manufactured guns for the U.S. Navy. The site has since been renamed the Washington

considerable advantage to us, because here again we were allowed government servants in the quarters and an official car for going back and forth to work. It made life a lot more bearable in what was a very, very busy job.

Q: I want to make a comment, because I think many times civilians see the appurtenances of office, and they wonder, or they may be critical, without having the faintest idea that when a man is pressured with the schedule that you had, that these are just minimum things you have to have truly to get along and do the job.

Admiral Stroop: That's quite true. As a matter of fact, these little perquisites that we got did make life more bearable and enabled me to do my job considerably better, or at least give more time to my official duties. These, of course, included not only the regular routine of the Bureau of Ordnance but a considerable amount of official entertaining and attendance at official functions. For example, we had quite a few dealings with foreign governments, and it was necessary that I have some acquaintance with the various foreign naval attachés in Washington. So we met them both officially and socially.

After I'd been in the Bureau of Ordnance about a year, the Secretary of the Navy set up a board known as the Franke Board, because it was headed by then-Under Secretary of the Navy Franke.[*] This board was to go over the organization of the bureaus, particularly the Bureau of Ordnance and the Bureau of Aeronautics, to see if possibly a better organization might be evolved for the material organization of the Navy. This board, after deliberating for several months and hearing many witnesses, came to the conclusion that the Bureau of Ordnance and the Bureau of Aeronautics should be combined in one bureau and be called the Bureau of Naval Weapons. A group was set up, consisting of two admirals and a number of key personnel from each bureau to work out the details of the organization.

Navy Yard and contains the residences of a number of active duty flag officers, including the Chief of Naval Operations.

[*] William B. Franke was Under Secretary of the Navy, 1957-59, and Secretary of the Navy, 1959-61.

A few months after that, I was told I would shift over when the organization became a fact and become the first Chief of the Bureau of Naval Weapons. The Bureau of Naval Weapons was established officially on the first of September, with a tentative date of 1 January for disestablishing the two former bureaus, giving a three-month opportunity to effect the changeover. Because of the Christmas holidays and the importance of the budget cycle, I soon decided that 1 December would be a better date. On 1 December 1959 we had a little ceremony where I was sworn in as the Chief of the Bureau of Naval Weapons, and the Bureau of Ordnance and the Bureau of Aeronautics were officially disestablished.

This new organization was quite large. We had probably 80,000 people in the field, and in Washington we had a headquarters of about 4,000 people, including 700 officers. Most of the officers were located in Main Navy building, although we had some annexes also down at the gun factory. The next two years were extremely busy ones.

I was quite gratified to find that the changeover into the Bureau of Naval Weapons was accomplished with a minimum of confusion. As a matter of fact, I had people in the field tell me that they really couldn't tell when the changeover occurred. This was a source of satisfaction to me, because we were handling emergencies every day, and I wanted to make sure that our people were responsive. I also wanted to make particularly sure that our service to the operating forces never faltered. So far as I could tell, it never did.

The budget of the new bureau amounted to, I believe about $9 billion, which was a very large part of the Navy's total budget.* About half of that was in the procurement area, where we bought airplanes, guns, ammunition, guided missiles, and all sorts of equipment pertaining to aviation and ordnance. In many ways it was one of the most responsible and important jobs in the Navy, and I considered myself quite honored and fortunate to have it. Naturally, I was extremely busy.

In the new organization I had to do a lot of delegating of authority and was able to do this, because I had a considerable number of fine flag officers who were capable of showing initiative and holding up their end of the work. I used these fine officers to reduce my frequent trips to Congress and found that most of them could handle the job quite well.

---

* The Navy's budget for fiscal year 1959 was $11.5 billion.

This took quite a lot of the load off my shoulders. I was also fortunate in having an excellent deputy, Rear Admiral William Schoech, whom I'd known ever since we were midshipmen together at the Naval Academy in the same squad.[*]

Q: You were still rear admiral?

Admiral Stroop: I held the rank of rear admiral, although I had about 11 rear admirals working for me in various capacities. I learned that I was to be nominated for vice admiral, but unfortunately this nomination never got cleared through the Secretary of the Navy, and up till the time I was detached remained in his "hold" basket.

There were many important decisions and procurements which occurred during this tour of duty, but I think the one which will go down in history as the most controversial and probably the most important was the procurement of the TFX, later called the F-111.[†] The individuals who were to evaluate this program from the Navy point of view, of course, came from the Bureau of Naval Weapons, from the old Bureau of Aeronautics side of the house. We had these people teamed up with their Air Force counterparts at Wright Field.[‡]

The program is now history, of course, but I well remember many of the sessions we had which were quite stormy, in that the personnel of the Bureau of Naval Weapons, with me as their spokesman, continually opposed the Navy part of the program and continually made recommendations against it. As a matter of fact, the uniformed side of the house and the Air Force were of the same opinion, but, as we know, after four reviews of the program, the recommendations of the uniformed services were turned down, or overruled,

---

[*] Rear Admiral William A. Schoech, USN. As a vice admiral, he served as Chief of Naval Material from 1963 to 1965.

[†] TFX stood for "tactical fighter experimental." The F-111, as it was later called, was a controversial fighter plane that Secretary of Defense Robert McNamara tried to develop in the 1960s for use by both the Air Force and the Navy. The Navy version eventually was transformed into the F-14.

[‡] Wright-Patterson Air Force Base, near Dayton, Ohio, was established in 1948 with the merger of Wright Field and Patterson Field. The work done at the base has long been in the engineering and material areas.

by the two service secretaries and the Secretary of Defense, and we were off and running with a very large, expensive program that was scheduled for disaster.

Q: Mr. McNamara was the Secretary of Defense?

Admiral Stroop: So far as I could ever determine, Secretary McNamara was the individual who insisted that this program go through and that the Navy and the Air Force have a common airplane.*

Q: Do you have any knowledge of your own as to why he was so intransigent on this subject?

Admiral Stroop: I don't have any direct knowledge. I've always felt that the final decision was to a considerable degree political. The reason I say this is that the Navy and the Air Force were unified in their recommendation that we not go ahead with a common program, and also we had complete agreement that the best proposal had been submitted by the competition, which was Boeing. We were overruled on both cases. That is, the Navy and the Air Force were ordered to go ahead with a common program, and the decision was reached at the level of the Secretary of Defense that the award should be made to General Dynamics. I believe history shows that the recommendations were right, and, of course, as we know now, the Navy part of the program was discontinued after about six airplanes had been delivered and many, many millions of dollars had been wasted on the program. It was an unfortunate event in the history of the Navy and the history of the Department of Defense, in my opinion.

Q: It probably went beyond the Secretary, up to the President.

Admiral Stroop: You said that; I didn't.

---

* Robert S. McNamara served as Secretary of Defense from 21 January 1961 to 29 February 1968.

Q: Well, that is from conversation and newspapers, and publicity. The public has no knowledge other than what appeared in papers and magazines.

Admiral Stroop: I have no real knowledge of this, of course. However, I am sure that the decision was discussed at White House level, and certainly the White House agreed with the final decision to award the contract to General Dynamics.

There was one other occasion when a recommendation of this type was overruled. This had to do with an experimental vertical takeoff and landing aircraft called the X-22. This was a rather small, minor research and development program and was of very small consequence compared to the TFX. As a matter of fact, initially it involved only about $16 million, although I suspect by now many times that sum has been spent on the program, which is still in existence.

In this particular case, the competitors were Douglas Aircraft and Bell. The evaluations by our very competent personnel in the Bureau of Naval Weapons gave the superior proposal to Douglas. However, the recommendations again of the Bureau of Weapons and the official recommendation of the bureau chief, myself, and the endorsements made by the Chief of Naval Operations, were all overruled at the level--this time--of the Assistant Secretary of Defense. The final award was made to Bell Aircraft, and they are still working on the program. All that I have recounted here became public knowledge when a year later Senator Stennis held a public hearing to inquire into the circumstances of this particular award.[*]

These were the only two cases that ever came to my attention where very serious and important recommendations for large procurement programs were reversed at a level beyond the chief of the bureau or the service chief.

Q: What was your reaction to it?

---

[*] Senator John C. Stennis (Democrat-Mississippi).

Admiral Stroop: Well, my reaction then--and always will be--is that the evaluations that were made in the bureau were completely honest, they were completely thorough, and the people who made them were the most competent people in the government to make them. The individuals who went through the process of considering the proposals were highly competent professionals. They had been in this business for many years and were thoroughly forthright. I might add, too, that the individuals who were involved in these evaluations had the complete respect of the industry. I was told many times that in very fierce competitions that the competitors always felt that they had an honest evaluation and were satisfied with the results, even through sometimes they were disappointed.

Q: They knew they were honestly made.

Admiral Stroop: That's right, and I can't ever recall thinking that we had made a mistake in an evaluation of this kind, simply because it was so thorough. There were so many people involved in it that there was always brought to bear the best possible professional, technical judgment, and honest evaluations and honest recommendations were made. I don't think that there is really any better way to judge and award important contacts of this kind than by going to a committee of experts who have the best interests of the operating services at heart and who will do a thoroughly competent job.

I might add that just before the award of the TFX contract was made, after the fourth time the proposals were restudied and presented, I was rather quickly detached from the bureau and therefore was not to take part in the final recommendation or final judgment. For this I was very glad. I was detached quite quickly in October of 1962 and ordered as Commander Naval Air Force Pacific Fleet, reporting on the first of November 1962.

The TFX/F-111 argument left a good many scars, particularly in the Navy. For example, the Chief of Naval Operations, Admiral George Anderson, who had backed me completely, was not reappointed as Chief of Naval Operations but was retired at the end of his first two-year term.* I believe that the TFX controversy had a good bit to do with this. Also, Vice Admiral Robert B. Pirie, the Deputy Chief of Naval Operations for Air, a friend and classmate of mine, decided rather quickly to retire at this time.† I know for a fact he was personally a casualty of the Navy's opposition to the TFX/F-111 program. Pirie was a fine officer, and up until this time had a service reputation which indicated he would probably go to four-star rank. After the difficulty with the TFX, it became obvious that he could not expect further promotion in the Navy, and he elected to retire voluntarily about the time that I was also detached from the Washington scene.

Q: Did it ever enter your mind to retire at this time?

Admiral Stroop: Well, obviously I did give it some thought, but fortunately I was far enough down on the totem pole so that I didn't get scarred quite as much. I say rather facetiously that the TFX caused the firing of the Chief of Naval Operations, early retirement of his Deputy Chief of Naval Operations for Air, and removal of his Chief of the Bureau of Naval Weapons from the Washington scene.

In my case, of course, the departure from the Washington scene also brought a promotion to three stars, the rank of vice admiral, and for that I was particularly happy. It was quite obvious that this had come along quite late in my naval career; I had only about four years, in fact, to do, and the chance for further promotion beyond vice admiral would be very slim.

On the other hand, I was being ordered into a very fine, important professional job, and I would have an opportunity to spend my final years on active duty in the Navy in the town where I felt I probably would retire. In addition to that, it enabled me to keep many of the important contacts I'd established in recent years in the Navy. I was entirely happy

---

* Admiral George W. Anderson, Jr., USN, served as Chief of Naval Operations from 1 August 1961 to 1 August 1963, the date of his retirement. His oral history is in the Naval Institute collection.
† Vice Admiral Robert B. Pirie, Jr., USN, served as Deputy Chief of Naval Operations (Air) from 26 May 1958 to 1 November 1962, the date of his retirement. His oral history is in the Naval Institute collection.

with the assignment, except that I was sorry that it had to result out of the large controversy involving the TFX, where the Navy came out second best. It was saddled with a program which was doomed for failure and which would cost the Navy and the taxpayer a great deal of money.

There was one incident that I failed to cover during my last year in the Bureau of Naval Weapons. This involved a trip to Europe, where I took a couple of staff officers and attended the Farnborough Aircraft Show in London, then went on to Stockholm, Sweden, where I visited with the Swedish ordnance people, Bofors. I then went to call on various military assistance groups in the Hague and Rome, Italy, and also visited an international plant which had just been established in Germany to build the NATO model of Sidewinder, which I participated in developing at the Naval Ordnance Test Station at China Lake. This trip was very important and interesting professionally, but it was also a personal pleasure because I took Mrs. Stroop along at private expense, and she enjoyed seeing a part of the world that we had never covered in my military service.

I was particularly glad to see the new little ordnance plant in Germany where the Sidewinders were being built and was quite impressed with the way it was being set up. It seemed to be a rather difficult type of operation in that several countries--Turkey, the Netherlands, Italy, Norway, and Great Britain--were cooperating in building one small missile, with parts being manufactured in each country and assembled in Germany. However, history shows us that the venture was a great success, and the NATO Sidewinders were proved out to be just as high quality as those which we were building in the United States.

In Rome I had the good opportunity to work a little bit with the Italian Navy and made an acquaintance with their chief of research and development, at that time Rear Admiral Michelagnoli.* This very fine, wonderful officer later became their fleet commander and finally their Chief of Naval Operations. At that time, the Italians were busy equipping some of their ships with guided missiles. The missiles they were to use were systems that had been developed by the United States Navy. I visited their government

---

* Ammiraglio de Squadra Alessandro Michelagnoli served as Italy's Chief of Naval Staff in the mid-1960s.

shipyard at La Spezia, Italy, and went aboard the Garibaldi, which was getting the Terrier missile system installed.*

Here again, I was pleasantly surprised that the Italian workmen were doing outstanding work. I talked privately with some American consultants who were on hand from the companies who had developed various parts of the system, and they told me that they had never seen any better work anyplace in the world. As a matter of fact, as each system was developed and checked out, each time it checked out perfectly, which was a lot better than we were able to do in our own country.

After Italy we stopped in Madrid, and I had an opportunity to see our three naval installations in Spain: an air station at Rota, an ammunition depot at Cartagena, and, of course, the naval headquarters in Madrid.

This trip to Europe and the various visits with the naval aviation activities was probably one of the highlights of my tour of duty in Washington.

Q: Before we leave your duties as the head of the Bureau of Naval Weapons, I want to read the commendation which you received, which I will quote as follows: "For meritorious service as Chief, Bureau of Ordnance, from March 14, 1958, to September 8, 1959, and as Chief, Bureau of Naval Weapons from September 9, 1959, to July 20, 1960. Through his keen foresight and judicious direction of the many competent resources within his cognizance, Rear Admiral Stroop provided vital research, development, technical and administrative facilities and knowledge in support of the fleet ballistic missile program, demonstrating an undeviating determination to utilize the total capabilities of his bureau in meeting the varied and complex problems and schedules imposed by the fleet ballistic missile development program. He made an important contribution toward the achievement of the final tactical weapon system on an accelerated schedule, which was five years in advance of the originally optimistic target date."

---

* The Italian light cruiser Giuseppe Garibaldi was built in the 1930s and then extensively modernized between 1957 and 1962. Her after 6-inch turrets were replaced, one by a twin Terrier missile launcher and the other by four Polaris missile tubes. She test-fired Polaris but did not carry it on an operational patrol.

Admiral Stroop was also awarded the Distinguished Service Medal, which cited as follows:

"For exceptionally meritorious service during the period September 9, 1959 to October 29, 1962 as the first Chief of the Bureau of Naval Weapons, exercising sound professional judgment, dynamic leadership and keen foresight, Admiral Stroop welded the Bureau of Ordnance and Bureau of Aeronautics into a smoothly functioning Bureau of Naval Weapons, providing the chief impetus through his own adeptness at getting things done. He efficiently solved some of the most complex management problems imaginable, causing the merger of the two bureaus to be completed seven months ahead of schedule. Operational support was not impaired at any time during the organizational malady.

"Vice Admiral Stroop's keen appreciation of both the human and physical problems involved was a major factor in the smoothness with which the consolidation was effected. His dedication to managing the bureau resulted in great strides being taken to reduce the lead time between the expression of an operational requirement and delivery to the combat forces of fully developed and effective weapons systems. Through his personal effort, multi-service weapon systems such as the F-4 aircraft had become a reality. His dedication to reducing the cost of the weapon systems acquisition has been directly reflected in the Department of Defense cost reduction achievement. By his exceptional devotion to duty, he rendered invaluable and distinguished service and contributed greatly to the improvement of weapons systems acquisition and management."

That's the end of the quote, Admiral. Do those words remind you of any part of the job that you might have overlooked reporting on?

Admiral Stroop: Well, I think I might comment that that citation was awarded about a year after I left Washington.

Admiral Stroop: Which one, the commendation, not the Distinguished Service Medal?

Admiral Stroop: The Distinguished Service Medal was awarded about one year after I left Washington by the Under Secretary of the Navy, Paul Fay[*]. I suppose it's a gratuitous observation, but there was no move at the time of my departure to award me the Distinguished Service Medal. It was only after some time had elapsed that apparently some decisions were made that the award was deserved.

As a matter of fact, my departure from Washington was quite precipitate. A new chief had not been selected or ordered in. I turned over command of the Bureau of Naval Weapons to my deputy, Rear Admiral Masterson, who had relieved Admiral Schoech about a year earlier. Admiral Masterson did not receive a set of orders as chief of the bureau. He was only acting and continued in an acting capacity for some time before his position was formalized. Also, in view of the hurry of the departure from Washington, I still believe this was somehow related to the upcoming TFX decision. There was not time for the usual amenities, such as, for example, a relieving ceremony in the office of the Secretary of the Navy. I read my orders in the office of the Assistant Secretary of the Navy, the Honorable Kenneth BeLieu, whose office was quite close to mine in the Main Navy building.[†] It was a very small, quiet, quick ceremony, considerably different from the one that had occurred two years earlier when I took over as Chief of the Bureau of Naval Weapons and the one that occurred four years earlier when I took over as Chief of the Bureau of Ordnance.

Q: Were you disgusted at the time?

Admiral Stroop: Well, I certainly left Washington with mixed emotions. I was most happy to get out from under the pressure of the job. I had felt since the administration had changed, there had been many frustrations, and I felt really that my usefulness in Washington had about ended.[‡] So that whatever disgust I might have had was balanced off

---

[*] Paul B. Fay, Jr., served as Under Secretary of the Navy from 16 February 1961 to 15 January 1965.
[†] Kenneth E. BeLieu served as Assistant Secretary of the Navy (Installations and Logistics) from 1961 to 1965. He was Under Secretary of the Navy for a period in 1965.
[‡] The administration of President John F. Kennedy took office on 20 January 1961.

by great relief to get out from under the Washington pressure, the frustrations, and go to a new location and a new job. On top of that, of course, was the promotion to vice admiral.

As a matter of fact, as a family, we were so happy to get out of Washington that as soon as I knew my orders were coming, I arranged for our youngest boy to be put in a school on the West Coast and actually flew out with him to enter the school. This was the Webb School at Claremont. Then, a few weeks later, I brought my wife and her mother to California and installed them in a hotel in Coronado. All of this was before I was relieved. I stayed on the West Coast to wrap up paperwork--that is, writing the fitness reports for senior officers of the bureau--and returned to Washington to spend only a few days, to have the change of command ceremony, and to start back to California.

One unusual feature of this whole operation was that for the first time in 43 years, it was Stroop who packed up the house and got the goods off and Mrs. Stroop who got out of the chore. She was already on the West Coast. Fortunately, I still had my two faithful stewards, the ones I'd had on the Princeton years before and on Okinawa, Boykin and Florendo, and they did all of the work. They got the household goods packed up, and then journeyed along with me to the new assignment in Coronado. The domestic arrangements, including storage and getting my family out and Patrick in a good private school in California, were very happy parts of this whole operation, and for that I was very glad. It was good to get away from Washington and to get back out with the operating forces.

Q: Sort of discouraging when you are doing the best job of which you're capable, and an honest and impartial one, to have the feeling that you're rewarded in reverse fashion for having done your best job. It isn't the first time it's happened too.

Admiral Stroop: Well, I know that's a true observation, and it certainly is philosophically quite correct. Unfortunately, the climate in Washington at that time was very bad. As a matter of fact, it was the worst I've ever seen it in all my experience in the Navy.

Q: You're speaking of the political climate?

Admiral Stroop: Well, the political climate and the arena in which you had to operate in the business of running the material side of the Navy. It just plain wasn't good, and it was not only frustrating, it was dangerous for an individual in my position who had the official responsibility for spending honestly and correctly very, very large sums of money. It was, indeed, unfortunate that I as an individual had all of this responsibility and yet was thwarted in doing the best possible job that I could do. So long as we're speaking philosophically, maybe it would be worthwhile to comment on some of the individuals I ran across in Washington.

Q: I think that's part of history.

Admiral Stroop: Especially on the civilian side. I was particularly impressed with the civilians who represented the Navy at the secretarial level before we changed administrations.

Q: Excuse me, now you're speaking of Kennedy and Johnson?

Admiral Stroop: Before that. The Republican side of the house. Eisenhower's . . .

Q: Oh, from Eisenhower, from the Republicans to the Democrats.

Admiral Stroop: That's right. I'm speaking of Eisenhower's administration.[*] I remember Tom Gates, for example, who was Under Secretary of the Navy and later became Secretary of the Navy and then Secretary of Defense.[†] He was an outstanding man. He was

---

[*] Dwight D. Eisenhower served as President of the United States from January 1953 to January 1961.
[†] Thomas S. Gates, Jr., served as Secretary of the Navy from 1 April 1957 to 7 June 1959 and as Secretary of Defense from 2 December 1959 to 20 January 1961.

thoroughly honest, competent, and he had great confidence in the people he put in responsible jobs, that is, people in uniform.

I remember one day he asked me about an evaluation I'd made with regard to a contractor. This happened to be the subroc contract, and he asked me why I was going to award the subroc contract to Goodyear.[*] Well, I took a few of my evaluation team over to his office, and they brought along some of the material they'd used in the evaluation and made what I thought was a rather dramatic presentation to the Secretary. I had a very smart young man describing the evaluation process, and at each stage he would put a document or a pile of documents on the Secretary's desk; these represented the studies that they'd gone through. Finally, when he had finished, you couldn't see the Secretary for the stack of documents that were on his desk. It was dramatic proof of just how much work we'd gone through to sift through the seven competitors for this important ordnance contract.

When it was all over, I wrapped up the meeting by saying, "Mr. Secretary, I hope that you will go along with my recommendation to award this contact to the company that we have selected as the winner--Goodyear."

He said, "That's your responsibility, not mine. All I want to know is the process used in determining this. I'm completely satisfied." And this, of course, was in complete contrast to the TFX business and the X-22 business, which I described a little earlier.

Mr. Gates was followed in the two jobs, Under Secretary and Secretary, by Bill Franke, and he was a man of the same mold. We became close personal friends and still are today, and we had a mutual trust. I knew that I could depend upon him to back me up to the hilt, and he knew that I would never come to him for any kind of backing that wasn't warranted. As a result, we were able to get along with the Navy's business in a forthright fashion.

---

[*] Subroc--a submarine-launched, rocket-propelled, intertially guided nuclear depth bomb. It was designed to be launched underwater from a submarine's torpedo tube, emerge into the air, fly to the location of an enemy submarine, re-enter the water, and then act as a depth bomb. The contract was awarded to Goodyear in 1958.

The Assistant Secretaries for Material, which were my immediate bosses, were of like caliber, and we understood each other thoroughly. Fred Bantz, for example, was one of these. He was the man who brought me back as Chief of the Bureau of Ordnance, and he fleeted up from Assistant Secretary for Material to Under Secretary, relieving Franke, who relieved Gates when he went down to the SecDef's office. When the administration changed, generally people with different philosophies came into government. For example, our first Secretary of the Navy under Kennedy was John Connally from Texas.[*]

Q: Of course, this happened right in the middle of your tour, didn't it?

Admiral Stroop: That's right. Connally came in as Secretary of the Navy, and it took a little while for us to get along and to understand each other. I remember my first experience with Connally had to do with the award of a large helicopter contract to Boeing Vertol. Time was pretty important here. We had been going over the proposals from competitors and had finally decided on Boeing. We had certain options which were about to expire, and also the equipment was badly needed by the operating forces, so time was of the essence. I went over to Mr. Connally's office, the way I had to Mr. Gates and Franke's office in the previous administration, and explained that I had gone over this thoroughly, that it had had a complete and thorough evaluation, that everybody was in agreement, including the Marines who were going to use the equipment, and that the award should go to Boeing Vertol.

I had hoped that Mr. Connally would just say, "Go right ahead and do it," the way it would have happened in the previous administration.

I was a little surprised when he said, "Well, I'd like to think about this a while." It took him at least a month to let us go ahead with the contract. He finally went along, in accordance with our recommendation, but in the meantime time had been lost, and certain values of the options were also lost.

---

[*] John B. Connally served as Secretary of the Navy from 25 January 1961 to 20 December 1961.

Q: Did you have to get his approval? Could you not have gone ahead and awarded it?

Admiral Stroop: Theoretically, I didn't have to get it. However, you must realize that the bureau chiefs under that system worked directly under the Secretary of the Navy. He was my immediate boss. I was responsible to him, and unless he acquiesced with the idea of me going ahead, I felt that I could not. At least I felt that it was almost my duty, and it had been going on for many, many years. The chiefs of the bureau on these important awards would just normally notify the Secretary of the Navy. The Secretary of the Navy would generally always concur with this, and it had gotten to be a system which had been worked up.

As a matter of fact, with this group of secretaries, I felt that I not only had to tell them, but I had to await their decision. If I'd gone ahead and reversed one of their decisions, or not waited for them to concur, why, my head would have been chopped off. I could have been detached summarily. So, in order to live in the climate, we had to go through this process, which I think was quite right, except that I think it was wrong to throw in unnecessary delays. And, of course, I think it was terribly wrong to reverse decisions that were made with the backing of complete technical competence, and to make wrong decisions at that high level. It would have been better, really, not to make any decision at all--just cancel the procurement--than to make the wrong one.

Well, it took a little while for me to work into the program and handling of these things with the new administration, but by the time Connally had been in there six months, we understood each other. We became quite close personal friends and still are. I think he learned to trust me and generally went along with what I would recommend. Of course, as history is now able to say, he lasted only about a year and then left Washington to become Governor of Texas.

There was another interesting aspect of this incoming administration. Connally was Secretary of the Navy, and Paul Fay was Under Secretary. Connally had been put in by

Johnson, the Vice President, and Paul Fay had been put in by Kennedy.[*] Fay was Kennedy's old torpedo boat pal from World War II days. He had had very little background or experience to qualify him for the job of Under Secretary. As a result, within a week after the new administration came in, I was informed officially that many of the matters that had been handled in the Under Secretary's office would always be brought directly to the Secretary. During the period that I was there, the Under Secretary, Paul Fay, had very little to do with the administration of the material side of the house.

One great shining light here was the new Assistant Secretary of the Navy for Installations and Logistics. He came in with the Democratic administration. His name was Ken BeLieu. Ken BeLieu had had a very interesting background. He had been a regular Army officer and gotten up to the rank of colonel. He had lost a leg in Korea and was retired from the Army on a physical retirement. He wound up at the time I knew him as staff director for the Government Preparedness Subcommittee in the Senate.[†] When the new administration came in, he was so highly thought of that he was appointed Assistant Secretary of the Navy for Installations and Logistics in the Democratic administration.

Ken BeLieu had this military background, and he understood operational problems. Also, he understood how the military worked, and, I think, basically he believed in the integrity and honesty of most military men. During this very difficult period he was a great help to me. I found that if I could go to Ken Belieu and give him a straight story and say that this was what the operating forces needed, this was the best equipment you could get, and this was the best company you could go to to get it, why, Ken BeLieu would go along with the decision. In cases where we had to make a direct award, without going through competition, I could always get his support when time was of the essence or when a company had a special capability that nobody else possessed, and the Secretary himself had to make what we call a D&F, determination and findings, that an award should be given to this particular company. Ken BeLieu was a great tower of strength, and I happen to know

---

[*] Lyndon B. Johnson served as Vice President of the United States from 20 January 1961 until he succeeded to the presidency on the assassination of John F. Kennedy on 22 November 1963.
[†] Lyndon Johnson served as Senate Majority Leader before becoming Vice President.

that he personally was responsible for the key recommendation that got me out of Washington and promoted to three stars.

Q: I like him then.

Admiral Stroop: Ken BeLieu is a fine man. He fleeted up and became Under Secretary of the Navy.

I also had a good bit to do with the Assistant Secretary of the Navy for Research and Development, and here was something unusual which I thought was interesting.[*] Jim Wakelin had been the Assistant Secretary for Research and Development under the Republicans, and he was the one holdover. He served for about two more years as Assistant Secretary and, as a coincidence, the present Assistant Secretary for Research and Development, Bob Frosch, also bridged that gap.[†] He was appointed by the Democrats and is still serving under the Republicans. So, for what it's worth, I give all three administrations credit for having sense enough to recognize quality and people available in spite of politics in the particular area of research and development.

I might comment just a little bit on some of the people in uniform that I served with during this period. Arleigh Burke was the Chief of Naval Operations during most of the period. As a matter of fact, I attended the ceremony at the armory in Annapolis when he relieved Admiral Carney.[‡] I was then Deputy Chief of the Bureau of Ordnance. I served, one way or another, with Arleigh Burke all during his six years as the Chief of Naval Operations. He, of course, was an outstanding man. He was a great leader. He had a great amount of physical courage, as demonstrated by his wartime record. Although he wasn't an

---

[*] James H. Wakelin, Jr., held the position from 1959 to 1964.
[†] Robert A. Frosch was Assistant Secretary of the Navy for Research and Development, 1966-73.
[‡] Admiral Robert B. Carney, USN, served as Chief of Naval Operations from 17 August 1953 to 17 August 1955.

aviator, he had served as Pete Mitscher's chief of staff during the war, and I felt he had a complete understanding of the problems of naval aviation.*

In addition to that, he was a postgraduate in ordnance and had an ordnance background. He could understand the problems I was having in the ordnance game, and Arleigh and I, although we had a few arguments, got along fine and understood each other. He was the type of man who insisted on getting into the details of any particular problem, and with his technical background and knowledge, had a great capacity for absorbing the information. Sometimes, many of us felt that he cluttered up his mind with too many details and worked too hard. He worked seven days a week and worked about a 12- to 14-hour day. But he was a fine man, and I'm happy to say served six years, the last two being unprecedented, as Chief of Naval Operations.

He was finally relieved by my friend and old shipmate, George Anderson. George was a fine, truthful, forthright individual. Maybe he was a little too forthright, because he couldn't bend with the wind. When the wind got strong and he got into arguments with the Secretary, the arguments became almost personal, and it was quite obvious that the President of the United States had to choose between his Chief of Naval Operations and his Secretary of Defense. Since he still had faith in his Secretary of Defense and didn't want to remove him, the Chief of Naval Operations had to go. George Anderson served only two years, and then, of course, as history shows us, he was given a sop as ambassador to Portugal, where he served for two years.

George is still around and enjoying life, living in Washington. We still see each other occasionally. A very fine man. It's unfortunate that he didn't have a better deal as Chief of Naval Operations, because he is most capable and, as far as the uniformed side of the house was concerned, he served very well. I think that about covers the personalities that I could comment on, unless you've got some questions.

Q: Well, I was just thinking, you were there at a most interesting time in history.

---

* Vice Admiral Marc A. Mitscher, USN, served as Commander Task Force 58, the fast carrier task force, in 1944-45.

Admiral Stroop: Yes, I suppose so. I was fortunate in my various Washington duties, being there as a lieutenant just before World War II, watching the events that led up to that, and then at the end of the war serving with Admiral King. And then I came back again during this particular period which had to do mostly with the Korean War. Of course, during all this period the Navy just got larger and the problems became more complicated. It was an interesting period.

Q: Admiral Stroop, the words in the commendation speak of complex problems in combining the two bureaus, and I wish that you would give me a little background of how the Navy Department went about forming this combination of the two bureaus.

Admiral Stroop: Well, the Bureau of Naval Weapons came about as a result of the recommendations of the Franke Board. Under Secretary Franke was the head of a board which had convened for several months and heard many, many witnesses. I appeared before it twice as Chief of the Bureau of Ordnance, and Admiral Dixon appeared before it many times as Chief of the Bureau of Aeronautics. The recommendation of the Franke Board was that the two bureaus be combined and be called the Bureau of Naval Weapons. The Secretary of the Navy approved this recommendation and actually went to Congress to obtain the necessary legislation and authorization, because the job of a bureau chief is a statutory job.

The bureau chief has the authority and the responsibility under Congress to obtain the funds and to administer the funds, and he's actually personally responsible for the funds. It's a personal responsibility which is rather unique in this government today. After some committee hearings and some rather sharp questioning, Congress did go along with the idea. I remember quite well one set of hearings before Mr. Vinson, head of the Armed Services Committee at the time. One of the questions he asked was what would be the rank of this new bureau chief. He was told by Under Secretary Franke's principal witness that he would remain a rear admiral. At the time of the amalgamation of the bureaus, of course, Franke had relieved Gates, and he was then Secretary of the Navy, so, as Secretary, he presided over the union of the two bureaus.

However, the mechanics were quite involved, because we had an extremely difficult job. Here were two very large organizations, spending a great deal of money, administering programs on a day-to-day basis. We didn't dare drop any bricks in the transition, if we could help it. Secretary Franke appointed Vice Admiral Clexton, the Chief of Naval Material, and Rear Admiral Martell, who was assigned the job full-time, to create on paper a new organization.*

This study took several months, from about May to September of 1959. The Chief of the Bureau of Aeronautics, Admiral Dixon, and I met with the board a number of times. We contributed several people to the study, and naturally we contributed extremely competent people, because we were vitally concerned. There were a lot of arguments. Sometimes I didn't agree with the recommendations that Martell made and the recommendations which finally came down in the official piece of paper. I was in a fortunate position when I was finally nominated to be the first chief. Those recommendations which I didn't agree with, I could immediately change. Or the decisions that had been made, I could change after I became chief of the bureau.

The immediate transition was accomplished in about a three-month period. The Bureau of Naval Weapons was officially established on the first of September 1959. Now, at that time it was just the chief and the deputy, who was Bill Schoech, and a small group of people. They ordered Bill in from sea duty.

As a matter of fact, we just had the study group that had been established, plus Admiral Martell, who had the job, and Admiral Clexton. We were told we had from September until the first of January. January 1960 was set as the target date. I turned over my duties as Chief of the Bureau of Ordnance to my deputy, and Admiral Dixon, of course, had continued as Chief of the Bureau of Aeronautics. Well, when we got into the job of filling out this organization--and this is what I might call a fleshing-out process--we had then available to us all the personnel, military and civilian, in the two bureaus. It was our job to fit them into the new organization the best possible way. In many cases we had to make some hard decisions when two similar groups were amalgamated. For example, we

---

* Vice Admiral Edward W. Clexton, USN, served as Chief of Naval Material from 1 February 1956 to 30 June 1960. Rear Admiral Charles B. Martell, USN.

had to choose between two senior persons for the number-one spot. And this happened all through the reorganization.

Q: You had the Civil Service to contend with too?

Admiral Stroop: We had Civil Service. I might point out that probably the most important job we had was selecting the assistant chiefs, the flag officers who were to head up the bureau divisions, and there were quite a few of these. The next most important job was posting the executive secretaries, because they were very important people. They had stature, they had tenure, they had personal ambitions.

Q: They were civilians?

Admiral Stroop: They were civilians and all female, so they were really a rough crowd to deal with.

Well, we got the assistant chiefs all appointed, and I participated in that. I gave Bill Schoech the nasty job of sorting out the secretaries, except I told him who I wanted. He and his assistant went through the whole bureau, about 4,000 people, and made up the new organization. Just the mechanics of rearranging offices and telephones and that sort of things--this was a tremendously big job. It cost about $800,000 just for that part of it.

Q: Was it eventually a good move?

Admiral Stroop: Yes, I think it was a good move. It worked well, it worked smoothly, and even the transition was smooth. As I said before, we had until the first of January to do this. However, it became apparent to me that we wouldn't accomplish very much in the month of December, due to leave and so forth. Also, the budget business for the following year was getting very important. Starting 1 January we would start hearings on the new budget as the first budget of the Bureau of Naval Weapons, which was to go into effect the following July. So I decided we would take 1 December as the target date, rather than 1

January. As a matter of fact, on 1 December I went over into the Secretary's office and officially relieved the two bureau chiefs. The Bureau of Naval Weapons, which had been in existence for three months, became an actual operating, responsible entity on that date.

Q: That must have been fantastic.

Admiral Stroop: We began 1 December 1959 with about a $9 billion budget. And that, generally, is the history of the organization. It was large. As a matter of fact, subsequent administration say it was too large. It was by far the largest bureau in the Navy and had the most money to administer.

It came about for a rather unusual reason. More and more, we found the business of the Bureau of Ordnance and the Bureau of Aeronautics were overlapping. Both bureaus were building a type of guided missile. The Bureau of Aeronautics had a guided missile that resembled an airplane, and the Bureau of Ordnance had guided missiles that more closely resembled guns. They used much the same types of equipment--guidance, for example--and carried the same explosive warheads. To some extent we were doing the same kind of a job. It was very difficult to keep this coordinated in two separate organizations, and yet there were good, sound reasons for what we were doing--at least good, sound rationale.

Traditionally, the Bureau of Ordnance had bought ordnance for airplanes and had provided fire control for airplanes. As their planes became more complicated and flew faster, ordnance became more complicated. It was essential, obviously, that one organization should procure all the weapons, as well as the vehicle, so that the match was there. In the area of fire control, traditionally the fire-control equipments for weapons, the Bureau of Aeronautics had built the vehicle, and the Bureau of Ordnance had built the fire control and tried to match them up. Again, as the systems became more complicated, the fire control not only controlled the weapons themselves but also flew the airplane. Here again, it was important that one organization handle it.

I recall when I went in as deputy chief, the Chief of the Bureau of Ordnance and the Chief of the Bureau of Aeronautics had been meeting for about a year and half trying to resolve just this one problem of fire control, and it never was resolved. Those were the kinds of problems that forced--or convinced--Secretary Franke and his board that the two bureaus should be combined. They realized they were getting a very large package. They realized that the organization would be complicated, but they felt that this was the best way to go.

Q: And you feel that it was?

Admiral Stroop: Oh, I feel that it was. We had another rather unusual . . .

Q: Well, I'm sure the success of it was because of you in the initial setup.

Admiral Stroop: Well, I had a lot of wonderful help. I had Bill Schoech, and I had my choice of flag officers in the Navy to pick from to put into the various important slots.

Q: But you were still the boss.

Admiral Stroop: Yes, but these people did an outstanding job. As I said before, we took over on the first of December, and the people in the field, and the people in the ships and the carriers and the squadrons didn't even know the difference. They sent in emergency dispatches, and they were answered right away. The reason for it was, of course, the goodwill and competence of the individuals we had. A man who was doing something one day, just because he's working for a different bureau, didn't lay down the bricks. He did the same thing the next day.

Q: But that was all leadership, as you well know.

Admiral Stroop: Well, it worked out quite well, and we did overcome a lot of the confusion and the duplication that was existing. I was particularly happy with the performance that the Assistant Chief for Research and Development turned in, Admiral

Ruckner.* Here was an outfit that dealt with basic science, with applied science, and with engineering, and I also wondered philosophically why this particular group of people, who were highly intelligent and very competent, should have melded into one organization faster than any other parts of the three bureaus. This was due, I think, largely to Admiral Ruckner himself, but also really to the fact that science and the laws of nature operate the same, whether it's in the Bureau of Ordnance or the Bureau of Aeronautics. So these people were able to get together and understand each other quicker and better than any other group.

I also noticed they were the first group to have organized social affairs. They were the first group that asked the chiefs to come to one of their social affairs, and I think this probably is significant.

Q: If it hadn't been properly organized from the administration standpoint, however, it could have become a monstrosity, with a third level just on top of the other two, instead of a melding of the two.

Admiral Stroop: Yes. Well, that's right, and that's what we, of course, wanted to avoid completely, and we did. We insisted right from the beginning that this wouldn't occur. It would be a unified structure, and it was. It was rather heartwarming to see generally how well people worked together and how they came to respect each other.

Q: I still claim that without leadership it wouldn't have happened.

Admiral Stroop: We traditionally had had in the Bureau of Ordnance a monthly senior personnel luncheon. I continued that when we had the new bureau, and I found it quite heartwarming to see how well these people took up together on a social basis. We would meet once a month at the gun factory and have a little program. The chief and deputy chief and all the assistant chiefs would be there, and it worked out quite well. As a matter of fact,

---

* Rear Admiral Edward A. Ruckner, USN, whose oral history is in the Naval Institute collection.

I personally felt that when they reorganized again and essentially separated the organizations, it was a step backward.*

Q: What do you mean, when they reorganized again?

Admiral Stroop: Well, the material bureaus no longer exist. They are now called systems command, and they now have an Ordnance Systems Command and an Air Systems Command.

Q: Under BuWeps?

Admiral Stroop: No, no. BuWeps has gone. BuOrd has gone. BuAer's gone, and the Bureau of Yards and Docks has gone.

Q: I hate to ask how long ago that was.

Admiral Stroop: Oh, about four years ago.

Now we come to the final period of my active duty career, the period as Commander Naval Air Force Pacific Fleet, which took place from November 1962 to November 1965.

As I stated earlier, I had made two trips to the West Coast in preparation for this move. On the first trip I brought our youngest boy out, Patrick, and established him at a school in Claremont, California, the Webb School. He was in the tenth grade at the time. Then, a few weeks later, I brought the rest of my family out, with the exception of the boy who had preceded us, and also brought my secretary from the Bureau of Naval Weapons, Miss Jean Child. I brought her along in order to make up the final fitness reports. Then I returned to Washington to have the final turnover. I had the personal job of getting our

---

* A reorganization effective 1 May 1966 abolished the Bureau of Naval Weapons and assigned its elements to three new commands: Naval Air Systems Command, Naval Ordnance Systems Command, and Naval Electronic Systems Command.

house all packed. This was handled by the two stewards, and then I drove west to California in our personal car, along with my administrative assistant, Commander Elk Kelley.[*]

We arrived in San Diego with about ten days to go before I took command of ComNavAirPac. Mrs. Stroop had been living in the El Cordova Hotel with the family at that time, and we stayed there until just before I took over. The change of command occurred around 1 December, when I relieved my old friend and long-time acquaintance, Vice Admiral Ekstrom.[†]

In the new job of Commander Naval Air Force Pacific Fleet, I had administrative responsibility for the nine attack carriers in the Pacific Fleet and all attached squadrons, the 15 patrol squadrons and wings of the Pacific Fleet, and the four antisubmarine warfare carriers. In addition, we had a few other ships, the large seaplane tenders which were still in commission in the Navy. We also had operational control of the several airfields on which our squadrons were located: a large field at North Island here in San Diego; Moffett Field at Sunnyvale; the field at Alameda; Lemoore, California; the field up at Whidbey Island, near Seattle; Barbers Point in Hawaii; Atsugi, Iwakuni, Naha in the Western Pacific; Sangley Point; and so forth.

Here again was a long-range and widespread responsibility, and it promised to be a most interesting job. It was one with considerable responsibility but one which I felt could be handled with a lot more satisfaction and less frustration than the one I'd just left. One of the principal advantages, of course, was that I was 3,000 miles from Washington. And my immediate boss was over 2,000 miles in the other direction; the Commander in Chief of the Pacific Fleet at the time was my old friend Admiral Sides.[‡] He was later to be relieved by

---

[*] Commander Edmond L. Kelley, USN, whose nickname "Elk" came from his initials.
[†] Vice Admiral Clarence E. Ekstrom, USN, served as Commander Naval Air Force Pacific Fleet from 21 October 1959 to 30 November 1962.
[‡] Admiral John H. Sides, USN, served as Commander in Chief Pacific Fleet, 30 August 1960 to 30 September 1963.

Admiral Oley Sharp, who was later to be relieved by Admiral Tom Moorer, and then Roy Johnson.*

My headquarters, of course, as Commander Naval Air Force Pacific Fleet were established in North Island, and my personal office was in the second floor of the administration building. We had a personal set of quarters--Quarters A, Naval Air Station, North Island--which was quite adequate. Here again, I brought my long-time personal staff from Washington: faithful Boykin and Florendo. Except at this time I made Boykin the chief steward on the flag plane, rather then the chief steward in the house, and kept Florendo on at the quarters. This gave Boykin a new experience and also permitted him to travel. He liked that, because he'd left his new wife back in Washington. She was a schoolteacher and didn't want to come out here. This change gave Florendo added responsibility as head of the domestic staff.

We found living, of course, much different from Washington, a lot less hectic. My quarters were only a few blocks from the office. I could walk back and forth. I was the senior naval officer present in the general San Diego area when Commander First Fleet was not in, and later on I became senior even to him when his relief occurred. I had a very fine position in the community and became a member of the Kiwanis Club. Since we had some idea of settling down here, I began taking a personal interest in community affairs. We found, of course, during this period that our earlier judgment that San Diego was a fine place to live was justified, and we began making plans to settle in San Diego permanently.

I might interject that if you can control your destiny in a military career and you can arrange for your final tour of duty to be in the place where you want to retire, why, this is an extremely fortunate arrangement. It makes the transition to retirement a whole lot easier and a whole lot pleasanter. It certainly has been pleasant in my case.

One of the tools or facilities I had at my command was a large four-engined airplane which we used to inspect various elements of the command. During the three years that I

---

* Admiral U. S. Grant Sharp, USN, served as Commander in Chief Pacific Fleet, 30 September 1963 to 26 June 1964. Admiral Thomas H. Moorer, USN, 26 June 1964 to 30 March 1965, and Admiral Roy L. Johnson, USN, 30 March 1965 to 30 November 1967. The oral histories of all three are in the Naval Institute collection.

was Commander Naval Air Force Pacific Fleet, I made numerous trips to the Western Pacific, to Hawaii, to Alaska, and--as infrequently as possible--back to Washington. I did have to go back on several selection boards, and also I went back to a congressional hearing when Senator Stennis's committee investigated the unhappy decision on the X-22.[*] This was about a year after I became Commander Naval Air Force Pacific Fleet.

Q: Is this the place that one should describe that congressional hearing?

Admiral Stroop: I don't think there's enough interest there, really. Senator Stennis, I think, had been unhappy all along that Senator McClellan had made such a Roman holiday out of the TFX hearing.[†] Now, here was a situation that had some of the same elements: that is, the uniformed people being overruled by the Office of the Secretary of Defense. The major difference, of course, in one case there was only about $16 million involved, and in the other case there was about $16 billion involved. So that was a terrific difference. I think Senator Stennis's philosophy here was that something was wrong, a wrong decision had been made, something that merited investigation. He would have the investigation clear up the record and would show Senator McClellan how an investigation could be accomplished and not be too embarrassing to the administration. They were both Democrats, you know.

This particular investigation was preceded by a three-hour questioning period by some advance investigators who came to San Diego to see what my testimony most likely would be, and to indicate to me generally what area of questioning they would have. I went back to Washington and appeared before the Stennis Committee. The questioning pretty much followed what they'd indicated it would be during the day that I was there, and I was present only one day. We had the senior man of the evaluating committee come in and put in the Senate record the evaluations as they had been made by the Bureau of Naval Weapons. Actually, the charts and the numerical scores and all the judgments became a matter of record. Of course, it was quite clear that the Douglas Company should have been given the award. The judgment of the chief of the bureau had been overruled by the Deputy

---

[*] Senator John C. Stennis (Democrat-Mississippi).
[†] Senator John L. McClellan (Democrat-Arkansas).

Secretary of Defense, whose name was Gilpatric.[*] He had actually signed a letter making his reversal a matter of official record. And that's about all there was to it.

The hearing was held. I completed my testimony in one day and came back to San Diego. As a result of the hearing, I don't know that anything particularly significant happened. The Office of the Secretary of Defense obviously got what might be considered a slap on the wrist. The most beneficial result of that hearing and the McClellan hearings was, of course, that--as far as I know--this procedure hasn't occurred again. The dangers, the mistakes that could be made by overruling this type of evaluation of judgment are bad and shouldn't be permitted to occur. In fact, basically, I think they're dishonest.

Q: They're not impartial; that's for sure.

Admiral Stroop: That's right. Anyway, this is what happened, and that was the X-22 hearing. By this time, Bell had been a year in the contract. They still have the contract, they're still developing the X-22, and it's a reasonably successful research and development program. I'm still of the opinion that the Douglas Company would have been able to have gotten along a lot faster and a lot cheaper and probably had a better product, but we'll never know.

My routine at AirPac consisted of office hours when I was in San Diego and quite a bit of travel. Actually, the needs for travel in the AirPac job were many, and I took advantage of them. A typical trip to the Western Pacific would last about three weeks. I could carry on the flag plane comfortably 11 passengers. They would be able to have meals aloft and bunks. Boykin always had a very fine galley. We could travel at night when making up for lost time. We could even hold conferences in the air, going from one place to another.

I usually would swing up through Alaska on the way out or on the way back, and also one way or the other stop at Hawaii to see the boss. Then I would go on to Japan, inspect the various elements of the command at Atsugi, have a conference with Commander

---

[*] Roswell L. Gilpatric served as Deputy Secretary of Defense, 1961-64.

Seventh Fleet, usually at the time of his scheduling conference. I would go down to Okinawa, stop at Iwakuni, Japan, where the Marines were based and also where we had one of our patrol squadrons.

Strangely enough, in this activity as Commander Naval Air Force Pacific Fleet, I still had a small type of Bureau of Naval Weapons responsibility, in that we dealt with foreign contractors overhauling aircraft in Japan and Taiwan. We had some rather sizable contracts at several locations there, so I would usually check in with the overhaul activity at Atsugi; the overhaul activity at Osaka, where our big seaplanes were overhauled; and also we had some contracts with the Air American overhaul activity in southern Taiwan. I would check in with that.

I usually dropped in at Hong Kong on these trips and gave the staff an opportunity for a couple of days of shopping. Then on down to Manila, where we would land at Sangley Point, spend two or three days there, and come back through Guam, look at the squadrons there in the airfield on Guam, come on back through Pearl and into San Diego. I probably made this swing six times in the three years that I was Naval Air Force Pacific Fleet.

We had in this job sub-commands. Had one at Alameda, a rear admiral. We had another one at Whidbey Island, a rear admiral. Had one in Kodiak, Alaska; sub-command in Hawaii. Commander Fleet Air Hawaii, also a rear admiral, happened to be another classmate of mine, Dutch Duerfeldt.[*] A sub-command based at Atsugi, Japan, just outside of Tokyo, also a rear admiral. He had a sub-command under him at Subic Bay.

The aircraft and ships of the Pacific Fleet were administered by me, but they were operated largely by the fleet commander. In other words, I had the job of providing the training, providing the personnel, and operating them when they were training on the West Coast. When they were deployed, they were, of course, under the operational control of the various fleet commanders: the First Fleet operating on the West Coast and the Seventh Fleet Commander operating in the Western Pacific. Even during these periods, of course, we retained administrative responsibility.

---

[*] Rear Admiral Clifford H. Duerfeldt, USN.

As senior officer present on the West Coast, I also had the opportunity and responsibility of taking care of many distinguished visitors--visitors at the secretarial level. My old friends such as Paul Fay came out to see me. The New Secretary of the Navy, Nitze, made his first trip out and visited us out here, and also many foreign visitors.* Some of my Chinese friends dropped by, particularly Admiral Ni, who was then personal chief of staff to the President of China, and some of the European contacts I had made. They also got as far as the West Coast. I found it a very fine professional job, one that was not too demanding. Since I was my own boss, I could prescribe my own working hours, and this enabled me to catch up on a little golf and hunting and fishing that had been pretty much neglected during the Washington years.

Q: Wasn't this the second assignment during which you had taken a large command when the Navy was somewhat at a peacetime operation and then seen it expand, as you did once in Korea, and this time was a period when in Southeast Asia?

Admiral Stroop: Yes, this is true. In both cases there was ascending action and increasing importance to the job that we had to do. And this, of course, made the job that I was doing more important.

One little aspect of this last period had to do with an emergency command of the First Fleet. I had been on a trip up in northern California with my boss, Admiral Sharp. We put in to Monterey, California, where we were spending the night, and got a dispatch from San Diego that Commander First Fleet, Vice Admiral Taylor Keith, a close personal friend and long-time acquaintance, was in the hospital with a heart attack.†

Since I was the senior flag officer on the West Coast immediately available, Admiral Sharp recommended that I take over command of the First Fleet as extra additional duty, and this I did. I found that could be handled fairly well. I had two complete staffs and two

---

* Paul H. Nitze served as Secretary of the Navy from 29 November 1963 to 30 June 1967.
† Vice Admiral Robert Taylor Scott Keith, USN, whose oral history is in the Naval Institute collection. Keith was hospitalized from 4 December 1963. On 25 January 1964 Vice Admiral Ephraim P. Holmes became Commander First Fleet. † Paul H. Nitze served as Secretary of the Navy from 29 November 1963 to 30 June 1967.

extremely competent chiefs of staff in each case, so I got in the habit of spending half a day on the flagship and half a day in my AirPac office. I'm happy to report that both chiefs of staff involved were finally selected for flag rank, Dick Fowler from AirPac staff and Walter Curtis from First Fleet staff.[*] As a matter of fact, Walter Curtis was just recently made vice admiral.

Admiral Stroop: From your comment I judge that you feel part of your success is because of the people who worked for you also becoming successful.

Admiral Stroop: Well, this is as it should be. If you're smart, you pick smart people to work for you, and those are the kind that get promoted.

Q: Plus the fact that you helped them develop. You gave them the opportunity.

Admiral Stroop: Well, if they're deserving, obviously, this is what you should do. It's a very happy circumstance.

The First Fleet job lasted about five weeks. During this period we had one fleet exercise and also a visit by Secretary of the Navy Nitze, who was making his first visit to the operating forces after assuming his new job as Secretary of the Navy. We had the very pleasant responsibility of entertaining him in Quarters A and then taking him out to the various ships and watching operations, and I particularly appreciated this. I got to know Mr. Nitze quite well and felt that he was a very capable Secretary. He came in well qualified. He had a fine background and, I thought, a fine attitude as Secretary of the Navy. As a matter of fact, he was a great improvement over the man he relieved, Secretary Korth.[†]

Q: I'm just laughing because the expression on your face can't go on tape.

Admiral Stroop: That's good.

---

[*] Captain Richard L. Fowler, USN; Captain Walter L. Curtis, USN.
[†] Fred H. Korth served as Secretary of the Navy from 4 January 1962 to 1 November 1963.

Actually, the job of Commander Naval Air Force Pacific Fleet settled down into a pleasant routine and one which I felt I could handle quite well. We were handicapped during the last year by the increasing tempo of affairs in Southeast Asia, and we found it becoming increasingly difficult to provide the aircraft, the personnel, and the ships that were needed out there. During the early part of the McNamara administration, training for naval aviators had been cut back. The purchase of new aircraft, the purchase of spare parts and overhaul monies for ships had been curtailed, and in all of these areas we were in a great deal of difficulty.

We had to go to extreme measures to keep our forces operating. We had to insist on quick turn-arounds of the ships, for the aircraft, and for personnel. It was an increasingly difficult period. I think probably, historically, the record will show that we were also quite short in ammunition distributed to the Western Pacific. The problem eventually took care of itself. As a matter of fact, when I turned over command to Admiral Connolly, I gave him a thumbnail report of these conditions which I have just described but said in the same breath that, although we were experiencing these difficulties, measures had been instituted at that time to take care of them.[*]

It was just a question of time catching up. After all, if you have an ammunition shortage or a spare parts shortage or an aircraft shortage, it takes about a year from the time you make a decision and get money obligated to see the results in tangible hardware and personnel. As a matter of fact, for aviators it takes two year. But when I turned over the force in 1965 to Vice Admiral Tom Connolly we still had some of these shortages, but measures to take care of them had been instituted, and as time went on, conditions did improve.

I think one of the things that bothered me most about my job as Commander Naval Air Force Pacific Fleet had to do with the losses of our pilots shot down by enemy action in Vietnam. I took a great personal interest in them and watched the course of rescues, the treatment of families, and so forth with a good bit of interest. It was, of course, and still remains a most regrettable and difficult situation.

---

[*] Vice Admiral Thomas F. Connolly, USN, served as Commander Naval Air Force Pacific Fleet from 30 October 1965 to 1 November 1966.

We had one happy occasion in this connection during the period that I was Commander Naval Air Force Pacific Fleet. We had a young pilot, a lieutenant named Klusmann, who was pilot of an RF-8 photographic aircraft. He was on a photographic mission over Laos when he was shot down and captured by the Pathet Lao.[*] He escaped after about, I believe, three months and after traveling several days through jungle on foot, during which one of his two companions was captured and, I guess, killed. He found friendly forces and was sent back here to the United States. It just happened that my boss at the time, Admiral Tom Moorer, Commander in Chief Pacific Fleet, was in San Diego when the report of Klusmann's return to friendly forces came in and was also here about two days later when Klusmann arrived in San Diego. This was a very heartwarming occasion, to see Klusmann return to his family and to watch his recovery. He was in pretty bad physical shape.

We found that Klusmann was an extremely valuable witness, and his debriefing was quite important to us in several areas. It gave us some idea of how the prisoners of war would be treated. It gave us guidance for the preliminary preparatory training that we conducted at our escape and evasion school in Warner's Hot Springs, and, I think, enabled us to have a little better understanding of the type of instructions, the type of reaction, that we might reasonably expect our prisoners of war to experience.

Well, in this regard I hesitate to expand too much, because a part of it probably still should be classified. But I do recall that Klusmann had had a very rough time in his interrogation. He had essentially been forced to write some statements that might have been considered improper. As a matter of fact, he didn't really know what he had written. The Communists, the Pathet Lao, were extremely smart in the way they accomplished their purpose. They finally got Klusmann to sign a piece of paper which was eventually released as a letter in Paris and which could be considered a little embarrassing.

---

[*] Lieutenant Charles F. Klusmann, USN, was attached to Detachment C of Light Photographic Squadron 63, flying from the carrier Kitty Hawk (CVA-63). On 6 June 1964 his RF-8 Crusader was shot down over the Plaine des Jarres region of Laos. On 1 September 1964 he escaped, along with several Laotians who had also been held captive.

Once this letter had been signed, Klusmann was taken out from under pressure. He was taken out of isolation and no longer subjected to daily interrogation and physical discomfort. He was put in a larger camp with other prisoners, none of whom, I believe, were naval aviators. These were ground force types, and most of them were Southeast Asian background. Klusmann, as he rehabilitated himself physically, made up his mind that he was going to escape and finally engineered an escape that was successful. He had a rather difficult time for a couple of days. He finally escaped with three people, one of whom was later captured, and finally found himself with friendly forces. He was evacuated from a forward area, I believe by helicopter, finally into Saigon and then back to the United States.

His physical condition was still not good. He required hospitalization and, of course, we were extremely anxious to get him for interrogation. He asked me personally for advice about what his attitude should be toward the interrogating. I told him that I wanted him to be completely frank and tell us everything. I felt that the information he had was more important than any disclosure he might make which could be considered a harm to himself or his case. I didn't think it through at the time that I told him this, but I realized later that this might have been considered improper advice, or at least it had all the aspects of a commitment on my part that if he were frank, he would come out all right.

Looking back on it, I am extremely happy that I did make this commitment. Klusmann was quite frank with us. He gave us an extremely accurate and detailed account of his experiences. We were able to take advantage of it and, as an individual, as a naval aviator and naval officer, he was completely rehabilitated. He went back to flying with his old squadron for a while at Miramar, then carried out orders to postgraduate school at Monterey, which had been in the mill even before he was shot down. After that he went back to active flying. I've seen him a couple of times and am happy to say that this former prisoner of war is doing all right and is a credit to the Navy.

Q: Did he go into combat again?

Admiral Stroop: As far as I know, he has not gone back into combat. His time at Miramar he was back in his old squadron just long enough to get back into flying again, then he went to Monterey for duty. He took a postgraduate course at Monterey, and then he got back to active flying in test work at Point Mugu. That's where he was the last time I heard about him.

Q: I wanted you to finish the tape with having you tell me what your present activities are.

Admiral Stroop: Well, my retirement took place on Saturday, and as I previously stated, we came up the hill and went home. We had a few friends in, and my two stewards came over and helped take care of them. I was still on active duty until midnight of the next day, so this was an official legal action. We got settled in our new house, and I took Monday off, as I recall.

I went to work as a consultant to the Ryan Company on Tuesday morning. As a matter of fact, I got a phone call from the executive vice president around 9:00 o'clock, wanting to know if I was going to come down that day. Of course, I did, and I've been going down there essentially daily ever since. I'm acting as a consultant to the Ryan Aeronautical Company; my official title is consultant to the president. At that time the Ryan Company was a majority stockholder in Continental Motors, and the president of Ryan was also the chairman of the board of Continental Motors. So I automatically became a consultant to Continental Motors, consultant to the chairman of the board, and I've held those two positions up until the 14th of December, when Continental Motors was separated from Ryan.

In addition to that, I am a consultant to the executive offices of North American Rockwell and some of their subsidiaries, notably the Rocketdyne Division at Canoga Park and Autonetics. I became a consultant or member of the advisers' board at the Naval Ordnance Test Station, later called Naval Weapons Center, at China Lake. This was a three-year tour of duty, and I worked at that for a full three years. I received an appointment from the director of the Navy laboratory in Washington, D.C., and became a member of his board of consultants. For about three years I met about once a quarter in that activity. That appointment has now become inactive, as has, of course, the China Lake appointment.

Currently, I have two laboratory consulting appointments. I am a consultant to Penn State University, where we have an ordnance research laboratory, and I meet with them physically at State College, Pennsylvania, once a year and do consulting work by telephone and letter in the interim. I am also a consultant to the Naval Undersea Research and Development Center right here in San Diego. This is located on the grounds of the old naval electronic laboratory. The technical director is my old friend, Dr. William B. McLean, who is the inventor of the Sidewinder and who was technical director at China Lake. I meet with them fairly frequently and enjoy that communication, as you can imagine, very much. It's physically easy to handle, since we are located on Point Lowell, and I enjoy the relationship. As a matter of fact, the tape recorder we're using right now came from there as a piece of borrowed equipment.

In these assignments I find that I still have plenty of opportunities to travel. I've made six major trips since retiring: one trip to Europe and five trips to the Far East, going over pretty much the same ground that I used to go over in the past, visiting in Taiwan and in Japan. This time, however, I included Bangkok on two trips and Singapore on two trips, and, of course, a couple of trips into Vietnam. Last October I went to Saigon and visited the Seventh Fleet at sea. So the intervening four years have been very active and have kept me out of mischief . . .

Q: Kept you looking very young, I might add.

Admiral Stroop: . . . and I have enjoyed it very much. I'm looking forward to continuing this kind of activity indefinitely. We're happily situated here in a modest little home on Point Lowell, which is quite comfortable and have enjoyed the presence of some of our children. With the opportunities to travel that I have, we managed to check in with all of them once or twice a year. Essentially, it's a very happy situation. I can only hope that my friends who are retiring after me can have the same kind of opportunity.

Q: Well, the Institute certainly appreciates your time. I think it will be a wonderful addition to their library, and I thank you. Besides the fact that I enjoyed it personally.

Index To

Reminiscences of

Vice Admiral Paul D. Stroop

U.S. Navy (Retired)

Air Force, U.S.
Inter-service squabble with the Navy in the late 1940s, 170; involvement in the controversial F-111 aircraft development program in the early 1960s, 222-224

Alcohol
The U.S. Army supplied oranges so President Franklin D. Roosevelt could have them when he drank old-fashioneds at the Yalta Conference in early 1945, 149

Anderson, Admiral George W., Jr., USN (USNA, 1927)
Served in the Bureau of Aeronautics as the fleet greatly increased its need for aircraft during World War II, 58, 134; early departure as CNO in 1963 was perhaps due to the TFX controversy, 225-226, 238

Antiair warfare
During the Battle of the Coral Sea in May 1942, the destroyer Dewey (DD-349) fired her guns at Japanese aircraft approaching the U.S. formation, 94-95; in the same battle, the guns of the aircraft carrier Lexington (CV-2) were unsuccessful against Japanese airplanes, 102-104

Antisubmarine Warfare
Old four-stack destroyers provided ASW protection when the aircraft carrier Saratoga (CV-3) deployed from San Diego to Pearl Harbor in December 1941, 67-69; combined U.S.-Taiwanese ASW exercises in the late 1950s, 214-215

Arkansas, USS (BB-33)
Underwent modernization in the mid-1920s, 10; gunnery practice in 1928, 11

Army Air Forces, U.S.
Provided a C-54 cargo plane so that U.S. military representatives could travel widely to inform high-ranking officers about the results of the Potsdam Conference in the summer of 1945, 160-162

Atomic Bomb
Fleet Admiral Chester Nimitz had advance word on the U.S. bomb to be dropped on Hiroshima, Japan, on 6 August 1945, 162-163

Ault, Commander William B., USN (USNA, 1922)
Was serving as air group commander for the aircraft carrier Lexington (CV-2) when he was lost at sea during the Battle of the Coral Sea in May 1942, 101

Australian Navy
Took part in the Battle of the Coral Sea in May 1942, 89, 91, 119

BF2C Goshawk
Curtiss-built fighter-bomber flown by Bombing Squadron Five-B in the mid-1930s, 26-27, 31-32

Bantz, Fred A.
    As Assistant Secretary of the Navy in the late 1950s, visited Stroop in the Far East, 216-217, 234

BeLieu, Kenneth B.
    Excellent administrator who served as Assistant Secretary of the Navy from 1961 to 1965, 230, 236-237

Berlin, Germany
    Condition of in July 1945 after having been repeatedly attacked by the Allies during World War II, 159-160

Blackburn, Rear Admiral Paul P., Jr., USN (USNA, 1930)
    Took command of the U.S. Taiwan Patrol Force in 1958, 217

Blick, Captain Robert E., Jr., USN (USNA, 1922)
    As a detailer for the Bureau of Aeronautics in 1943, inadvertently gave Mrs. Stroop some incorrect information concerning his next duty station, 135-136

Boe, Lieutenant Commander Nils W., USN
    As commanding officer of VF-193, he was involved in carrier operations in 1952, during the Korean War, 185-187

Bogan, Lieutenant Commander Gerald F., USN (USNA, 1916)
    Served as an instructor for flight training at Pensacola in the late 1920s, 15-16

Bombing
    Attacks on Japanese and U.S. aircraft carriers during the Battle of the Coral Sea in May 1942, 93-94, 100-106, 118

Bombing Squadron Five-B (VB-5B)
    Operations from the aircraft carrier Ranger (CV-4) in the mid-1930s, 25-29; introduction of the Curtiss BF2C in 1934, 26-27; participation in war games, 31; navigation by instruments was rudimentary in the mid-1930s, 31-32; operations from the carrier Saratoga (CV-3) in the mid-1930s, 35-36

Bowen, Lieutenant John B., Jr., USN (USNA, 1930)
    Service on the staff of Commander Carrier Division One in the early part of World War II, 63-64, 99; abandoned ship from the aircraft carrier Lexington (CV-2) during the Battle of the Coral Sea in May 1942, 111

Boxer, USS (CV-21)
    Had a serious fire on board in August 1952 while off Korea, 191

Bradley, Captain Willis W., Jr., USN (USNA, 1907)
    Commanded the heavy cruiser Portland (CA-33) in the mid-1930s, 40-41

Bremerhaven, Germany
　　Condition of in July 1945 after having served as the site of submarine building during World War II, 158-159

Budgetary Concerns
　　The Bureau of Aeronautics testified to Congress around 1940 about the cost of upcoming aircraft, 49-50

Bureau of Aeronautics
　　Had a relatively small staff in the late 1930s, 47; exercised wide-ranging control of naval aviation, 47-48; role in the late 1930s programming upcoming aircraft needs, 49, 51, 53-54; testimony before Congress, 49-51, 53, 57-58; assignment of aircraft to squadrons and shore stations, 51-53; made plans for the wartime increase in the number of aircraft needed, 55-56; merged with the Bureau of Ordnance in 1959 to form the Bureau of Naval Weapons, 220-221, 228-229, 239-243

Bureau of Naval Weapons
　　Formed in 1959 by the merger of the Bureau of Aeronautics with the Bureau of Ordnance, 220-221, 228-229, 239-243; was staffed with several capable flag officers, 221-222; work on the TFX/F-111 project in the early 1960s, 222-226; work on the X-22 V/STOL aircraft, 224, 248-249; process of evaluating various competing design proposals before awarding contracts, 224-225, 233; trip to Europe by bureau chief Stroop in 1962, 227-228

Bureau of Ordnance
　　Received excellent leadership from Rear Admiral Frederic S. Withington as bureau chief in the mid-1950s, 203-206; comprised a large shore establishment, 207; daily routine for the bureau chief in the late 1950s, 219-220; merged with the Bureau of Aeronautics in 1959 to form the Bureau of Naval Weapons, 220-221, 228-229, 239-243

Burke, Admiral Arleigh A., USN (USNA, 1923)
　　Visited the island of Okinawa with his wife in the late 1950s, 213, 215-216; qualities that served him well as CNO, 1955-61, 237-238

Butterfield, Commander Horace B., USN (USNA, 1922)
　　Commanded the small seaplane tender Mackinac (AVP-13) in 1942-43, 136-137

C-54 Skymaster
　　Army Air Forces cargo plane used by U.S. military officers as they traveled widely to report the results of the Potsdam Conference in the summer of 1945, 160-162

Callaghan, Rear Admiral Daniel J., USN (USNA, 1911)
　　Served in the heavy cruiser Portland (CA-33) in the mid-1930s, later killed in World War II, 44

Carrier Division One
Staff officers when Rear Admiral Aubrey Fitch took command in 1941, 63-64; deployment of the carriers Lexington (CV-2) and Saratoga (CV-3) in the months just before World War II, 64-65; reaction to the Japanese attack on Pearl Harbor in December 1941, 65-66; staff embarked in the Saratoga in December 1941 and deployed to Hawaii, 67; took over aviation type command duties at Hawaii in December 1941, 83; the staff embarked in the Lexington in April 1942 and remained on board until the ship sank in the Battle of the Coral Sea in May, 87-116

Catapults
Floatplane operations on board the heavy cruiser Portland (CA-33) in the mid-1930s, 37-39

Catoctin, USS (AGC-5)
Amphibious force flagship that provided support for the Yalta Conference in early 1945, 147-148, 150

Chester, USS (CA-27)
Heavy cruiser that transported survivors of the Battle of the Coral Sea from Tongatabu to San Diego in May 1942, 118-119, 122-123; made a hurried voyage westward in June but was too late to take part in the Battle of Midway, 122

Chillingworth, Lieutenant Commander Charles F., Jr., USN (USNA, 1925)
As commanding officer of the destroyer Dewey (DD-349) during the Battle of the Coral Sea in May 1942, ordered his ship to fire at Japanese aircraft approaching the U.S. formation, 94-95

China
Site of briefings by U.S. military officers on the results of the Potsdam Conference in the summer of 1945, 161

See also Taiwan Patrol Force, U.S.

China Lake, California
See Naval Ordnance Test Station, Inyokern, California

Chincoteague, USS (AVP-24)
Small seaplane tender that serviced aircraft from an advance base at Vanikoro Island during World War II, 141-142; attacked by Japanese aircraft in July 1943, 142-144

Churchill, Winston
British leader who took part in the Yalta planning conference in early 1945, 150-151, 153; lost election for Prime Minister in the summer of 1945, 161

Clark, Admiral Joseph J., USN (Ret.) (USNA, 1918)
Criticized Admiral Raymond Spruance for his cautious use of aircraft carriers during World War II, 85-86; served as Commander Seventh Fleet during the Korean War, 193-194

Classified Information
In August 1945 Stroop carried the top-secret plans for the invasion of Japan from Guam to Washington, D.C., 163-165

Clexton, Vice Admiral Edward W., USN (1924)
As Chief of Naval Material in 1959, oversaw the creation of the new Bureau of Naval Weapons, 240

Collisions
The aircraft carrier Princeton (CV-37) had a slight brush with an oiler in early 1952, 179-180

Commercial Ships
The Matson Lines passenger ship Lurline took Mrs. Stroop to Hawaii in 1936 and 1940, 43, 59; aircraft of the U.S. Taiwan Patrol Force took pictures of commercial ships during operations in the late 1950s, 212

Communications
By radio during the Battle of the Coral Sea in May 1942, 92-95, 97-99, 101; visual signaling by Stroop prior to leaving the aircraft carrier Lexington (CV-2) at the end of the Battle of the Coral Sea in May 1942, 110

Congress
In 1922 Stroop received an appointment to the Naval Academy from his Alabama congressman, 2; involvement by Congress in the procurement of aircraft for the Navy around 1940, 49-50, 53, 57-58; Carl Vinson of the House Naval Affairs Committee had an impressive knowledge of naval matters, 50-51, 57; passed the legislation that created the Bureau of Naval Weapons in 1959, 239; in 1963 conducted hearings on the award of the contract for the X-22 aircraft, 248-249

Connally, John B.
As Secretary of the Navy in 1961, was slow in making up his mind on a helicopter procurement contract, 234-236

Cooke, Commander Charles M., Jr., USN (USNA, 1910)
While attached to OpNav in the late 1930s, consulted with the Bureau of Aeronautics on the number of aircraft to be projected in upcoming war plans, 55-56

Coral Sea, Battle of
Carrier versus carrier action in May 1942 that resulted in the sinking of the aircraft carriers Shoho and Lexington (CV-2), destroyer Sims (DD-409), and oiler Neosho

(AO-23), and damage to the carrier Yorktown (CV-5), 85, 87-117; strategic significance of the battle, 119-121

Cornwell, Lieutenant Commander Delbert S., USN (USNA, 1922)
Service on the staff of Commander Carrier Division One in the early part of World War II, 63, 83-84, 99

Crace, Rear Admiral John G., RN
British officer who commanded Australian forces during the Battle of the Coral Sea in May 1942, 89, 91, 119

Croatan, USS (CVE-25)
Was used in 1945 for pilot training and Magic Carpet duty, 166-167

Cuba
Seaplanes of Patrol Squadron Ten sometimes operated out of Cuba in the early 1930s, 19-20

Curtiss, USS (AV-4)
Seaplane tender that served as the flagship for Commander Aircraft South Pacific in 1942-43, 128-129, 133-134; tended seaplanes at Espiritu Santo in the New Hebrides, 136

Damage Control
Inadequate damage control readiness in the aircraft carrier Lexington (CV-2) when she was attacked by Japanese bombs and torpedoes during the Battle of the Coral Sea in May 1942, 104-109; the aircraft carrier Boxer (CV-21) had a serious fire on board in August 1952 while off Korea, 191

Denfeld, Admiral Louis E., USN (USNA, 1912)
Was relieved as Chief of Naval Operations in 1949 because of his role in the inter-service squabble with the Air Force, 170

Dewey, USS (DD-349)
During the Battle of the Coral Sea in May 1942 fired on Japanese planes approaching the U.S. formation, 94-95

Dixon, Rear Admiral Robert E., USN (USNA, 1927)
Led one section of the attack force from the aircraft carrier Lexington (CV-2) during the Battle of the Coral Sea in May 1942, 93-94, 99-100, 105; sent the famous message, "Scratch one flattop," 94; as Chief of the Bureau of Aeronautics in 1959, was involved in the merger with the Bureau of Ordnance, 239-240

Edwards, Ensign Heywood L., USN (USNA, 1926)
Was on the U.S. Olympic team in 1928, later killed in World War II, 14

Engineering Plants
   The aircraft carrier Saratoga (CV-3) ran short of fuel oil while approaching Pearl Harbor in December 1941, 69-70

Espiritu Santo, New Hebrides
   Served in 1942-43 as the base for Commander Aircraft South Pacific and for seaplane patrols, 128-129, 133, 136

Essex, USS (CV-9)
   Early relief of Captain Walter Rodee in September 1952, 190-191; use of the "pinwheel" technique to dock the ship at Yokosuka, Japan, in the early 1950s, 192-193

F-111
   Controversial multi-service aircraft development program in the early 1960s, 222-226

F4U Corsair
   Use of in the air group of the aircraft carrier Princeton (CV-37) during her deployment off Korea in 1952, 183-187, 189

Families of Servicemen
   The Stroop family made frequent moves over the years, 15, 24, 29-30, 59, 63, 135-136, 145, 171-172, 177, 194-195, 202, 208, 218-219, 231, 245-246; comfortable family life in Coronado, California, in the mid-1930s because the fleet didn't deploy, 33, 42; survivors from aircraft carrier Lexington (CV-2), lost in the Battle of the Coral Sea in May 1942, asked their wives to order new uniforms for them, 121-122; the Stroop family enjoyed Navy quarters in Okinawa in the late 1950s, 209-210, 217-218

Fay, Paul B.
   After being picked for the job by John F. Kennedy, he served as Under Secretary of the Navy from 1961 to 1965, 230, 235-236, 251

Fire
   Did great damage to the aircraft carrier Lexington (CV-2) when she was attacked by Japanese bombs and torpedoes during the Battle of the Coral Sea in May 1942, 104-109; the aircraft carrier Boxer (CV-21) had a serious fire on board in August 1952 while off Korea, 191

First Fleet, U.S.
   Stroop took temporary command in 1963-64 after Vice Admiral Taylor Keith had a heart attack, 251-252

Fitch, Rear Admiral Aubrey W., USN (USNA, 1906)
   Commanded Patrol Wing Two for a period in 1940, 59-63; as Commander Carrier Division One in late 1941, deployed from San Diego to Pearl Harbor following the Japanese attack, 66, 68; attended the ceremony at which Admiral Chester Nimitz took

command of the Pacific Fleet in December 1941, 74; took over type commander functions in December 1941, 83; embarked in the Lexington (CV-2) in April 1942 and remained on board until the ship sank in the Battle of the Coral Sea in May, 85, 87, 90-91, 97, 99, 107-113, 115-116; signed off on the action report after the battle, 118; took over Air Force Pacific Fleet type commander functions at Pearl Harbor in June 1942, 122-124; served as Commander Aircraft South Pacific from October 1942 to December 1943, 124-125, 128-129, 132-134

Fletcher, Vice Admiral Frank Jack, USN (USNA, 1906)
Passed tactical command to Rear Admiral Aubrey Fitch during the Battle of the Coral Sea in May 1942, 85, 115; embarked in the aircraft carrier Yorktown (CV-5) for the battle, 89, 91, 116

Flight Training
Various stages, conducted at Pensacola in 1928-29, 15-17

Forrestal, James V.
As Under Secretary of the Navy, made an inspection trip to the South Pacific in September 1942 and recommended command changes, 124-125, 127; as Secretary of the Navy, established the concept of the General Line School following World War II, 172-173; as the first Secretary of Defense in the late 1940s, developed the concept for the Weapons Systems Evaluation Group, 201, 205-206

Franke, William B.
As Under Secretary of the Navy in the late 1950s, chaired a board that recommended combining the Bureau of Aeronautics with the Bureau of Ordnance, 220-221, 233, 239-240, 242-243

Fuel Oil
The aircraft carrier Saratoga (CV-3) ran short of fuel oil while approaching Pearl Harbor in December 1941, 69-70

Gallery, Lieutenant Daniel V., Jr., USN (USNA, 1921)
Colorful officer who served as executive officer of Torpedo Squadron Nine in the early 1930s, 17-18, 21; called floatplane duty "purgatory," 36

Gardner, Rear Admiral Matthias B., USN (USNA, 1919)
Visited Guadalcanal in the October 1942 while serving as chief of staff to Commander Aircraft South Pacific, 130-132; attended the Potsdam Conference in the summer of 1945, 156, 166

Gates, Thomas S.
Did an outstanding job while serving as Secretary of the Navy and Secretary of Defense in the late 1950s and early 1960s, 232-233

General A. E. Anderson, USS (AP-111)
Transported the Stroop family between the West Coast and the Far East in the late 1950s, 208-209, 218-219

General Board
Shortly before World War II, was involved in plans for the number of aircraft needed by the Navy, 55-56

General Line School, Monterey, California
Pleasant living conditions for those on the staff in the late 1940s, 170-171; set up after World War II to provide further training for reserve officers commissioned during the war, 172-175; the Navy worked at establishing good relations with the nearby civilian communities, 174

German Navy
Disposition of its assets by the victorious Allies in the summer of 1945, 158-159

Germany
Devastated condition of the defeated nation in the summer of 1945, 157-159

Ghormley, Vice Admiral Robert L., USN (USNA, 1906)
Was relieved as Commander South Pacific Force in October 1942, 127-128

Great Britain
Prime Minister Winston Churchill represented the nation at Allied planning conferences in 1945, 150-151, 153, 161; quality of military staff work at Yalta, 152-153; desire to continue receiving Lend-Lease aid after the end of hostilities in 1945, 164

Guadalcanal
Had shore-based Navy planes in late 1942, after their carriers had been sunk, 129; underwent heavy bombardment from Japanese warships in October 1942, 130-132

Gunnery--Naval
Japanese warships bombarded Guadalcanal in the October 1942, 130-132

Gymnastics
Stroop excelled in the sport at the Naval Academy in the mid-1920s, then became an alternate on the U.S. team for the 1928 Olympic Games, 3-4, 11-14

Halsey, Vice Admiral William F., Jr., USN (USNA, 1904)
As Commander Aircraft Battle Force, shifted headquarters from San Diego to Pearl Harbor in 1941, 64; went to sea and left the administrative functions in Pearl, 83, 123; took command of the South Pacific Force in October 1942, 124-125, 127, 132-134; as Commander Third Fleet in the autumn of 1944, was given approval to speed up the capture of the Philippines, 154-156

Healy, Lieutenant Commander Howard R., USN (USNA, 1922)
Was killed while serving as the damage control officer in the aircraft carrier Lexington (CV-2) during the Battle of the Coral Sea in May 1942, 105

Helicopters
Used for the rescue of downed U.S. aviators from North Korea in 1952, 183-188; As Secretary of the Navy in 1961, John Connally was slow in making up his mind on a helicopter procurement contract, 234-235

Hobbs, Commander Ira E., USN (USNA, 1925)
Commanded the small seaplane tender Chincoteague (AVP-24) in the South Pacific in World War II, 141-144

Hollingsworth, Captain William R., USN (USNA, 1926)
Took command of the aircraft carrier Princeton (CV-37) in August 1952, 189

Holloway, Vice Admiral James L., Jr., USN (USNA, 1919)
As Chief of the Bureau of Naval Personnel in the mid-1950s was involved in flag officer assignments, 203, 207-208

Hoover, Vice Admiral John H., USN (USNA, 1907)
In his role as Deputy CinCPac, hosted a conference at Pearl Harbor in August 1945, 164-165

Horne, Rear Admiral Frederick J., USN (USNA, 1899)
While on the General Board shortly before World War II, was involved in plans for the number of aircraft needed by the Navy, 55-56, 58

Hoskins, Lieutenant John M., USN (USNA, 1921)
Served as an instructor for flight training at Pensacola in the late 1920s, 16

Instrument Flying
Air navigation by electronic means was rudimentary in the mid-1930s, 31-32

Intelligence
Reports on Japanese naval movements connected with the Battle of the Coral Sea in May 1942, 88-91, 97-99; American intelligence personnel listened to Japanese radio transmissions during the battle, 97-98

Iowa, USS (BB-61)
Provided a helicopter to rescue a downed aviator from North Korea in July 1952, 185-187

Italian Navy
Association with the U.S. Navy on weapons acquisition projects in the early 1960s, 227-228

Japan
   In August 1945 Stroop carried the top-secret plans for the invasion of Japan from Guam to Washington, D.C., 163-165

Japanese Navy
   Attacked Pearl Harbor in December 1941, 65-67; a Japanese submarine torpedoed and damaged the aircraft carrier Saratoga (CV-3) in January 1942, 84; fought in the Battle of the Coral Sea in May 1942, 89-106, 117-118; heavy bombardment of Guadalcanal in the October 1942, 130-132; mounted air attacks on the small seaplane tender Chincotague (AVP-24) in July 1943, 142-144

Keith, Vice Admiral Robert Taylor Scott, USN (USNA, 1928)
   Had to step down as Commander First Fleet because of a heart attack in December 1963, 251

Kimmel, Admiral Husband E., USN (USNA, 1904)
   As the Navy budget officer in the late 1930s was slow in approving the purchase of airplanes for the new carrier Wasp (CV-7), 53-54, 74; attended the ceremony at Pearl Harbor in December 1941 when Admiral Chester Nimitz took command of the Pacific Fleet, 54, 74; relieved of command in mid-December 1941, 73-76

King, Fleet Admiral Ernest J., USN (USNA, 1901)
   Service on the General Board of the Navy shortly before World War II, 56; members of his CominCh planning staff in 1944, 145-146; took U.S. delegates on a sight-seeing tour during a break from the Potsdam Conference in July 1945, 158-159

Kinkaid, Rear Admiral Thomas C., USN (USUA, 1908)
   Commanded a cruiser division involved in the Battle of the Coral Sea in May 1942, 89; his flagship, the cruiser Minneapolis (CA-36), rescued a number of survivors from the aircraft carrier Lexington (CV-2) before she sank as a result of the battle, 113-116

Klusmann, Lieutenant Charles F., USN
   Flew a U.S. Navy RF-8 Crusader photo reconnaissance aircraft that was shot down over Laos in June 1964, 254; subsequently escaped in September of that year, 254-256

Korean War
   When returning from the Korean War to San Diego in the summer of 1951, the crew of the aircraft carrier Princeton (CV-37) selected a girl with muscular dystrophy as homecoming queen, 177-179; operations of the Princeton and her air group during the ship's 1952 deployment to Korea, 180-188; limitations on bombing of North Korea, 182; rescue of downed aviators from North Korea, 183-187; Naval Reserve aviators who had served in World War II again performed capably during the Korean War, 188-189; the aircraft carrier Boxer (CV-21) had a serious fire on board in August 1952 while off Korea, 191

Laos
A U.S. Navy RF-8 Crusader photo reconnaissance aircraft was shot down over Laos in June 1964, 254-256

Leary, Rear Admiral Herbert Fairfax, USN (USNA, 1905)
Was embarked as Commander Task Force 14 in the aircraft carrier Saratoga (CV-3) when she was torpedoed in January 1942, 84

Lend-Lease Program
The British wanted U.S. aid to continue, even after the end of hostilities in 1945, 164-165

Lexington, USS (CV-2)
Site of officer of the deck qualification by Stroop in the mid-1930s, 34; with Rear Admiral Aubrey Fitch and his staff embarked, in May 1942 this carrier took part in the Battle of the Coral Sea, which resulted in her sinking, 87-102; the Pearl Harbor Navy Yard installed additional guns in the spring of 1942, 89; description of bomb and torpedo attacks against the ship, 102-106, 117-118; poor damage control readiness, 104-108; the crew abandoned ship after the determination she could not be saved, 107-114; explosion of after the crew had left, 112, 114; the destroyer Phelps (DD-360) torpedoed the carrier to finish her off, 114-116

Lurline, SS
Matson Lines passenger ship that took Mrs. Stroop to Hawaii in 1936 and 1940, 43, 59

MacArthur, Brigadier General Douglas, USA (USMA, 1903)
Accompanied the U.S. Olympic team to Amsterdam in 1928, 13

Mackinac, USS (AVP-13)
In 1943-44 served as a support ship for seaplane patrols out from Vanikoro Island, 136-138, 141; had an SOC seaplane assigned, 137-138; description of the officers and enlisted men in the crew, 138-139; recreation for the crew, 139-140

Mare Island Navy Yard, Vallejo, California
Repaired the small seaplane tender Mackinac (AVP-13) in 1943, 143-144

Marine Corps, U.S.
Defense of Wake Island against the Japanese in December 1941, 78-80; Rear Admiral Aubrey Fitch's Marine orderly was helpful on board the aircraft carrier Lexington (CV-2) during the Battle of the Coral Sea in May 1942, 110-112, 126; Marine pilots were killed during a Japanese bombardment of Guadalcanal in October 1942, 131-132

Martell, Rear Admiral Charles B., USN (USNA, 1930)
Was involved in creating the organization for the new Bureau of Naval Weapons, which went into effect in 1959, 240

McCain, Rear Admiral John S., USN (USNA, 1906)
Relieved as Commander Aircraft South Pacific in October 1942, 124, 126-128; as Chief of the Bureau of Aeronautics in 1942-43, 134

McClellan, Senator John L.
In the early 1960s held congressional hearings on the awarding of the contract for the F-111 aircraft, 248-249

McNamara, Robert S.
As Secretary of Defense in the early 1960s, was heavily involved in the TFX/F-111 aircraft development program, 222-226

Medical Problems
President Franklin D. Roosevelt was weak and partially paralyzed when he took part in the Yalta Conference in early 1945, 152; When returning from the Korean War to San Diego in the summer of 1951, the crew of the aircraft carrier Princeton (CV-37) selected a girl with muscular dystrophy as homecoming queen, 177-179

Miami, Florida
Seaplanes of Patrol Squadron Ten sometimes operated out of Miami in the early 1930s, 19-20

Michener, James A.
Author who based his novel Tales of the South Pacifig on the island of Vanikoro, where the small seaplane tender Mackinac (AVP-13) was based in World War II, 139

Midway, Battle of
The heavy cruiser Chester (CA-27) made a hurried voyage westward from California in June 1942 but was too late to take part in the battle, 122

Midway Island
Construction around 1940 of U.S. aviation facilities, 60-61

Minneapolis, USS (CA-36)
Heavy cruiser that rescued survivors from the aircraft carrier Lexington (CV-2) in the aftermath of the Battle of the Coral Sea in May 1942, 112-116

Monterey, California
See General Line School, Monterey, California

National War College, Washington, D.C.
In 1950-51 the college had a population of top-notch students from the various services, 176

Naval Academy, Annapolis, Maryland
Stroop was initially rejected in 1922 because he wasn't the minimum height, 2; summer training cruises in the early 1920s, 3; midshipmen did well in gymnastics

competitions, 3-4; academics in the mid-1920s, 5-6; restrictions on midshipmen, 6; social life for midshipmen, 7; post-graduation aviation training for the class of 1926, 8-10

Naval Air Force Pacific Fleet
As a type command, had a broad range of responsibility for ships, aircraft, and shore stations in the early 1960s, 246-256; the pace stepped up with the onset of the Vietnam War in the mid-1960s, 253-256

Naval Ordnance Test Station, Inyokern, California
Development work on aviation ordnance in the early 1950s, 195-200

Naval Postgraduate School, Monterey, California
Moved from Annapolis to Monterey in 1951, 172, 175

Naval Reserve, U.S.
Reserve aviators who had served in World War II again performed capably during the Korean War, 188-189

Navigation
Air navigation by electronic means was rudimentary in the mid-1930s, 31-32

Newhart, Second Lieutenant Harold G., USMC (USNA, 1927)
Was a gymnast on the U.S. Olympic team in 1928, 4, 11-12

Nimitz, Fleet Admiral Chester W., USN (USNA, 1905)
Took command of the U.S. Pacific Fleet at Pearl Harbor in late December 1941, 54, 74, 77-78; was a fortuitous choice to run the fleet after the losses at Pearl Harbor, 76-77; speculation about what approach he might have taken toward the Wake relief expedition of December 1941, 82-83; supported Admiral Raymond Spruance in his use of aircraft carriers during World War II, 85-86; received a briefing in August 1945 on the results of the Potsdam Conference, 162-163

Nitze, Paul H.
As Secretary of the Navy, paid a visit to the First Fleet in the early 1960s, 252

North Atlantic Treaty organization
Involvement of NATO nations in various weapons acquisition programs in the early 1960s, 227-228

North Island Naval Air Station, Coronado, California
In 1935 Lieutenant Commander Felix Stump led a flight that took the wrong course in landing at the station, 30-31; contained the headquarters for ComNavAirPac in the early 1960s, 247

North Korea
    Bombing missions against this nation in 1952, 182, 189; rescue of downed aviators from North Korea in 1952, 183-187

Okinawa
    Served as the home base for the commander of the U.S. Taiwan Patrol Force in the late 1950s, 209-210, 217-218; base for patrol force aircraft, 211, 213; visited by Admiral Arleigh Burke, Chief of Naval Operations, in the late 1950s, 213, 215-216

Olympic Games
    Stroop was an alternate on the U.S. gymnastics team for the 1928 Olympics, 3-4, 11-14

PBY Catalina
    Flying boat that operated from advance bases in the South Pacific in World War II, 142

Pan American World Airways
    Construction of seaplane facilities at Midway Island in the late 1930s, 61-62

Patrol Squadron Ton (VP-10)
    Operations from the seaplane tender Wright (AV-1) in the early 1930s, 19-21

Patrol Wing Two
    Operated out of Pearl Harbor in 1940, 59-60, 62; monitored the construction of outlying bases, 60-61

Pay and Allowances
    The pay of U.S. Navy personnel was cut 15% during the Depression in the 1930s, 22; flight pay for aviators, 33

Pearl Harbor
    The Navy yard overhauled the heavy cruiser Portland (CA-33) in 1936, 42-46; had the headquarters for Patrol Wing Two in 1940, 59-60; attacked by the Japanese in December 1941, 65-67; damage resulting from the attack, 71-73; role of Admiral Husband Kimmel, 54, 74-75; the Navy yard installed new guns in the aircraft carrier Lexington (CV-2) in the spring of 1942, 89; the heavy cruiser Chester was the first warship to arrive following the Battle of Midway in early June 1942, 122

Pearson, Lieutenant (j.g.) John B. Jr., CC, USN (USNA, 1923)
    Was a gymnast on the U.S. Olympic team in 1928, 4, 11-12

Pensacola Naval Air station
    Site of Navy flight training in 1928-29, 15-17

Phelps, USS (DD-360)
Torpedoed the aircraft carrier Lexington (CV-2) to finish her off following the Battle of the Coral Sea in May 1942, 114-115

Philippine Islands
At the Quebec Conference of September 1944 the Allies moved up their timetable for invasion of the Philippines, 154-156; site of operations for a portion of the U.S. Taiwan Patrol Force in the late 1950s, 211-212

Photography
Group pictures of the participants in the planning conference held at Yalta in the Crimea in early 1945, 150-152; aircraft of the U.S. Taiwan Patrol Force took pictures of commercial ships during operations in the late 1950s, 212; a U.S. Navy RF-8 Crusader photo reconnaissance aircraft was shot down over Laos in June 1964, 254-256

Pirie, Captain Robert B., USN (USNA, 1926)
While serving as DCNO (Air) in the early 1960s, opposed the Navy version of the controversial TFX, possibly costing him a fourth star, 226

Planning
In the late 1930s, OpNav consulted with the Bureau of Aeronautics on the number of aircraft to be projected in upcoming war plans, 55-56; members of the CominCh planning staff in 1944, 145-146; Roosevelt, Stalin, and Churchill met at Yalta on the Crimea in early 1945, 146-153; quality of staff work at Yalta by the various nations, 152-153; at the Quebec Conference of September 1944 the Allies moved up their timetable for invasion of the Philippines, 154-156; in August 1945 Stroop carried the top-secret plans for the invasion of Japan from Guam to Washington, D.C., 163-165

Portland, USS (CA-33)
Operation of the aviation detachment on board this heavy cruiser in the mid-1930s, 36-42, 44-46; catapult operations, 37-39; use of the floatplanes for scouting, 41; overhaul at the Pearl Harbor Navy Yard in 1936, 42-46

Potsdam Conference
Devastated condition of defeated Germany in the summer of 1945, 157-158; the Soviets held private meetings with U.S. representatives during the conference in July 1945, 158; after the conference a delegation of military officers was sent around the world to report the results, 160-162

Princeton, USS (CV-37)
When returning from the Korean War to San Diego in the summer of 1951, the crew selected a girl with muscular dystrophy as homecoming queen, 177-179; had a slight collision with an oiler in early 1952, 179-180; operations during the ship's 1952 deployment to Korea, 180-188; presentation of awards to crew members, 190

Prisoners of War
    U.S. naval aviators were shot down and captured in the mid-1960s while participating in the Vietnam War, 253-256

Promotion of Officers
    Promotion exams on professional subjects were suspended for officers of the U.S. Navy during World War II, 81

Pye, Vice Admiral William S., USN (USNA, 1901)
    Temporarily commanded the U.S. Pacific Fleet in December 1941, 73-74, 78-80, 83

Quebec Conference
    Held in September 1944, its most important result was a decision on when the Allies should invade the Philippines, 154-156; living arrangements for the participants, 156

RF-8 Crusader
    Photo reconnaissance aircraft shot down over Laos in June 1964, 254-256

Raborn, Lieutenant (j.g.) William F., Jr., USN (USNA, 1928)
    Served in the aviation detachment of the heavy cruiser Portland (CA-33) in the mid-1930s, 36, 45-46

Radar
    Use of during the Battle of the Coral Sea in May 1942, 95-97, 100

Radio
    Air navigation by electronic means was rudimentary in the mid-1930s, 31-32; communications during the Battle of the Coral Sea in May 1942, 92-95, 97-99, 101

Ramsey, Lieutenant Commander Paul H., USN (USNA, 1927)
    Led the fighter planes from aircraft carrier Lexington (CV-2) during the Battle of the Coral Sea in May 1942, 95-96

Ranger, USS (CV-4)
    Small aircraft carrier that went into service in 1934, 24-28; pilots' landing experiences, 27-29; transfer from Norfolk to San Diego in 1935, 29-30; participation in war games, 31; fleet operations in the mid-1930s, 33

Rescue at Sea
    Boats from various ships picked up survivors from the aircraft carrier Lexington (CV-2) when her crew abandoned her in the aftermath of the Battle of the Coral Sea in May 1942, 111-112

Rescue on Land
    Recovery of downed U.S. aviators from North Korea in 1952, 183-187; pickup of a Navy pilot who escaped from captivity in Laos in 1964, 254-256

Research and Development
   Work done on aviation ordnance in the early 1950s by theNaval Ordnance Test Station, Inyokern, California, 195-200

Riedl, Lieutenant (j.g.) Harold A., USN
   Pilot rescued by helicopter after he was shot down in North Korea in July 1952, 185-187

Rodee, Captain Walter F., USN (USNA, 1926)
   Was relieved of command of the carrier Essex (CV-9) in September 1952 so he could handle a family emergency, 190-191

Roosevelt, President Franklin D.
   Participation in the planning conference held at Yalta in the Crimea in early 1945, 146-147, 149-152; shocking physical condition at Yalta, 151-152; appeared to have inadequate staff work on his behalf while at Yalta, 152-153

Ruckner, Rear Admiral Edward A., USN (USNA, 1932)
   Did an excellent job as Deputy Chief of Naval Material in the early 1960s, 243-244

SOC Seagull
   Curtiss-built floatplane that operated from the heavy cruiser Portland (CA-33) in the mid-1930s, 36-42, 45-46; catapult operations, 37-39; a SOC was assigned to the small seaplane tender Mackinac (AVP-13) during World War II, 137-138

Salvage
   Recovery of U.S. warships sunk by the Japanese attack on Pearl Harbor in December 1941, 72-73

Saratoga, USS (CV-3)
   Temporarily provided a base of operations for Bombing Squadron Five-B in the mid-1930s, 35-36; steamed from California to Pearl Harbor in December 1941 after getting news of the Japanese attack, 65, 67-69; ran short of fuel oil while approaching Hawaii, 69-71; started for Wake Island in December 1941 but turned back, 78-83; damaged by a Japanese torpedo in January 1942, 84, 86

Schoech, Rear Admiral William E., USN (USNA, 1928)
   Did an excellent job as Deputy Chief of the Bureau of Naval Weapons when it was formed in 1959, 222, 240-241, 243

Shepherd, Captain Tazewell T., Jr., USN (USNA, 1943)
   Commanded the amphibious assault ship Princeton (LPH-5) in the mid-1960s, 178

Sherman, Rear Admiral Forrest P., USN (USNA, 1918)
   As a member of Fleet Admiral Chester Nimitz's staff in August 1945, gave Stroop a load of top-secret war plans to carry to Washington, D.C., 162-163

Sherman, Captain Frederick C., USN (USNA, 1910)
>Commanded the aircraft carrier Lexington (CV-2) when she was attacked and sunk by Japanese aircraft during the Battle of the Coral Sea in May 1942, 103, 105, 107-109, 112-113, 116; trip back to the United States after the battle, 119, 123

Ship Handling
>Use of the "pinwheel" technique to dock aircraft carriers at Yokosuka, Japan, in the early 1950s, 192-193

Shoho (Japanese Aircraft Carrier)
>Sunk in the Battle of the Coral Sea in May 1942, 92-93

Shokaku (Japanese Aircraft Carrier)
>Role in the Battle of the Coral Sea in May 1942, 92, 99-101

Sides, Vice Admiral John H., USN (USNA, 1925)
>Did effective work as head of the Weapons Systems Evaluation Group in the late 1950s, 205-206

Soviet Navy
>The U.S. Taiwan Patrol Force tracked ships of the Soviet Navy during operations in the Western Pacific in the late 1950s, 212-213

Soviet Union
>Participation in the planning conference held at Yalta in the Crimea in early 1945, 146-154; travel conditions in the Crimea, 154; Soviet soldiers took a heavy-handed approach when occupying Germany in 1945, 157-158; held private meetings with U.S. representatives during the Potsdam Conference in July 1945, 158

Spruance, Admiral Raymond A., USN (USNA, 1907)
>Use of aircraft carriers while commanding the Fifth Fleet in 1944-45, 85-86

Stalin, Joseph
>Soviet leader who took part in the Yalta diplomatic conference in early 1945, 150-151

Stennis, Senator John C.
>In the early 1960s held congressional hearings on the awarding of the contract for the X-22 aircraft, 248-249

Strategy
>The Yalta Conference in early 1945 dealt with political issues rather than military ones, 150, 153-154; at the Quebec Conference of September 1944 the Allies moved up their timetable for invasion of the Philippines, 154-156

Stroop, Vice Admiral Paul D., USN Ret.) (USNA, 1926)
Boyhood in Ohio and Alabama, 1; parents of, 1; as a Naval Academy midshipman, 1922-26, 2-7; was an alternate on the 1928 Olympic team, 3-4, 11-14; wife of, 7, 11, 15, 22-24, 29-30, 42-43, 59, 122, 124, 135-136, 144-145, 171-172, 194-195, 200, 202, 208, 216, 227, 231, 246; spent the summer of 1926 in aviation training, 6-10; duty as a junior officer in the battleship Arkansas (BB-33), 1926-28, 10-11; wedding of in 1926, 11; children of, 11, 15, 23-24, 29, 43, 59, 63, 145, 169, 171, 202, 208, 217, 231, 245, 257; flight training at Pensacola in 1928-29, 15-17; served from 1929 to 1932 in squadrons based on the tender Wright (AV-1), 17-21; as a student at the Naval Postgraduate School in Annapolis, 1932-34, 21-24; Stroop's mother-in-law lived with the family for many years, 24, 29, 43, 59, 171, 208, 231; served in Bombing Squadron Five, 1934-36, 24-36; served in the aviation detachment of the cruiser Portland (CA-33) in 1936-37, 36-46; duty at the Bureau of Aeronautics in Washington, 1937-40, 46-59; served in 1940 on the staff of Commander Patrol Wing Two, 59-63; on the staff of Commander Carrier Division One in 1941-42, 63-121; on the staff of Commander Air Force Pacific Fleet in 1942, 122-125; on the staff of Commander Aircraft South Pacific in 1942-43, 125; in 1943-44 commanded the small seaplane tender Mackinac (AVP-13), 134-142; as a member of the CominCh planning staff in 1944-45, 145-166; commanded the escort carrier Croatan (CVE-25) briefly in 1945, 166-167; served briefly on the staff of Commander Fifth Fleet in 1945-46, 167-168; duty on the Pacific Fleet Staff, 1946-48, 168-169; served as executive officer of the General Line School, 1948-50, 169-175; attended the National War College, 1950-51, 175-176; commanded the aircraft carrier Princeton (CV-37) in 1951-52, 176-189; commanded the aircraft carrier Essex (CV-9) briefly in 1952, 190-194; commanded the Naval Ordnance Test Station, Inyokern, California, in 1952-53, 194-200; duty in 1953-54 as a member of the Weapons Systems Evaluation Group, Department of Defense, 201-206; as Deputy Chief of the Bureau of Ordnance, 1954-57, 206-207; as Commander Taiwan Patrol Force, 1957-58, 209-218; served in 1958-59 as Chief of the Bureau of Ordnance, 219-220; served from 1959 to 1962 as Chief of the Bureau of Naval Weapons, 219-245; service from 1962 to 1965 as Commander Naval Air Force Pacific Fleet, 246-256; temporary additional duty as Commander First Fleet, 1963-64, 251-252; activities following Navy retirement in 1965, 256-257

Stump, Lieutenant Commander Felix B., USN (USNA, 1917)
In 1935 Stump led a flight that took the wrong course in landing at North Island Naval Air Station, 30-31

SubRoc
Awarding of the procurement contract for this nuclear depth bomb to Goodyear in 1958, 233

TFX
See F-111

Taiwan
The port of Kaohsiung served as a base for the destroyer tender supporting the U.S. Taiwan Patrol Force in the late 1950s, 210-211

Taiwan Patrol Force, U.S.
Okinawa served as the home base for the force commander in the late 1950s, 209-210, 217-218; mission of keeping Taiwan Straits neutral, 210-211; operation of patrol force aircraft, 211-212; tracking of ships of the Soviet Navy, 212-213; connections with the Taiwanese Navy in the late 1950s, 213-215

Taiwanese Navy
Interaction with the U.S. Navy in the late 1950s, 213-215

Tangier, USS (AV-8)
Seaplane tender that was part of an abortive relief expedition toward Wake Island in December 1941, 78-80, 82

Tongatabu, Friendly Islands
Survivors from the Battle of the Coral Sea in May 1942 gathered here afterward to regroup, 115-118

Torpedo Squadron Nine (VT-9)
Based on the seaplane tender Wright (AV-1) in the late 1920s and early 1930s, 17-19

Torpedoes
A Japanese submarine used torpedoes to damage the aircraft carrier Saratoga (CV-3) in January 1942, 84, 86; used successfully by the Japanese Navy against the aircraft carrier Lexington (CV-2) during the Battle of the Coral Sea in May 1942, 101-105, 116-118; the destroyer Phelps (DD-360) torpedoed the aircraft carrier Lexington (CV-2) to finish her off following the Battle of the Coral Sea, 114-115

Towers, Vice Admiral John H., USN (USNA, 1906)
Served as Chief of the Bureau of Aeronautics, 1939-42, 47-49, 58; took command of Air Force Pacific Fleet in October 1942, 125

Training
Summer cruises for Naval Academy midshipmen in the mid-1920s, 3; aviation training at the Naval Academy for the new graduates of the class of 1926, 8-10; flight training at Pensacola in 1928-29, 15-17; prospective naval aviators trained at the Del Monte Hotel in Monterey, California, during World War II, 172; the General Line School was set up after World War II to provide further training for reserve officers commissioned during the war, 172-175

Uniforms--Naval
Survivors from aircraft carrier Lexington (CV-2), lost in the Battle of the Coral Sea in May 1942, asked their wives to order new uniforms for them, 121-122

VB-5B
See Bombing Squadron Five-B (VB-5B)

VT-9
>See Torpedo Squadron Nine (VT-9)

V/STOL
>See Vertical/Short Takeoff and Landing

Vanikoro Island
>Used as base in 1943 by the small tender Mackinac (AVP-13) when she was supporting seaplane patrols, 136; used by author James Michener as the basis for his Tales of the South Pacific, 139; civilian residents, 139-140

Vertical/Short Takeoff and Landing
>Navy development work on the X-22 in the 1960s, 224; congressional hearings on the X-22 in 1963, 248-249

Vietnam War
>Pilots experienced a higher heart rate when making carrier landings than when attacking enemy targets, 28; the onset of the war in the mid-1960s put additional demands on Commander Naval Air Force Pacific Fleet, 253

Vinson, Representative Carl
>As chairman of the House Naval Affairs Committee in the late 1930s, had an impressive knowledge of naval matters, 50-51, 57-58; was involved in the legislation that created the Bureau of Naval Weapons in 1959, 239

Visual Signaling
>Stroop sent a message by semaphore prior to leaving the aircraft carrier Lexington (CV-2) at the end of the Battle of the Coral Sea in May 1942, 110

Wake Island
>The Navy sent a relief expedition to the island in December 1941 but recalled it because of the potential threat from the Japanese, 78-83

Wakelin, James H., Jr.
>Served as Assistant Secretary of the Navy for Research and Development from 1959 to 1964, under both Republican and Democratic administrations, 237

War Plans
>In the late 1930s, OpNav consulted with the Bureau of Aeronautics on the number of aircraft to be projected in upcoming war plans, 55-56; in August 1945 Stroop carried the top-secret plans for the invasion of Japan from Guam to Washington, D.C., 163-165

Wasp, USS (CV-7)
>Rear Admiral Husband Kimmel, the Navy's budget officer, was slow in the late 1930s to purchase planes to outfit this new carrier, 53-54

Watkins, Vice Admiral Frank T., USN (USNA, 1922)
Commanded the General Line School at Monterey, California, in the late 1940s, 171, 174

Weapons Systems Evaluation Group
Role in the early 1950s in evaluating new weapons, 201-206

Withington, Rear Admiral Frederic S., USN (USNA, 1923)
Did an excellent job of leading the Bureau of Ordnance in the mid-1950s, 203, 206-207

Wright, USS (AV-1)
Tender that served various naval aviation squadrons in the late 1920s and early 1930s, 17-21

X-22
Experimental vertical takeoff and landing aircraft under development by the Navy in the 1960s, 224; congressional hearings on the contract held in 1963, 248-249

Yalta Conference
Living arrangements for the participants of the conference held in the Crimea in early 1945, 146-149; dealt with political issues rather than military ones, 150, 153-154; photographs of principals, 150-152; quality of staff work by the various nations, 152-153

Yokosuka, Japan
Use of the "pinwheel" technique to dock aircraft carriers at Yokosuka in the early 1950s, 192-193

Yorktown, USS (CV-5)
Took part in the Battle of the Coral Sea in May 1942, 87-89, 91-92, 94-96, 100, 105, 107; members of the Carrier Division One staff boarded the Yorktown at Tongatabu after their previous flagship, the Lexington (CV-2) had been sunk, 115-116

Zuikaku (Japanese Aircraft Carrier)
Role in the Battle of the Coral Sea in May 1942, 92, 99-101